Disability Law and Policy

Disability Law and Policy

Edited by Wesley Keller

MURPHY & MOORE
www.murphy-moorepublishing.com

Murphy & Moore Publishing,
1 Rockefeller Plaza,
New York City, NY 10020, USA

ISBN: 978-1-63987-165-0

Cataloging-in-Publication Data

Disability law and policy / edited by Wesley Keller.
p. cm.
Includes bibliographical references and index.
ISBN 978-1-63987-165-0
1. People with disabilities--Legal status, laws, etc. 2. People with disabilities--Government policy. 3. People with disabilities--Civil rights. 4. Discrimination against people with disabilities--Law and legislation. I. Keller, Wesley.

K637 .D57 2022
342.087--dc23

For information on all Murphy & Moore Publications
visit our website at www.murphy-moorepublishing.com

MURPHY & MOORE

Contents

Preface

This book has been a concerted effort by a group of academicians, researchers and scientists, who have contributed their research works for the realization of the book. This book has materialized in the wake of emerging advancements and innovations in this field. Therefore, the need of the hour was to compile all the required researches and disseminate the knowledge to a broad spectrum of people comprising of students, researchers and specialists of the field.

The disability law seeks to protect disabled persons from various forms of discrimination, increase measures for their effective participation and inclusion in society, and ensure equality of opportunity and adequate accessibility. The responsibility has been placed on the government to facilitate the rights of disabled persons such as the right to equality, dignity, and respect for their integrity, right to protection, right to live in a community, etc. The disability policy requires the private employers to frame an equal opportunity policy, appoint a liaison officer, identify posts for disabled persons, prohibit discrimination, and conform to accessibility norms. This book unravels the recent studies on disability law and policy. It picks up individual topics and explains their need and contribution in the context of a growing economy. This book will provide comprehensive knowledge to the readers.

At the end of the preface, I would like to thank the authors for their brilliant chapters and the publisher for guiding us all-through the making of the book till its final stage. Also, I would like to thank my family for providing the support and encouragement throughout my academic career and research projects.

Editor

1

From pillar to post: Legal solutions for children with debilitating conduct disorder

Trynie Boezaart & Ann Skelton

This material is based upon work supported financially by the National Research Foundation. Any opinion, findings and conclusions or recommendations expressed in this material are those of the authors and therefore the NRF does not accept any liability in regards thereto.

Introduction

The rights of children with disabilities have gained recognition in international and South African law in the past two decades. This chapter considers the relevant international and regional instruments, and examines the provisions relating to children with disabilities in the Constitution and the new Children's Act 38 of 2005. The Mental Health Care Act 17 of 2002 is included when considering children with mental health disabilities. However, legal instruments and statutes cannot, in and of themselves, change the lives of children. That requires planning and provisioning by government to ensure that children have access to the services that the law promises to them. This chapter begins with a description of two current case studies of children with debilitating conduct disorder, who have been sent 'from pillar to post', and yet have never received any therapeutic intervention. The failure of the state to provide appropriate services for them demonstrates the gap between law and practice. The chapter concludes with a consideration of legal solutions that may contribute to closing that gap.

Case studies

The two case studies discussed below pertain to two different boys who have both been diagnosed with conduct disorder. We describe this as 'debilitating' conduct disorder because it has severely disrupted the lives of the boys. It has led to their removal from their families, caused them to be shifted from care facility to psychiatric hospital and back again, has resulted in them being charged with crimes, and has cut them off from education.[1] To protect their identities, they are referred to by the initial of their first names, A and G.

The case of 'A'

A is 14 years old. He is physically small, looking more like a child of 11 or 12 years. A and his brother were placed in a children's home in May 2007 when their mother died and it became apparent that their father could not care for them. During 2009, A was referred by the children's home to a psychiatric hospital on several occasions. His diagnosis indicated that he suffers from conduct disorder, ADHD, dysthmic disorder, severe MR and abnormal EEG. He has a low IQ and is developmentally delayed.[2] On each occasion he was stabilised, provided with medication, and then discharged back to the children's home. The children's home repeatedly complained that they were unable to care for him due to his disruptive behaviour. In October 2009, the Children's Home laid a charge of malicious damage to property against A. He was transferred to a secure care facility for child offenders, pending a referral to a psychiatric hospital to determine if he was mentally fit to stand trial in terms of sections 77 to 79 of the Criminal Procedure Act 51 of 1977. The personnel at the secure care facility were concerned about his vulnerability but also found him to be aggressive. The report from the facility indicates that they kept him sedated for most of the time that he was there. He spent a month at this facility, before being referred back to the psychiatric hospital where he had frequently been admitted on previous occasions. In April 2010, his behaviour became erratic and the police were asked to intervene. On appearing at the criminal court, he was referred to the children's court. The magistrate ordered that he be held at a Place of Safety pending the children's court investigation, but the facility refused to receive him and he had to spend a night in the police cells. He was then taken back to the psychiatric hospital. The children's court magistrate,

1 According to the American Psychiatric Association *Diagnostic and statistical manual of mental disorders* (2000) Table 44–2 (commonly known as the DSM IV) the onset of conduct disorder can be mild, moderate or severe. Severe conduct disorder is characterised by many conduct problems in excess of those required to make the diagnosis, or conduct problems which cause considerable harm to others.

2 ADHD is the acronym used for Attention-Deficit/Hyperactivity Disorder, MR stands for Magnetic Resonance, EEG is used for Electroencephalography and IQ is intelligence quotient.

dismayed and frustrated by the failure of the state to provide for A, requested that the Centre for Child Law intervene. The Centre brought an urgent High Court application for a curator *ad litem* to be appointed to assist A. The tasks of the curator were to:

(1) investigate the circumstances surrounding the placement of A in alternative care and to determine which legal rights of the child are being infringed;
(2) institute, conduct and finalise legal proceedings on behalf of A in respect of the determination and/or enforcement of any of A's rights through further litigation or otherwise on behalf of A;
(3) take all necessary steps, including signing on behalf of A and ratifying all steps on behalf of A, in order to protect the legal rights of A and to protect his best interests;
(4) negotiate on behalf of A with interested parties and with private or provincial or national governmental institutions or officials for the appropriate treatment and accommodation of A;
(5) settle any disputes subject to the approval by a Judge in chambers;
(6) and compile a report.

The case of 'G'

G is 16 years of age. The history of G is even more disturbing than that of A. From G's early childhood, he suffered neglect and erratic parenting. He was given up for adoption by his mother at the age of six, but when he was ten she 'reclaimed' him. He was removed from her care by social workers after she had threatened to kill G and herself, and he was then placed in a Place of Safety. His adoptive parents refused to take him back and he remained at the Place of Safety for approximately six months after which they referred him to a psychiatric institution owing to their inability to manage his behaviour. The institution diagnosed G as having severe conduct disorder. He was discharged shortly thereafter and taken back into the care system but behavioural problems soon emerged, and saw him being moved from one placement to another. G was 15 years of age when he was arrested for malicious damage to property whilst in the care of a psychiatric institution. G was remanded to a secure care facility pending the finalisation of the matter. However, such placement broke down resulting in G being detained at New Lock prison in a single cell for 23 hours a day, where he spent several months. A social worker was tasked to draft a pre-trial report in respect of G making suitable recommendations as to the diverting of G away from the criminal justice system. However, her conclusion was that 'there is no infrastructure to deal with severe conduct disorder and aggressive behaviour in children'. G was acquitted owing to a finding of criminal incapacity, despite a panel of psychiatrists testifying to the contrary, and released into the care of a shelter for children. The placement option broke down very rapidly and G was once again drifting between different placements, eventually ending up at a psychiatric institution. The attorney assisting G during his criminal trial contacted the Centre for Child Law and requested the Centre to intervene. Another urgent application was brought requesting similar relief to that granted in the case of A.

What is conduct disorder?

Children with conduct disorder are likely to show physical aggression or threats of harm to people as well as destruction of their own property or that of others (including setting things on fire). Acts of theft or deceit are also common and frequent violation of age-appropriate rules (such as staying out at night, being truant, running away).[3] Conduct disorder is associated with many other psychiatric disorders including ADHD and depression. Rule breaking and rebellious behaviour is common during childhood and adolescence but in children with conduct behaviour this becomes a pervasive pattern of behaviour that violates the rights of others.[4]

The cases of A and G revealed that mainstream residential facilities such as children's homes struggle to manage children with conduct disorder in the environments and with the programmes that they currently provide. On the other hand, institutions providing mental health care services maintain that they too cannot control such behaviour and that the behaviour itself is not associated with a pathological disease of the mind.

The curator *ad litem,* in his report pertaining to G, has drawn on the work of an expert on child and youth care work in order to make suitable recommendations. This expert report is attached to the curator's report as an annexure and forms part thereof. The expert states that:

> [m]any children referred to residential care facilities are diagnosed as 'conduct disordered' ... in the context of consistent nurturing and holding environments, re-education processes can be affected and competencies

[3] American Psychiatric Association (n 1 above) table 44–2, diagnostic criteria for conduct disorder.

[4] B Sadock & V Sadock *Kaplan & Sadock's synopsis of psychiatry: behavioural sciences/ clinical psychiatry* (2007) 1221.

> can be built in children with such and other diagnoses that can ameliorate their symptoms or result in more socially productive behaviour patterns being developed.[5]

It is evident from the above that if provided with the correct therapeutic programmes, these children can make progress.

These case studies are not isolated cases

The curator began his investigation into the cases of just two children, A and G. However, as his investigation into these two cases unfolded, many other children were brought to his attention who had been diagnosed as suffering from conduct disorder, or were believed by professionals working with them to be conduct disordered. Some of these children are currently in mental health facilities, whilst others are in schools of industries or children's homes. It would appear that in Gauteng, there is a need for at least one specialised facility for 20 children suffering from conduct disorder, and indications are that the need is greater.[6] This chapter will return to the possible solutions in this particular case, but it is necessary to elaborate on the South African legal framework pertaining to children with disabilities.

International instruments

The United Nations Convention on the Rights of the Child

The 1989 United Nations Convention on the Rights of the Child (CRC) was the first human rights treaty explicitly prohibiting discrimination against children on the basis of disability.[7] The Preamble to the CRC recognises that in all countries in the world, there are children living in exceptionally difficult conditions, and that such children need special consideration. Article 2 of the CRC imposes an obligation on state parties to respect and ensure the rights afforded to children in the CRC without discrimination of any kind,

[5] M Allsopp 'Expert opinion on secure residential and treatment services' (appended to the report of the Curator *ad litem* in the case of *Centre for Child Law v MEC Health and Social Development, Gauteng* North Gauteng High Court case no 37850/2010, annexure GM 19') 211.

[6] Report of the curator *ad litem* in the case of *Centre for Child Law v MEC Health and Social Development, Gauteng* North Gauteng High Court case no 37850/2010 234–326.

[7] General Comment No 9 (2006) para 2.

irrespective of, *inter alia*, a child's disability. South Africa has ratified the CRC on 16 June 1995.[8]

Article 2 is specifically important in the sphere of the rights of children with disabilities, since its explicit prohibition of discrimination on the ground of disability implies that such children are entitled to all the other rights afforded to children who do not suffer from a disability. These would include the right of access to institutions, services and facilities responsible for the care or protection of children that conform with the standards established by competent authorities, particularly in the areas of safety, health, in the number and suitability of their staff, as well as competent supervision (article 3(3)); the right, in the case of a child who is capable of forming his or her own views, to express those views freely in all matters affecting the child (article 12(1)); the right to the development of institutions, facilities and services for the care of children as part of appropriate assistance to their parents and legal guardians (article 18(2)); the right to a periodic review of the treatment to a child who has been placed by the competent authorities for the purposes of care, protection or treatment of his or her physical *or mental*[9] health and all other circumstances relevant to his or her placement (article 25); the right to education (article 28) and the right to have education directed to a child's personality, talents and *mental* and physical abilities to their fullest potential (article 29(1) (a)).

Apart from the general rights highlighted above, article 23 is specifically dedicated to the rights of children with disabilities.[10] It consists of four paragraphs: The first paragraph requires state parties to recognise that a physically or mentally disabled child should enjoy a full and decent life, in conditions which ensure dignity, promote self-reliance and facilitate the child's active participation in the community.[11] The second paragraph

[8] J Sloth-Nielsen 'Chicken soup or chainsaws: some implications of constitutionalisation of children's rights' in R Keightley (ed) *Children's rights* (1996) 6. It is interesting to note that the CRC was the first international human rights document ratified by the (then) Government of National Unity on 16 June 1995. See J Sloth-Nielsen & B Van Heerden 'New child care and protection legislation for South Africa? Lessons from Africa' (1997) 8 *Stellenbosch Law Review* 261 and P Mahery 'The United Nations Convention on the Rights of the Child: maintaining its value in international and South African law' in CJ Boezaart (ed) *Child law in South Africa* (2009) 323.

[9] Own emphasis.

[10] No reservations or declarations have been entered specifically to art 23 of the CRC: General Comment No 9 (2006) para 4.

[11] According to General Comment No 9 para 11 '[t]he core message of this paragraph is that children with disabilities should be included in the society'.

encapsulates the right of the disabled child to special care and requires state parties to encourage and ensure the extension of assistance, for which application is made and is appropriate to the child's condition, to the child and those responsible for his or her care or protection. The extension of assistance, however, is made subject to available resources.[12] The third paragraph recognises the special needs of a disabled child and requires that assistance as indicated in the second paragraph, must be provided free of charge – whenever possible – and must be designed to ensure that a disabled child has effective access to and receives education, training, healthcare services, rehabilitation services, preparation for employment and recreation opportunities in a manner which is conducive to the child achieving the fullest possible social integration and individual development, including his or her cultural and spiritual development. The final paragraph promotes international co-operation to improve state parties' capabilities and skills and to widen their experience.

Article 23 has been criticised as giving children with disabilities no absolute right to assistance, as access to services is made subject to conditions such as whether children are eligible and apply for such services, and is subject to available resources.[13] It has been argued that the other provisions of the CRC, such as those highlighted earlier, hold more promise for the vindication of the rights of children with disabilities.[14] There is little doubt that a major source of hardship to people, and especially children, with disabilities comes from the fact that enjoyment of sectoral rights depends upon resource allocations. It has been suggested that one way to increase allocations is by adopting 'reasonable accommodation' laws and policies.[15]

State parties are required to submit an initial report, followed by periodic reports, to the UN Committee on the Rights of the Child (Committee on RC) which gives an indication of measures taken to give effect to the rights of children embodied in the CRC. As far back as 1996, the Committee on RC summarised the general concerns that arose from its examination of state parties' reports with regard to article 23. The Committee on RC recognised the prevalence of certain negative attitudes which hamper the implementation

[12] See General Comment No 9 para 14(a).

[13] H Combrinck 'The hidden ones: Children with disabilities in Africa and the right to education' in J Sloth-Nielsen (ed) *Children's rights in Africa: A legal perspective* (2008) 307.

[14] As above.

[15] B Abramson 'Article 2: the right of non-discrimination' in A Alen *et al* (eds) *A commentary on the United Nations Convention on the Rights of the Child* (2008) 123–124.

of the rights of disabled children, such as isolation from society. It suggested that the promotion of these children's rights should be further advanced through, for instance, support to parents' organisations and to community-based services and a sustained programme for moving children from institutions to a good family environment.[16]

In their reports to the Committee on RC, state parties have to provide information on a range of aspects relating to article 23. This includes information on the measures taken to ensure an effective evaluation of the situation of disabled children, including the development of a system of identification and tracking of disabled children, the establishment of any appropriate monitoring mechanism, the assessment of progress and of difficulties encountered, as well as any targets set for the future. It also requires information on the consideration given to the inclusion of disabled children together with children without disabilities in institutions, services and facilities, including within the education system.[17]

It is interesting to note that in the process of drafting article 23, the drafters expressed fundamental philosophical differences of opinion on specific provisions of the article. Some believed that the care of disabled children was the responsibility of governments and that care should be provided free of charge. Others argued that parents and close relatives have the primary responsibility but that the state and private organisations might be called on to provide certain services. A third group believed that the state should be involved substantially but that the CRC should recognise the needs of poor countries in providing assistance to disabled children and should mandate some forms of assistance for these children.[18] Article 23 in its current form appears to be a compromise of these divergent points of view as it establishes the basic principles that are to guide assistance to disabled children within the context of available family resources augmented by national and international assistance.[19]

[16] See UNICEF *Implementation handbook of the Convention on the Rights of the Child* (2007) 300.

[17] UNICEF (as above) 295.

[18] United Nations Economic and Social Council E/CN.4/1983/62 (25 March 1983) *Report of the Working Group on a Draft Convention on the Rights of the Child* 13 para 59; L LeBlanc *The Convention on the Rights of the Child: United Nations law making on human rights* (1995) 103.

[19] LeBlanc (n 18 above) 103.

The Convention on the Rights of Persons with Disabilities

The Convention on the Rights of Persons with Disabilities (CRPD) adopted in December 2006 and opened for signature in March 2007, represents an international response to the long history of discrimination, exclusion and dehumanisation of persons with disabilities. The CRPD is a complement to existing international human rights treaties. It does not recognise any new human rights of persons with disabilities, but rather clarifies the obligations and legal duties of states to respect and ensure the equal enjoyment of all human rights by all persons with disabilities.[20] As far as children with disabilities are concerned, the CRPD builds upon and elaborates on the provisions of article 23 of the CRC.

Although the CRPD applies to all persons with disabilities,[21] which would include children, the rights of and protection for children with disabilities are specifically highlighted in various parts of the CRPD. The Preamble, for instance, recognises that children with disabilities should have full enjoyment of all human rights and fundamental freedoms on an equal basis with other children, while article 3(h) incorporates, as a substantive principle, respect for the evolving capacities of children with disabilities and respect for the right of such children to preserve their identities. Article 7 is solely devoted to children and places additional obligations on state parties, similar to provisions in the CRC,[22] in the following terms:

> 2. In all actions concerning children with disabilities, the best interests of the child shall be a primary consideration.
> 3. State parties shall ensure that children with disabilities have the right to express their views freely on all matters affecting them, their views being given due weight in accordance with their age and maturity, on an equal basis with other children, and to be provided with disability and age-appropriate assistance to realise that right.

[20] United Nations *From exclusion to equality: realizing the rights of persons with disabilities* (2007) 5.

[21] Art 1 of the Convention denotes persons with disabilities as those who have long-term physical, mental, intellectual or sensory impairments which in interaction with various barriers may hinder their full and effective participation in society on an equal basis with others. Also see F Bhabha 'Disability equality rights in South Africa: Concepts, interpretation and the transformation imperative' (2009) 25 *South African Journal of Human Rights* 218.

[22] Arts 3 & 12 of the CRC.

A range of other obligations are also imposed on state parties in respect of children with disabilities, such as the adoption of child-focused legislation and policies (article 16); securing registration of births and the rights of children to a name, nationality and to know and be cared for by their parents (article 18); ensuring that children have equal rights with respect to family life and that they are not separated from their parents against their will (article 23); ensuring that children are not excluded from free and compulsory education and that education is delivered in the most appropriate language and means of communication, especially in the case of children who are blind, deaf or deafblind (article 24); providing health services to children to minimise and prevent further disabilities (article 25); and ensuring that children have equal access with other children to participation in play, recreation and leisure and sporting activities (article 30).

The CRPD approach to disability also emphasises the significant impact that attitudinal and environmental barriers may have on the enjoyment of persons with disabilities. For instance, a child with an intellectual disability might have difficulties in school because of teachers' attitudes toward him or her, inflexible school boards and possibly parents who are unable to adapt to students with different learning capacities. Changing those attitudes and environments that make it difficult for disabled persons to participate fully in society therefore becomes vital.[23]

In order to enable persons, including children, with disabilities to attain and maintain maximum independence, full physical, mental, social and vocational ability, and full inclusion and participation in all aspects of life, state parties are required, in terms of article 26, to organise, strengthen and extend comprehensive habilitation and rehabilitation services and programmes, particularly in the areas of health, employment, education and social services. These services and programmes are to begin at the earliest possible stage, based on a multidisciplinary assessment of individual needs and strengths. State parties are also required to promote the development of initial and continuing training for professionals and staff working in habilitation and rehabilitation services.

In respect of legal capacity, article 12 requires state parties to provide for appropriate and effective safeguards to prevent abuse in accordance with international human rights law. The safeguards are to ensure that measures relating to the exercise of legal capacity respect the rights, will and preferences

[23] United Nations (n 18 above) 13.

of the disabled person, are free of conflict of interest and undue influence, are proportional and tailored to the person's circumstances, apply for the shortest time possible and are subject to regular review by a competent authority.

In terms of the Optional Protocol to the CRPD, the Committee on the Rights of Persons with Disabilities is empowered to receive and consider communications from or on behalf of individuals or groups of individuals subject to its jurisdiction who claim to be victims of a violation by a state party of the provisions of the CRPD.

The CRPD has been hailed as the most rapidly negotiated human rights treaty in the history of international law, and it does create a basis for some optimism in this regard.[24]

African Charter on the Rights and Welfare of the Child

South Africa, as a member state of the African Union (or Organisation of African Unity as it was then called), is also a party to the African Charter on the Rights and Welfare of the Child,[25] (ACRWC) which was adopted in 1990. The ACRWC came into force on 29 November 1999, almost ten years later.[26] South Africa has ratified the ACRWC on 7 January 2000. It is regrettable that this regional document has battled to gain the attention and support it deserves from African countries.[27] The ACRWC is a valuable document which acknowledges and enhances children's rights on this continent.[28]

Article 3 of the ACRWC sets out the principle of non-discrimination on various grounds – similar to the CRC, but unfortunately omits the aspect of disability as a ground in respect of which a child may not be discriminated against. However, it is doubtful that this means that such children may be the

[24] Combrinck (n 13 above) 310.

[25] This document was the first so-called regional human rights instrument which exclusively focused on the rights of the child. See G Van Bueren *The international law on the rights of the child* (1995) 22.

[26] See also F Viljoen 'The African Charter on the Rights and Welfare of the Child' in Boezaart (n 8 above) 331.

[27] On the basis of art 47(3) of the African Children's Charter, the treaty has come into operation 30 days after the reception of the ratification by the 15th Member State, which took nine years. See BD Memzur 'The African Children's Charter versus the UN Convention on the Rights of the Child: a zero-sum game?' (2008) 23 *SA Publiekreg/Public Law* 1. See also Viljoen (n 26 above).

[28] DM Chirwa 'The merits and demerits of the African Charter on the Rights and Welfare of the Child' (2002) 10 *The International Journal of Children's Rights* 157.

subject of discrimination as the first part of article 3 confers the right to non-discrimination to 'every child'.

Article 13, conferring rights upon disabled children,[29] to a certain extent mirrors the provisions of article 23 of the CRC, although it is less detailed. Both instruments contain the limitation that protection for disabled children is subject to available resources. On a positive note, assistance under the ACRWC is not dependent on the circumstances of the parent or caregiver – as is the case under article 23 of the CRC. It has been argued that this could be to the advantage of a disabled child as states are allowed to consider the circumstances of the child's situation and not those of his or her parents. This could imply a higher level of protection, since it widens the group of persons eligible for state assistance.[30]

The list of facilities and services to which a disabled child should have access does not contain education, healthcare services and rehabilitation services which are provided for in the CRC. Education is, however, dealt with under article 11 of the ACRWC, but it has been pointed out that the omission of a reference to education in article 13 is regrettable because the educational needs of children with disabilities are different from children without disabilities.[31] Article 13 contains an additional provision not found in article 23 of the CRC. Paragraph 3 aims to strengthen mobility for children with disabilities and their access to public institutions and facilities.[32]

The direct operation of the ACRWC has been weakened by shortcomings in its implementation mechanisms. However, this does not detract from the fact that it contributes substantially to the evolving body of international human rights principles pertaining to children with disabilities. Moreover, African courts on a national level may be able to draw on this body of principles as an interpretative aid.[33]

[29] The article refers to 'handicapped' children.

[30] Combrinck (n 13 above) 311.

[31] As above.

[32] The paragraph even includes access to public highways. It reads as follows: 'The State Parties to the present Charter shall use their available resources with a view to achieving progressively the full convenience of the mentally and physically disabled person to movement and access to public highways, buildings and other places to which the disabled may legitimately want to have access to.'

[33] Combrinck (n 13 above) 312. It is agreed with Viljoen (n 26 above) 332 that international child law does not replace, but rather, supplements the protection of children on a national level.

Status of international law

In this context, it is important to establish the relationship between international law and national law. In this regard, a distinction can be drawn between the system of monism and the system of dualism. According to the monistic system, international law is integrated into the national law of a country and the courts apply the rules of international law directly.[34] The dualistic system regards international law and the national law of a country as two distinct systems of law. Incorporation of international law into the national law of a country is an absolute prerequisite for its application by the courts of the country concerned.[35] Therefore, individuals, in our case children, cannot derive rights and obligations directly from the treaty. South Africa in essence[36] subscribes to the system of dualism, meaning that incorporation is necessary.[37]

The Constitution of the Republic of South Africa deals specifically with the application of international law.[38] Section 39(1)(b) explicitly states that when interpreting the Bill of Rights, a court, tribunal or forum is obliged[39] to consider international law;[40] and section 233 states that 'when interpreting any legislation, every court *must*[41] prefer any reasonable interpretation of

34 According to J Dugard *International law – a South African perspective* (2007) 47–48, the whole body of international law, which is binding on a country, cannot be applied directly by the national courts of a country. Thus, the absolute monist view is put in perspective by the so-called 'harmonisation theory', where in the case of conflict between international law and the national law of a country, the judge should apply their own jurisdictional rules. However, see General Comment No 5 (2003) on *General Measures of Implementation of the Convention on the Rights of the Child* (arts 4, 42 and 44, para 6), UN Document CRC/GC/2003/5) para 20 that 'in case of any conflict in legislation, predominance should always be given to the Convention, in the light of art 27 of the Vienna Convention on the Law of Treaties.'

35 Dugard (n 34 above) 47.

36 Pertaining to the status of international law, sec 231(4) of the Constitution states that an '[i]nternational agreement becomes law in the Republic when it is enacted into law by national legislation; but a self-executing provision of an agreement that has been approved by Parliament is law in the Republic unless it is inconsistent with the Constitution or an Act of Parliament'. This seldom happens in South Africa.

37 See Chapter 14 of the Constitution, secs 231–233, that deals with international law.

38 See Mahery (n 8 above) 323.

39 'must'.

40 It is interesting to note that for the purpose of interpretation, the South African Constitution allows reference to international human rights law in general, and that it is not limited to treaties to which South Africa is a party. I Currie & J de Waal *The Bill of Rights Handbook* (2005) 160.

41 Own emphasis.

the legislation that is consistent with international law over any alternative interpretation that is inconsistent with international law'.

Skelton has pointed out that the courts also pay attention to guidelines developed in reference to a treaty.[42] For example, the Committee on RC produces on a regular basis *General Comments* which provide guidance for state parties with regard to the interpretation of the Children's Convention[43] and moreover Concluding Observations (including recommendations) as a response to the reporting duty of a state party.[44] Such input of a monitoring body, like the Committee on RC, is not binding on the courts.[45] Nevertheless, since a treaty is not a static document, it is submitted that any additional documentation to an international document is an aid to interpretation and should be taken into consideration by the courts.

From the above, it becomes evident that the contents and standards of the CRC, the CRPD and the ACRWC, to which South Africa is a party, have to be included in the national legislation dealing with children. In other words, the rights of children as dealt with in the treaties have to be reflected in national legislation. It is therefore not surprising that the government endorsed the principles contained in these international instruments in the White Paper on an *Integrated National Disability Strategy* (1997).[46] The White Paper aimed at initiating a process to develop specific policies and legislation to promote and enhance the human rights of South Africa's 5–12% moderate to severely disabled persons. However, was this goal achieved for children?

Constitutional imperatives

The South African Constitution states that children have a right to family care or parental care, or to appropriate alternative care if removed from the family environment.[47] In the landmark case of *Government of the Republic of*

[42] A Skelton 'Constitutional protection of children's rights' in Boezaart (n 8 above) 272.

[43] Mahery in Boezaart (n 8 above) 316.

[44] Mahery in Boezaart (n 8 above) 325.

[45] Mahery in Boezaart (n 8 above) 323.

[46] See General Comment No 9 para 1 that 'more should be done to create the necessary political will and real commitment to investigate and put into practice the most effective actions'.

[47] Sec 28(1) (b).

South Africa and others v Grootboom and others[48] the court interpreted this to mean that children will be cared for primarily by their immediate or extended family members,[49] and only if the child is, for example, removed from the parents is the state then directly liable for their care.[50] Section 28(1) *(b)* of the Constitution has more than one purpose. It primarily aims to protect families from arbitrary interference, so that children are not separated from their parents or family except on substantial grounds and where it is in their best interests.[51] However, sometimes families fail to care for children properly, or even abuse and neglect them. In such circumstances, children may be removed[52] and placed in alternative care.

Alternative care must provide the children being cared for with a therapeutic programme appropriate to their needs,[53] and the facilities must conform to certain minimum standards.[54] The quality of care provided to children living separately from their parents came under scrutiny in the case of *Centre for Child Law & Others v MEC for Education, Gauteng, & Others.*[55] This case dealt with the rights of children who had been removed from their parents via care and protection proceedings and had been placed in a school of industries. The application revealed that the children were living in parlous conditions[56] and with no access to psychological support or therapeutic

48 *Government of the Republic of South Africa and others v Grootboom and others* 2002 5 SA 703 (CC).

49 General Comment No 9 (n 46 above), para 77.

50 General Comment No 9 (n 46 above), para 78.

51 A Friedman *et al* 'Children's rights' in S Woolman *et al Constitutional law of South Africa* (RS 2007/2010) 47–18.

52 The grounds for finding children in need of care and protection are set out in sec 150 of the Children's Act. The procedures for initiating care and protection proceedings are set out in sec 155 and the orders that children's courts may make in the case of children found in need of care and protection are described in secs 156–159.

53 Sec 191(2) of the Children's Act provides that '[a] child and youth care centre must offer a therapeutic programme for the residential care of children outside the family environment ...'. A Skelton 'Child and youth care centres' in CJ Davel & A Skelton (eds) *Commentary on the Children's Act* (2007) 13–7, has pointed out that '[i]t is well established in South African policy that children in residential care should not merely be receiving food and accommodation, but are entitled to proper programmes as an integral part of residential care'.

54 The minimum standards for child and youth care centres are set out in part V of annexure B to the Regulations to the Children's Act GN R 261 in *GG* 33076 of 1 April 2010.

55 *Centre for Child Law & Others v MEC for Education, Gauteng & Others* 2008 1 SA 223 (T).

56 The court describes the conditions at 226G – 227A. They included lack of adequate clothing or bedding, concrete floors, broken windows, no heating, and the court mentioned that at that time of year the night time temperatures dropped to below zero.

services. With regard to the lack of psychological and therapeutic services, the court remarked that an underlying premise of the system is that children are sent to schools of industry precisely to receive care and rehabilitation, and that psychological and social support is a critical ingredient of state care. It was common cause that the industrial school had neither a psychologist nor a social worker.[57] The judgment expresses frustration at this point, as Murphy J states as follows:

> I have to pause here, perhaps in a moment of exasperation to ask: what message do we send the children when we tell them they are to be removed from their parents because they deserve better care, and then wholly neglect to provide that care? We betray them, and we teach them that neither the law nor State institutions can be trusted to protect them. In the process we are in danger of relegating them to a class of outcasts, and in the final analysis we hypocritically renege on the constitutional promise of protection.[58]

The court made a far-reaching order which included psychological and support services for the children.

The case studies of A and G demonstrate that they, as well as other children suffering from debilitating conduct disorder, are not receiving the services that they require. This is a failure to meet legislative promises, because as we demonstrate in the next part of this chapter, the obligation to provide appropriate therapeutic programmes in child and youth care centres is clearly provided for in the Children's Act.

Applying the Children's Act to children with disabilities

General principles

From the onset of the Law Commission's endeavour to develop a new model for a children's code for South Africa, it was agreed that throughout the proposed model, mention would be made of children in especially difficult circumstances, such as children with disabilities or suffering with chronic

[57] *Centre for Child Law & Others v MEC for Education, Gauteng & Others* 2008 1 SA 223 (T) 229B–C (n 55 above).

[58] *Centre for Child Law & Others v MEC for Education, Gauteng & Others* (n 55 above), 229D–E.

illness.[59] The Children's Act (the Act) now provides the primary legal framework for the realisation of every child's constitutional rights, such as family care, parental care or appropriate alternative care, social services, protection from maltreatment, neglect, abuse or degradation and that the best interests of a particular child are of paramount importance in every matter concerning that child.[60] It is an explicit objective of this Act 'to recognise the special needs that children with disabilities may have'.[61] It is therefore not surprising that the rights of children with disabilities are addressed upfront under the general principles of this particular Act. Subsection 6(2) *(d)* dictates an approach upholding the basic principle of non-discrimination that goes to the root of our Constitution[62] and international law.[63] The Act states unequivocally that a child must be protected from unfair discrimination on the ground of his or her disability or the disability of a family member of the child. Subsections 6(2) *(e)* and *(f)* unveil the application of the twin principles relating to development.[64] On the one hand, children should be encouraged to maximise their potential. On the other hand, it is recognised that children are vulnerable and that they need protection. Children with disabilities are extremely vulnerable and they particularly need an enabling environment due to the special needs they might have: Subsection 6(2) *(f)* mandates that a child's disability must be recognised and an enabling environment must be created to respond to the special needs that the child has. When the Act lists the factors that must be considered when applying the best interests standard,[65] 'any disability that a child may have', is specifically stated.[66]

[59] South African Law Commission '*The Review of the Child Care Act* (April 1998)' Issue Paper 13, Project 110, para 2.6, 10, para 4.2.6, 26–27 and para 4.2.7, 27–28, in line with General Comment No 5 (2003) para 30.

[60] Sec 2(b) of the Children's Act 38 of 2005. All references to sections will be to that of the Children's Act unless stated else wise.

[61] Sec 2(h).

[62] See eg secs 1, 7 & 9 of the Constitution of the Republic of South Africa, 1996.

[63] See eg the Preamble and art 2 of the United Nations Convention on the Rights of the Child and the Preamble and art 3 of the African Charter on the Rights and Welfare of the Child.

[64] South African Law Commission Issue Paper 13 Project 110 (n 59 above) para 2.1, 7.

[65] CJ Davel 'General principles' in Davel & Skelton (n 53 above) 2–4 to 2–8 on the best interests standard and 2–9 to 2–12 on the paramountcy thereof.

[66] Sec 7(1)*(i)*.

Section 11(1) obliges that due consideration must be given to provide children with disabilities with parental care, family care or special care when that is appropriate.[67] Section 11(1) also obliges the participation of disabled children in social, cultural, religious and educational activities, recognising the special needs that such a child may have.[68] This is an extremely bold step while the education system currently fails to provide sufficient access to basic education for learners with disabilities.[69] Very importantly, the same section also obliges providing the child with conditions that ensure dignity, promote self-reliance and facilitate participation in the community.[70] In this context section 11(3) is also relevant; because it provides that a child with a disability has the right not to be subjected to medical (social, cultural or religious) practices that are detrimental to his or her health, well-being or dignity. Lastly, section 11(1) obliges providing the child and the child's care-giver with the necessary support services.[71]

In the chapter on 'General Principles' section 13 provides for information on health care and section 13(2) explicitly provides that the information provided for children in terms of this section must be relevant and in a format accessible to children, giving due consideration to the needs of disabled children.[72] The chapter on the children's courts ensures accessibility for

[67] Sec 11(1)*(a)*.

[68] Sec 11(1)*(b)*.

[69] *The Citizen* newspaper reported that the Western Cape Forum for Intellectual Disability filed papers in the Cape High Court to order the Western Cape provincial and national governments to take 'reasonable measures' to meet the educational needs of severely disabled children. According to the Forum's chairperson, Fatima Shabaodien, the state had set up and funded special schools for children with moderate to mild disability, with an IQ of 35 to 70. However, children with an IQ of less than 35 were not admitted to the special schools, and according to her, the state made no direct schooling provision for them, even though their needs were greater. See 'Court challenge on disabled kids' education' http://www.citizen.co.za/index/article.aspx?p Desc=130090,1,22 (accessed 10 June 2010). "*Western Cape Forum for Intellectual Disability v Government of the Republic of South Africa and other* 2011 5 SA 87 (WC)".

[70] Sec 11(1)*(c)*.

[71] Sec 11(1)*(d)*. However, research studies in Gauteng and Mpumalanga revealed that more than 50% of children who are eligible for care dependency grants do not receive even that: 'Strategy for the Integration of Services for Children with Disabilities' Department of Social Development (Draft August 2009) 32.

[72] Sec 13(1) provides that every child has the right to –

'(a) have access to information on health promotion and the prevention and treatment of ill-health and disease, sexuality and reproduction;

(b) have access to information regarding his or her health status;

disabled people, including children, by providing that the children's court must be held in a room that is accessible to disabled persons and persons with special needs.[73]

Child and youth care centres

It is submitted, that the content of section 191, providing for child and youth care centres, is of particular importance in relation to the case studies. This section introduces a new concept of residential care for children.[74] A child and youth care centre is a facility for the provision of residential care to more than six children outside the child's family environment in accordance with a residential care programme suited for the children in the facility.[75] The term 'child and youth care centre' moves away from categorising facilities to avoid the stigmatisation caused by placing children in certain facilities to deal with their 'problems'.[76] Such a child and youth care centre may in addition to its residential care programmes provide for appropriate care and development of children with disabilities.[77] The Minister of Social Development[78] *must* develop a comprehensive national strategy aimed at ensuring an appropriate spread of child and youth care centres throughout the Republic providing the required range of residential care programmes in the various regions giving due consideration to children with disabilities (or chronic illness).[79] It is our view that section 191(2)*(i)*, which provides for 'the reception, development and secure care of children with behavioural, psychological and emotional difficulties' is the provision of care required for children with conduct disorder.

(c) have access to information regarding the causes and treatment of his or her health status; and
(d) confidentiality regarding his or her health status and the health status of a parent, caregiver or family member, except when maintaining such confidentiality is not in the best of the child'.

73 Sec 42(8) *(d)*.

74 Skelton in Davel & Skelton (n 53 above) 13–7.

75 See sec 191(1) for the facilities that are excluded in the definition of child and youth care centres.

76 Sec 13(1) (n 72 above).

77 Sec 191(3) *(a)*.

78 After consultation with interested persons and the Ministers of Education, Health, Home Affairs and Justice and Constitutional Development.

79 Sec 192(1).

Children in need of care and protection

Although some children are adequately cared for by their own parents, this is not the situation in our case studies. Often, children with debilitating conduct disorder are removed from their parents due to their unwillingness or, in many cases, their inability to care for the children. In some cases, poor and inconsistent parenting may have contributed to the disorder. In such cases, the children may be in need of care and protection, often requiring alternative care. If a children's court finds that a child that is in need of care and protection has a physical or mental disability, the court may order that the child be placed in a facility for the care of children with disabilities, if it is in the best interests of the child to be cared for in such a facility.[80]

Drop-in centres

Where children are living on their own (as G's case illustrates) or living on the street fending for themselves, assistance provided to them through drop-in centres becomes relevant. A drop-in centre is a facility providing basic services aimed at meeting the emotional, physical and social development needs of vulnerable children.[81] The Minister of Social Development[82] *must* develop a strategy aimed at ensuring an appropriate spread of drop-in centres throughout the Republic, giving due consideration to children with disabilities (or chronic illnesses).[83] The MEC for social development may, from money appropriated by the relevant provincial legislature, provide and find drop-in centres for a particular province.[84] However, the funding of drop-in centres must be prioritised and made accessible to children with disabilities.[85]

Partial care facilities

Where children are living with parents or family members but additional assistance for part of the day partial care may of assistance. It is often the case that such assistance is needed due to the requirement for constant care and supervision of children with conduct disorder. Partial care is provided

[80] Sec 156(1)*(g)*. See C Matthias and N Zaal 'The child in need of care and protection' in Boezaart (n 8 above) 163–179.

[81] Sec 213(1).

[82] After consultation with interested persons and the Ministers of Finance, Health, Provincial and Local Government and Transport.

[83] Sec 214(1).

[84] Sec 215(1).

[85] Sec 215(4)*(b)*.

when a person, with or without reward, takes care of more than six children on behalf of the parents or care-givers during specific hours of the day or night or for a temporary period.[86] The Act envisages that the Minister of Social Development develops[87] a comprehensive national strategy aimed at ensuring an appropriate spread of partial care facilities throughout the Republic giving due consideration to children with disabilities.[88] The funding of partial care facilities *must*[89] be prioritised and must be made accessible to children with disabilities.[90] When providing for the norms and standards that partial care facilities have to adhere to, the Act stipulates additional requirements that partial care facilities for children with disabilities (or chronic illness) have to provide. These facilities *must*[91] be:

(a) accessible to children with disabilities;
(b) meet the needs of children with disabilities; and
(c) employ suitably trained staff and provide training on –
  (i) the needs, health and safety of disabled children;
  (ii) appropriate learning activities and communication strategies for such children; and
  (iii) basic therapeutic interventions.[92]

The Act leaves the door open for a specific facility to provide special programmes appropriate to the developmental needs of the children in that facility,[93] thus catering for children with special needs.

National Child Protection Register

The Act deals with the establishment of a National Child Protection Register. The Director-General must keep and maintain this register[94] consisting of a part A and a part B.[95] Part A of the register is

[86] Sec 76. But it excludes the care of a child by a school, a school hostel or a hospital.

[87] After consultation with interested persons and the Minister of Education, Finance, Health, Provincial and Local Government and Transport.

[88] Sec 77(1): 'must'.

[89] The wording of the Act. Own emphasis.

[90] Sec 78(4)*(b)*.

[91] The wording of the Act. Own emphasis.

[92] Sec 79(3).

[93] Sec 79(4).

[94] Sec 111(1).

[95] Sec 111(2).

intended to be the so-called 'child register', and its goals extend to both child protection service delivery, as well as for the purposes of forming the basis of a national monitoring system for victims of abuse and neglect.[96] It is therefore important that, for planning and delivering services for children with conduct disorder, the state needs to properly assess the need and make provision for children with any disability, including conduct disorder. For this reason, the Act provides that the record contained in part A must detail the fact that the child concerned has a disability, if that is the case, and the nature of the disability.[97]

The Mental Health Care Act

The Mental Health Care Act 17 of 2002 in the context of care and rehabilitation only finds operation where a person has been found to be mentally ill. The Mental Health Care Act defines mental illness as: '[A] positive diagnosis of a mental health related illness in terms of accepted diagnostic criteria made by a mental health care practitioner authorised to make such diagnosis.'

According to the definition, it is within the discretion of the medical sciences (a mental healthcare practitioner) to make such diagnosis. As a result, children suffering from conduct disorder are not provided with care or therapy owing to the view held by mental health practitioners that such disorder is not a mental illness.

Social assistance

For parents who have the capacity and are willing to care for their own children with disabilities, section 7 of the Social Assistance Act 13 of 2004 provides for a care dependency grant, which will be paid up until the child turns 18 years of age. Persons eligible for the grant are a 'parent, foster parent or caregiver of a child who requires and receives permanent care or support services due to his or her physical or mental disability.' The grant is

[96] J Sloth-Nielsen 'Protection of children' in Davel & Skelton (n 53 above) 7–12.

[97] Sec 114(1)*(a)* read with sec 114(2)*(a)*(iii); sec 114(1)*(b)* read with sec 114(2)*(b)*(iii) and sec 114(1)*(c)* read with sec 114(2)*(c)*(iii).

payable to South African citizens or permanent residents.[98] The grant is means-tested,[99] and a state medical officer must assess the child before the grant will be approved. The amount of money is relatively small, however.[100]

Legal solutions

The curator *ad litem* for A and G, in his report for G,[101] set out a model for the secure care of children with conduct disorder, drawing on an expert report.[102] He then made the following recommendations:

> Firstly, he invited the respondent, namely the Minister of Health and Social Development (hereafter the MEC), to accept the proposals in his report regarding a model of care for children with conduct disorder, or alternatively to make counter-proposals regarding such model within 15 court days of receipt of the report. Secondly, he recommended that the MEC must urgently make a decision regarding the registration of an existing twenty-bed facility in Pretoria,[103] as a child and youth care centre providing for the reception, development and secure care for children with behavioural, psychological and emotional difficulties in terms of section 191(2)(i), read with section 193(1) of the Children's Act, Act 38 of 2005. Alternatively, the MEC was required to identify another suitable child and youth care centre that should be so registered. This alternative recommendation rests on the presumption that there is another suitable facility available. A further alternative was offered, should there not be such an alternative: The MEC must in that case make a decision regarding the urgent establishment of a facility for the therapeutic care of children who have been diagnosed with conduct disorder.

[98] The case of *Khosa v Minister of Social Development; Mahaule v Minister of Social Development* 2004 6 SA 505 (CC) established that permanent residents, as well as South Africans, are eligible for social grants.

[99] The parent/caregiver must not earn more than R129 600 per year, or have a joint income with a partner of more than R259 200 per year. Foster parents seeking the grant will not have their income taken into consideration.

[100] From April 2010, the amount payable is R1080 per month.

[101] M Allsopp (n 5 above).

[102] Sadock & Sadock (n 4 above).

[103] The identified facility is Paul Jungnickel Home, which has an empty wing containing a 20 bed facility, and which was visited by the curator during his investigations.

Whether a facility is selected or established, the curator further recommended the earmarked facility should be assessed by an independent child and youth care expert, to determine if it is suitable for the required programme.

The curator also recommended that the MEC, after consultation with the relevant role-players, must provide a detailed plan of action to the High Court, regarding the provision of suitable therapeutic care in the identified twenty-bed or other suitable child and youth care centre for the therapeutic care of G and A and other children in the province of Gauteng with conduct disorder, within 30 court days of receipt of this report. The plan should include timeframes for the achievement of the goals set out in the plan of action.

With regard to the immediate care needs of G and A, the curator recommended that the MEC, after consultation with the relevant role-players and himself, must provide an appropriate temporary-care placement for G and for A pending the further steps to be taken in respect of my recommendations.

Finally, the curator drew on the provisions of section 192(2) of the Children's Act (read with section 191), and requested the MEC to provide to him a provincial strategy on the establishment and/or identification of child and youth care centres in the Gauteng province, including those that cater for the reception of, development and secure care of children with behavioural, psychological and/or emotional difficulties, specifically those with conduct disorder. He explained that he deems this necessary because it appears from his investigations that the issues identified in the report were widespread and systemic. He required the provincial strategy, which should include timeframes for the realisation of such child and youth care facilities, be provided to him within 60 court days of this report.

As we can observe from these recommendations, the cases of A and G provided a platform to engage with government about providing an appropriate care facility with therapeutic services for them and for others in Gauteng who fall into the same category.[104] It is always important to give the state an opportunity to resolve issues without resorting to the courts, and the curator's recommendations provided space for the necessary dialogue to take place. By providing several alternatives, the curator was respecting the separation of powers between the courts (seeing that he is court-appointed)

[104] See General Comment No 9 (2006) para 18 calling for a comprehensive national plan of action, including plans and strategies for children with disabilities.

and the executive. In other words, he did not attempt to dictate to the MEC exactly how she should carry out her mandate, but provided options and alternative solutions within the scope of that mandate. Unfortunately the MEC failed to respond directly, and did not provide the plan that was asked for. The department of Health and Social Development in Gauteng has, however, designated the Paul Jungnickel Home to receive the children with conduct disorder. There are only 20 beds, and already some children have been turned away. If some children are left without appropriate care and other services, it is possible that this issue might end up before the courts. As we have seen from the *Centre for Child Law and Others v MEC for Education, Gauteng and Others*[105] (the case about the School of Industry), the courts can order the state to provide appropriate services.

Impact litigation is a way of using the law to bring about changes in the law not only for the particular person concerned, but for all the people who are similarly situated. This is so because, in South African law, court cases create precedents that are binding on lower courts or courts at the same level in that province. Thus the law can be developed not only through law reform, but also through case law. This is a particularly important tool for closing the gap between the law and practice. The law may promise a great deal, but this is of little use unless we can hold the government accountable to deliver on those promises. Strategic impact litigation offers a way to do this.

The case studies used in this chapter have focused on residential care for children with conduct disorder. However, a strategic litigation approach can also be used in other situations where children with disabilities are not able to access services to which they are entitled. Litigation is not a panacea for all problems, however, and in every case, there is a need to first try to engage with the responsible government departments. In some cases, this will be sufficient to resolve the situation. If not, the courts can be approached to uphold and protect the rights of children with disabilities.

[105] *Centre for Child Law and Others v MEC for Education, Gauteng and Others* 2008 1 SA 223 (T) (n 55 above). "See also *Western Cape Forum for Intellectual Disability v Government of South Africa and Another* 2011 5 SA 87 (WC)".

2

The rights of persons with disabilities in Botswana: Policy and institutional framework

Bonolo Ramadi Dinokopila

Introduction

On 13 December 2006, the much expected United Nations Convention for the Rights of Persons with Disabilities (CRPD) was adopted. The convention has generated tremendous expectations that it can bring succour to persons living with disabilities (PWDs) the world over. An analysis of the convention reveals it as a significant step towards the effective promotion and protection of the rights and welfare of PWDs, whose rights have been historically marginalised. Sadly, Botswana is not a party to the CRPD and due to this development, Botswana's legal, institutional and policy framework with regards to the protection of the rights of PWDs have been brought to question.

This chapter takes a look at Botswana's legal, policy and institutional framework in so far as the promotion and protection of the rights of PWDs are concerned. After this introduction, the chapter will briefly highlight some of the cultural barriers that PWDs face in Botswana and may continue to face as well as the impact of such cultural practices on the promotion and protection of the rights of PWDs. This will be followed by a review of constitutional protection of human rights in Botswana. The third part of the chapter will proffer an analysis of Botswana's profile comprising of an overview of disability policies and institutions tasked with the promotion and protection of the rights of PWDs in Botswana. This will be accompanied by a discussion of the effectiveness or lack thereof of such policies and institutions particularly with regards to progress of implementation of the identified policies. The chapter will highlight that Botswana has made progress in so far as the promotion and protection of the rights of PWDs is concerned but it has since become apparent that the time is right that Botswana move away from the welfare system *viz* PWDs, towards a more robust rights-based approach. By way of conclusion the chapter will identify possible implementation gaps and how such gaps may be addressed.

Culture and disability: the case of Botswana

Until the early 1980s, many PWDs around the world did not enjoy much protection from states[1] and their rights were not as given much attention as the rights of their 'able bodied' counterparts. Over time, there has been increased movement towards the adoption of proper policies that best take into account the needs of PWDs.[2] As various programmes from governments and other international organisations took root, and measures were taken to ameliorate the harsh conditions that PWDs found themselves in, one thing that was noted was that 'true community involvement in such initiatives remained difficult to achieve.[3] This, as it turned out, was because of lack of a proper understanding of the manner in which communities viewed disability. This is largely because '[c]conceptions of disability and the associated rehabilitation practices vary widely across societies, and are influenced by the unique socio-political and cultural histories of those societies'[4] It is also beyond doubt that the conceptions of disability are influenced by societal perceptions that are a factor to consider when addressing matters affecting the rights of PWDs.

As Harley rightly points out, differences in perspectives on disability and rehabilitation between nations or communities have been linked to, among other things, differences in cultural beliefs and perceptions about disabilities.[5] It is submitted that these cultural perceptions or conceptions

1 S Reynolds & B Ingstad 'Help for people with disabilities: Do cultural differences matter?' (1998)19 *World Health Forum* 42.

2 As above.

3 As above.

4 DA Harley 'Disability and rehabilitation in Zimbabwe: Lessons and implications for rehabilitation practice in the U.S – disability and rehabilitation in Zimbabwe' (2002) *Journal of Rehabilitation* 1.

5 As above.

about disability are important if one is to understand the strides that a country – in this case Botswana – has made in so far as protecting the rights of PWDs.

Traditional conceptions and understanding about disability are prevalent even in modern day Botswana. *Batswana*[6] also have certain perceptions about disability and tend to view disability as a limitation on a person's capacity or ability. The Setswana word for a PWD is *'Segole'* and in that sense the term has come to be attributed to mean that someone is incapable of doing what the community views as normal. To that extent, communities will normally shun a *'Segole'*. What some people would consider to be misconceptions about disability in Botswana are, in the minds of some Batswana, representative of the realities surrounding disability. Thus, PWDs in Botswana are often looked upon as incapacitated and are most of the time described as having been bewitched by some other member of the community or they tried and failed to bewitch someone. For example, an elderly woman with a mental illness is sometimes viewed by the community as a witch. To that extent, the reason for her mental condition is attributed to the fact that she had attempted to bewitch someone and failed.

Misperceptions and the accompanying taboos regarding people with disabilities in Botswana could be credited as being one of the big contributory factors to understanding disability as a result of supernatural sanctions in Botswana. This is because the disobedience of *meila* is usually said to attract a '… supernatural sanction, where the consequences of disobedience follow automatically, without the direct intervention of any specific human agency.'[7] Schapera asserts that although these 'taboos are trifling in character and not taken *very* [emphasis placed] seriously by the people themselves,' they are indeed taken seriously and do have a sizeable influence on the way *Batswana* conceive and understand disability. The understanding of and misconceptions with regards to disability are mostly discernible and are most evident after the birth of a child with disability.

A child born with a disability is usually regarded as either having been born of parents who were bewitched or as an indication that the mother did not adhere to the taboos relating to confinement, in particular, having sex whilst breastfeeding. Children born with a disability are normally referred to as *'mepakwana'*, a derogatory term that translates to mean that the father went into the house of a wife who just gave birth and the two proceeded to

6 This is a term that denotes the plural of the people of Botswana with the singular being a *Motswana*.

7 I Schapera *A handbook of Tswana Law and Custom* (1994) 39.

have sex before the traditionally set time limitations. This is regardless of the fact that the child was not born with a disability and did not become disabled as a result of the sex. Consequently, such children are normally hidden from the public as their parents and relatives alike are embarrassed by their disability. In most cases, they are neglected and sometimes 'imprisoned' by their own families under the pretext that they are being protected from harm. From an early age, children who have disabilities are excluded from most daily activities and lack the opportunity to socialise with other members of the community. This exclusion of children from mainstream activities largely impair the development of their social skills.[8]

In Botswana, disability is usually associated with stigma. In some communities, there are '... entrenched beliefs that blame the birth of a child with disability on anything from parents' adultery to divine punishment'[9] and it is difficult to totally rid people of such perceptions. The effects of these cultural perceptions on disability have had a negative impact on the rights of PWDs in Botswana and to a certain extent continue to do so. Due to the social neglect and general exclusion from social life that PWDs have experienced over time, they remain amongst the most marginalised and poverty stricken members of society. This is largely because they are not afforded normal social benefits like health and education which in turn relegates them to the peripheries of the working society, and further impeding their development. This results in them living in poverty for the better part of their lives, and never having an opportunity to learn to live and lead productive lives.

The marginalisation of PWDs is not at all a phenomenon peculiar to Botswana. Estimates of PWDs in the world vary widely, ranging from estimates of around 350 million to around 600 million (about 1 in every 10 people)[10]. This trend is often more visible in developing countries such as Botswana, where around 80% of the world's PWDs are reported to be residing[11] and where they usually form part of the poorest, most vulnerable and marginalised sections of their societies. They are usually forced to begging due to poverty combined with high levels of illiteracy. It is not

[8] 'Giving Children with disability hope' *Sunday Standard* (online edition) available at www.sundaystandard.info/article.php?NewsID=8339&GroupID=4 (accessed 6 October 2010).

[9] As above.

[10] See World Heath Organisation: www.who.int/disabilities/introduction/en/index.html (accessed 6 October 2010).

[11] As above.

usually common to see many PWDs as beggars in the streets of Botswana. This is largely attributable to the fact that most people with some form of disability are confined in rural areas where the stigma associated with disability is perpetuated, and with no relief on sight.

However, over the years slight changes in public attitudes and perceptions of PWDs were witnessed. Consequently, society perception and attitudes with regards to PWDs has slightly improved as many have come to acknowledge that PWDs are not creatures of witchcraft. This is largely attributable to the fact that the government has had to put in place measures necessary for the promotion and protection of the rights of PWDs and it has become clear that the misconceptions about disability are likely to be dealt away if the public could be made to appreciate that PWDs are not necessarily a burden as they have come to be understood.

An overview of the legal and institutional protection of human rights in Botswana

Botswana has been hailed as a shining example of democracy in Africa[12] and as a country where the rights and freedoms of individuals are protected and fulfilled. Sections 3 to 15 of the Constitution[13] make provision for civil and political rights. Section 3 of the Constitution is the umbrella provision of the rights embodied in Chapter of the Constitution.[14] It provides that '... every person in Botswana is entitled to the fundamental rights and freedoms of the individual, that is to say, the right, whatever his or her race, place of origin, political opinions, colour, creed or sex, but subject to respect for the rights and freedoms of others and for the public interest ...'.[15]

Specific rights are then provided for under sections 4 to 15 of the constitution. The rights under the chapter include the right to life,[16] the right

12 See generally, A Cook & J Sarkin 'Is Botswana the miracle of Africa? Democracy, the rule of law, and human rights versus economic development' (2010) 19 *Transnational Law & Contemporary Problems* 458–488, 466.

13 2009 Botswana Constitution.

14 EK Quansah 'Law, religion and human rights in Botswana' (2008) 8 (2) *African Human Rights Law Journal* 486, 491.

15 As above. See a purposive interpretation of the Constitution in *Dow* v *Attorney General* [1992] BLR 119 where the Court interpreted the Constitution to have prohibited discrimination on the basis of sex despite the same not being included in the grounds of discrimination under the Constitution.

16 Constitution of Botswana, sec 4.

to personal liberty,[17] protection from slavery and forced labour,[18] protection from torture and other cruel, inhuman, or degrading treatment or punishment,[19] freedom of expression,[20] protection from discrimination,[21] the right to privacy[22] and protection from deprivation of property,[23] freedom of conscience[24] as well as protection of the law.[25] The constitution of Botswana does not make any reference to economic, social and cultural rights and as such socio-economic rights are not given the same constitutional protection as civil and political rights. Even though there is no specific mention of people with disabilities in the constitution, the rights guaranteed under the constitution, such as the right to non-discrimination provided for under section 15, may be used to protect the rights of PWDs.

On an international level, Botswana is party to several international and regional human rights instruments. These include the International Covenant on Civil and Political Rights (ICCPR), the Convention on the Elimination of All Forms of Discrimination against Women (CEDAW), Convention on the Rights of the Child (CRC), the African Charter on the Rights and Welfare of the Child (ACRWC) and the African Charter on Human and Peoples' Rights (African Charter). Botswana is neither party nor signatory to the International Covenant on Economic, Social and Cultural Rights (ICESCR) and to the CRPD. Due to the dualist nature of Botswana's legal system, treaty provisions do not become part of the laws of the Botswana unless

17 As above, sec 5

18 As above, sec 6

19 As above, sec 7; See *Petrus & Another* v *The State* [1984] BLR 14, addressing the issue of corporal punishment and holding that corporal punishment was inhuman and degrading treatment contrary to internationally acceptable standards.

20 Constitution of Botswana, sec 12

21 As above, sec 15; see generally CM Fombad 'The Constitutional protection against discrimination in Botswana' (2004) 53 *The International and Comparative Law Quarterly* 139–170.

22 Constitution of Botswana, sec 9; See *Kanane* v *The State* [2003] 2 BLR 67 wherein the Court of Appeal was of the view that gay men do not represent a group or class which required protection. Refusing to decriminalise same sex relations or declaring such sections of the penal code as constitutional, the Court held further that the time had not arrived for the adoption of progressive trends taking place elsewhere. See further EK Quansah 'Same-sex relationships in Botswana: Current perspectives and future prospects' (2004) 4(2) *African Human Rights Law Journal* 201; KN Bojosi 'An opportunity missed for gay rights in Botswana: *Utjiwa Kanane* v *The* State' (2004) 20 *South African Journal on Human Rights* 466–481; MM Chilisa 'Two steps back for human rights: A critique of the *Kanane* case' (2007) 1 *The Botswana Review of Ethics, Law & HIV/Aids* 45–52.

23 Constitution of Botswana, sec 8

24 Constitution of Botswana, sec 5: See Quansah (n 14 above) 486–504.

25 Constitution of Botswana, sec 5

specifically incorporated through an Act of parliament.[26] As such, treaties creating rights and obligations ratified by Botswana are not enforceable before the courts immediately upon ratification. However, section 24 of the Interpretation Act provides that such treaties may only be used in the interpretation of the law where the wording of the statute is ambiguous.[27] Customary international law is applicable in Botswana in so far as it is not inconsistent with any piece of domestic legislation.[28]

As aforementioned, Botswana is not party to the CRPD nor has it signed the Convention. Instead of incorporating the provisions of the various instruments in its various pieces of legislation, Botswana has chosen to promote and protect the rights of PWDs through policy measures, a move that continues to baffle many considering its healthy financial status. The following discussion highlights the various measures and policies that the Government has adopted in the bid to safeguard the rights of PWDs.

The policy and institutional framework for the promotion and protection of the rights of PWDs in Botswana

The Policy framework

Unlike many jurisdictions, Botswana has no specific piece of legislation that offers a comprehensive legal protection for PWDs in accordance with the provisions of the constitution. Instead, the Government has adopted several policies that are said to be aimed at securing the promotion and protection of the rights of PWDs in Botswana. Such policies include the 1996 National Policy on Care for People with Disabilities (which policy is the main policy on matters relating to the rights of PWDs),[29] the Botswana National Policy on HIV/AIDS[30] as well as the Botswana National Policy on Education.[31]

[26] *Attorney-General v Dow* [1992] BLR 119; *Kenneth Good v The Attorney-General* [2005] 1 BLR 462.

[27] As above.

[28] *Amadou Oury Bah* v *Libyan Embassy* 2006 (1) BLR 22 (IC) 25; *Republic of Angola* v *Springbok Investments* 2005 (2) BLR 159.

[29] Multisectoral national policy available at http://www.gov.bw/en/Citizens/Sub-Audiences/People-with-Disabilities-/National-Policy-on-Care-for-People-with-Disabilities/ (accessed 13 August 2010).

[30] Available at http://www.hsph.harvard.edu/population/aids/botswana.aids.93.pdf (accessed 10 August 2010).

[31] See generally, Botswana Federation of Trade Unions (BFTU) *Policy on Education in Botswana* (2007) available at http://library.fes.de/pdf-files/bueros/botswana/04922.pdf (accessed 15 September 2010).

The 1996 National Policy on Care for People with Disabilities

This multisectoral policy outlines 'the national response to the demand for a co-ordinated delivery of service and care for people with disabilities in Botswana.'[32] The purpose of the Policy is therefore to guide those interested in disability issues, in order to involve them in the process effectively.

The nine principles of the Multisectoral National Policy are aimed at promoting the quality of life for PWDs in Botswana. To that end the policy, through its principles – advocate for the recognition and protection of the rights of PWDs and the dignity of every individual, their participation in the basic entities of society, the family social grouping and community, ensuring that PWDs are able to and strive for a self-sufficient society. This is supposed to be done through the creation of an environment within which all peoples, including those with disabilities, can develop their abilities to the fullest possible extent.[33] The Multisectoral policy recognises the challenges which are being faced by PWDs and the contribution of PWDs to economic activity, growth and development. The policy describes the role of the various government ministries, the private sector, NGOs, local organisations, community leaders as well as PWDs in the national response.[34]

It is through this policy that the various ministries are assigned roles and their envisaged contribution to the implementation of the policy is also highlighted. It is important to mention that the principles that constitute the Multisectoral Policy are based on the guidelines contained in the various National Development Plans of Botswana, the United Nations World Programme of Action Concerning Disabled Persons and the different government ministries' knowledge of the nature of disability issues in the context of Botswana.[35]

The policy is woefully inadequate and cannot be used as a tool for judicially enforcing the rights of PWDs. In 2008, Global Consult noted that the 'current National Policy on Care for People with Disabilities is outdated and out of sync with global trends on disability issues'.[36] The fundamental flaw of this policy is its failure to define 'disability'. Due to this anomaly, the scope and coverage of the policy remain uncertain which uncertainty compromises

[32] 1996 National Multisectoral Policy para1.4.

[33] 1996 National Multisectoral Policy para 4.2.

[34] As above, paras. 4.3–4.4.

[35] As above, para 1.6.

[36] Global Consult (2008) 'National Disability Strategy (MultiSectorial Strategic Plan)' 14.

the extent to which the various stakeholders and the society at large could better utilise it. In addition, the title of the policy is misleading. The title suggests that the policy is meant to guide the provision of 'care' to those with disabilities. This approach is in stark contrast with the modern approaches to disability issues such as the social model of disability. The other shortfall of the policy is that the structures for co-ordinating the implementation of the policy, as provided therein, are very weak and their role and functions are not clearly spelt out. In recognition of developments elsewhere and increased efforts to protect the rights of persons with disabilities, the government embarked on an amendment of the 1996 National Policy on Disability. This policy will be, in the near future, replaced by the National Policy on the Rights of Persons with Disabilities (2010) which is still in draft form.

The Draft National Policy on the Rights of Persons with Disabilities[37]

The National Policy on the Rights of Persons with Disabilities (Draft Policy) is still in draft form. The Draft Policy is put forward as '[t]the country's long-term policy towards a socially inclusive society that recognises the rights and human dignity of PWDs to realise their full potential and lead a satisfying life'.[38] It is formulated as a basis for appropriate social interventions and legislation to guarantee social inclusion, the mainstreaming of disability issues towards the promotion and protection of the fundamental rights as well as the respect for the dignity of PWDs.

The policy is divided into four main chapters. Chapter is titled 'introduction to the policy' and provides background information on disability in Botswana and its likely impact. Chapter highlights the policy objectives and its purpose as to guide policy makers and stakeholders on disability issues, in order to involve them in its effective implementation. The policy has five major objectives. The core of the objectives being to foster, among others, the meaningful participation of PWDs in family life in a meaningful, purposeful and dignified manner, mainstreaming disability for social inclusion and guaranteeing equal access by persons with disabilities of all advantages of social life.

The policy has eight guiding principles for responding to the concerns and needs of PWDs. These include the respect for inherent dignity, individual

[37] 2010 Botswana Government national policy.

[38] Botswana Government, Draft Reviewed Policy (2010) under Application of Policy.

autonomy including the freedom to make one's own choices, equality opportunities for all and the principle of non-discrimination.

The policy further identifies eleven policy priorities. The eleven priority areas are accessibility, information and public education, participation of PWDs and care providers, capacity building, prevention and management of disabilities, care and support, research, employment, HIV and AIDS and disability, gender and disability specific programmes. These top priority areas are commendable since they are in line with modern notions on disability especially with the CRPD. The policy can be seen as centred on the social model of disability and recognises PWDs as a distinct social group and aims at ensuring that all barriers to them accessing information, education, employment and social opportunities are removed.

Chapter of the draft policy, which forms the bulk of the draft policy, deals with the implementation mechanism and strategies. It advocates that the provision of social services will be integrated into ongoing activities of all stakeholders particularly government ministries in order to optimise the use of human resources. Like the 1996 Multisectoral Policy, the Draft National Policy provides for a multisectoral approach in so far as sharing responsibilities is concerned. The policy recognises the various stakeholders in the disability movement in Botswana which the various government ministries and the caregivers such as the Disabled Persons Organisations (DPOs).

Chapter of the draft policy deals with monitoring and evaluation mechanisms. It is through this chapter that the government undertakes to establish focal points with a clearly defined mandate and with adequate human and financial resources to deal with matters related to implementation of the policy. There is further an undertaking on the part of the government to implement appropriate interventions and strategies in order to effectively address disability issues through communities, local authorities, the private sector networks and civil society organisations, and to enhance their capacity for effective outreach.

The Draft National Policy sets out to mainstream disability issues in all government responses with the aim of nurturing the inclusion of PWDs in the social, cultural and economic activities. However, a closer look at the Draft National Policy shows that the issue of culture and the role that culture plays in the promotion and protection of the rights of PWDs has not been given sufficient attention by the crafters of the policy. This is notwithstanding the fact that there are still remnants of communities that still believe in the notion that disability comes as a result of witchcraft or possible supernatural sanctions.

The interesting thing however is that the draft policy mirrors the provisions of the CRPD. The policy's strategic directions, which guides the policy implementation, provides for and recognises that PWDs have, among others, the right to life, the right to non-discrimination, equality before the law the rights to privacy, freedom from torture or cruel, inhuman or degrading treatment as well as the right to liberty. It should be noted that such 'rights' are not rights *per se* but are strategic directions that the government undertakes to adhere to so as to protect and promote the full realisation of all human rights and fundamental freedoms for all PWDs.

The implications of this rather peculiar approach are that the adoption of legislation is likely to be delayed as the policy might camouflage the fact that there is need to have disability legislation in Botswana. The undesirability of this approach is further fortified by the fact that the 'rights' contained in the policy are not enforceable before a Court of law and are not rights *per se*. As such, the policy cannot be used as an effective tool of judicially enforcing the rights of PWDs. What is comforting though is that the draft policy makes reference to the adoption of legislation on disability.

Further to the above, policies have the tendency of being minimally used and their minimal usage is usually by government officers as opposed to the private sector. To that end, it is submitted that the policy is insufficient and that the government should have taken the opportunity to pass disability legislation as opposed to adopting another policy.

Other Relevant policies

As indicated above, Botswana has chosen a policy route as opposed to legislative or specific mention of persons with disabilities in the constitution. There are other policies that are also used or are meant to be used by the government to streamline disability issues. Such policies include the Tertiary Education Policy, the Revised National Education Policy as well as the National Policy on HIV/AIDS. However, they are also inadequate in so far as promoting and protecting the rights of PWDs are concerned. For example, in response to the HIV and AIDS pandemic, Botswana adopted the Botswana National Policy on HIV/AIDS which policy is to be implemented by the National AIDS Council. It is worth mentioning that the National AIDS Policy as it stands today is not disability specific.

The first education policy in Botswana was enacted in 1977 but it was not until the second policy on education adopted in 1999 that special education provisions were specifically introduced. Prior to the inclusion of the special education provisions, a small number of nongovernmental organisations (NGOs) had already been providing education for a few children with specific disabilities.[39] The Draft National Policy now sets out a plan for the development of the special education programmes that are to foster the integration of children in the mainstream schools. This it is hoped will assist with the social integration of children with disabilities except where the child has severe learning problems or disabilities in which case they are to be taught in special units.[40] The revised national policy on education places emphasis on the quality of education at the primary level, assurance of the quality of education provided and the importance of ensuring that education is relevant to children and their communities, including children with special education needs.[41] It is due to this policy that there is a marked improvement on the provision of education to children with disabilities. It has also been highlighted that the National Policy on Vocational Education 'recognises that priority should be given to disadvantaged groups, including disabled students and women, and that special training programs may need to be developed'.[42]

The institutional framework

Whilst the constitution guarantees the right to equality and non-discrimination, the reality of the situation in most jurisdictions is that these rights are more of paper rights than realisable rights to PWDs.[43] It is therefore imperative that in addition to the laws and policies that have been put in place to protect the rights of PWDs, institutions are equally strengthened to ensure that such rights are transformed into a reality. That is why the CRPD is one of the few instruments to specifically contain a provision dealing with the national implementation and monitoring of its implementation. Article 33 of the CRPD enjoins states to establish institutions or focal points for matters relating to the implementation of the CRPD and the '[P]arties shall, in accordance with their legal and administrative systems, maintain,

[39] S Chabra *et al* 'Inclusive education in Botswana: The perceptions of school teachers' (2010) 20 *Journal of Disability Policy Studies* 219– 228, 220.

[40] As above.

[41] As above.

[42] As above.

[43] V Jere 'The right to equality in the work place for persons with physical disabilities in Malawi: Does the Convention on the Rights of Persons with Disabilities offer any hope?' unpublished LL.M thesis, University of Pretoria, 2008 3.

strengthen, designate or establish within the State Party, a framework, including one or more independent mechanisms, as appropriate, to promote, protect and monitor implementation of the present Convention'.

The government of Botswana, a few years after attaining independence began to gauge the need for helping PWDs. In the early 1970s, the Government commissioned a study on different disabilities that were prevalent in the country in order to analyse the situation. The Ministry of Health in response to the findings of the above mentioned project, and realising the need to provide services, introduced the Special Services Unit for the Handicapped (Special Services Unit) in 1975. The Special Services Unit has now been developed into Rehabilitation Services Division under the Ministry of Health (MOH).[44] This Division is now responsible for ensuring that the policies and interventions aimed at promoting and protecting the rights of PWDs are implemented. Further, the MOH through its Rehabilitation Services Division remain responsible for the implementation of rehabilitation services in the country;[45] strengthen the community based rehabilitation services under the Primary Health Care programmes so as to achieve more effective delivery of services.[46] The MOH is further responsible for providing assistance to NGOs so as to ensure that the services that they are eligible for Government assistance.[47] To that end, the division is responsible for the co-ordination, training as well as supervision of the relevant stakeholders.

The 1996 National Policy on Care for People with Disabilities has detailed the functions that the various key ministries should play in the implementation of the policy. For example, the Ministry of Education is tasked with the duty of ensuring that special education forms an integral part of regular and formal education,[48] provision of guidelines for use by Local Authorities and NGOs on matters pertaining to establishing and managing special education provisions and to provide support to NGOs providing special education.[49] Further, the Ministry of Education was tasked with ensuring that schools were provided with specialists on all areas of special

[44] See Government of Botswana National Policy on Care for People with Disabilities available at http://www.gov.bw/en/PrintingVersion/?printid=2827 (accessed 14 October 2010).

[45] 1996 National Multi-sectoral Policy para 4.3.1.3.

[46] As above.

[47] As above.

[48] 1996 National Multi-sectoral Policy para 4.3.1.2.

[49] As above.

education in order to assist the children and adults with learning difficulties.[50] It was in furtherance of these duties that the Special Education Division was set up within the ministry. The division has been set up for the purposes of planning and overseeing the educational needs of the people with special needs.

Other key ministries include the Ministry of Labour and Home Affairs. The ministry is tasked with ensuring that issues pertaining to the rights of PWDs should be taken into consideration when formulating all the policies and laws on social welfare to safeguard the interests and needs of disabled persons.[51] The then Ministry of Works, Transport and Communication was mandated to further the social integration of people with disabilities through transport communication policies,[52] support infrastructural developments undertaken by Government with regards to PWDs[53] and to provide national leadership and supervision for support of PWDs as users of the built environment.

The Ministry of Local Government, Lands and Housing is supposed to ensure that the development plans and policies designed by local authorities have adequate provisions for PWDs. The ministry established the Department of Social Welfare and Community Development in the early 1970s. The services delivered by the department, although not specifically targeting PWDs, benefit all those in need. The ministry is also in charge of the District Councils (Local Municipalities) which are also mandated to provide social welfare services to the whole population, PWDs inclusive, as well as to ensure that rehabilitative programmes derived from the policy are fully implemented. These districts are by far the closest to those PWDs found in rural communities and are able to provide such services to them so as to ensure that they are well taken care of.

As aforementioned, Botswana does not have any national human rights commission established in accordance with the Paris Principles. Instead under the 1996 National Policy on Care for People with Disabilities, there was established a National Coordinating Committee on Disability (NCCOD). The NCCOD was established with the aim that it will serve to ensure that the government ministries formulate strategic policies that are to

[50] As above.

[51] 1996 National Multi-sectoral Policy para 4.3.1.5.

[52] As above, para 4.3.1.6.

[53] As above.

better provide PWDs services in accordance with the National Policy.[54] Additionally, the NCCOD is tasked with monitoring the implementation of the 1996 National Policy, monitor, evaluate programmes that are developed within its framework and advise Government ministries on the provision of assistance to NGOs within the disability movement.[55] The NCCOD is therefore made up of senior government officers from the various ministries involved in disability issues, representatives of key non-governmental organisations and private individuals with or without disability who have exhibited a high level of interest, concern and dedication regarding care for disabled persons.[56] The NCCOD is at the moment inactive and it is only now that it is being revived to allow for better co-ordination of the policies and projects adopted and carried out under the auspices of the 1996 National Policy.

Notwithstanding the fact that there have been clear laudable attempts by the government to ensure that its policies mirrored the multisectoral policy objectives as embodied in the 1996 National Policy, there are still some implementation gaps. For example, the Disability and HIV and AIDS Trust (DHAT)[57] consolidated Report pointed out that:

> Major interventions around HIV and AIDS prevention, care, support and mitigation are being carried out, but little or none has targeted the disabled people as a special category. This is so because ASOs and government/municipal health departments have not considered disability as their issue and that HIV and AIDS programmes are a one size fits all.[58]

Perhaps that explains why in March 2010, the Government announced the establishment of the Coordinating Office for People with Disabilities (COPD) within the Office of the President. The office was established after the:

> Government recognised disability as a social phenomenon and that there was need for appropriate interventions to create a wholesome physical

[54] 1996 National Multisectoral Policy para 4.4.2.

[55] As above, para 4.3.3.

[56] As above, para 4.3.2.

[57] DHAT, an NGO based in Botswana dealing with issues of HIV and AIDS and disability rights in Botswana and advocate for the implementation of policies or interventions that are human rights sensitive.

[58] Disability and HIV and AIDS Trust (DHAT) consolidated Report 2007–2009, executive summary (on file with author).

> and social environment conducive to the achievement by persons with disabilities of their maximum human potential in private and public life.[59]

This office has the onerous task of developing and coordinating the implementation of policies and programmes aimed at empowering PWDs, guided by 1996 National Policy on Care for People with Disabilities.[60] The office is also responsible for liaising with stakeholders, including relevant government ministries, and people with disabilities on assisting and administering best practices for assisting the disabled.[61] Further, the office is also charged with monitoring whether other ministries or stakeholders are really providing PWDs with the services they deserve.[62] Currently the office, which is a single office housed within the office of the President, has a staff compliment of one person who is the coordinator and is a person with disability. The Office of the President is currently working with health facilities around the country to locate and develop a database of people with disabilities. Since the office is still at its embryonic stages, it is premature to assess its effectiveness. It is nonetheless worth pointing out that the one already visible shortcoming is that the office is currently not an implementation office but a referral office. People with disabilities who cannot make it all the way to the office are usually advised to seek assistance from the Ministry of Local Government.

Equally, the Revised National Policy undertakes to appoint a Coordinator for Disability Rights, or some other coordinating body, within the Office of the President, which office will handle matters relating to implementation of the Draft National Policy by organs of Government and other agencies. Further, the Draft National Policy aims at establishing an independent Commission on the Rights of Persons with Disabilities to promote, protect and monitor the fundamental rights and freedoms of PWDs, and to monitor the implementation of this Policy.[63]

59 Office for People with Disabilities available at http://www.gov.bw/en/Citizens/Citizen-News/Office-for-People-with-Disabilities (accessed 14 August 2010).

60 As above.

61 As above.

62 As above.

63 Earlier drafts of the policy indicates that the role of the National Commission for Disability will be to implement the policy on disability and coordinate the mainstreaming of the interventions of the policy, implement the policy, monitor and evaluate the impact of the policy and its programmes as well as to create an Advisory Committee to advice the ministries on strategies, policies and formulation of the new ones.

Civil Society organisations and disability rights in Botswana

One of the important actors in the disability movement is civil society organisations. Although government remain instrumental in the implementation of the 1996 National Policy on care for PWDs, the civil society play an important role in the national drive.

Botswana has a network of NGOs and community based groups that are focused on various thematic issues relating to disability rights. The various NGOs are coordinated by the Botswana Council for the Disabled (BCD) which is the umbrella body for those NGOs dealing with issues relating to disability. Furthermore and since the BCD is largely sponsored by the government, it provides support services as well as co-ordination of NGOs forming part of its network or NGOs providing rehabilitation services to PWDs. Its main role is co-ordinate the activities of its members, monitor the activities of its members and lobby the government in relation to matters pertaining to the rights of PWDs.

To that end and due to its representative nature, the BCD is the mouthpiece of members of the network. It maintains that it played a significant role in the promotion of the rights of PWDs in Botswana and it has emerged during the interviews conducted that the BCD was instrumental in the creation of the DPO within the Office of the President, and, as one of the major stakeholders, has been greatly involved in the drafting of the Revised Disability Policy.

It has also begun lobbying the government for the ratification of the Convention which they hope will get the government to ratify the CRPD. The reality of the situation however is that BCD is limited in its reach due to finances and most obviously lack of trained personnel in the various thematic areas relating to the rights of PWDs. For example, at the time of this study the BCD did not have any member of staff trained in law, a factor which makes it difficult for it to interrogate most legal issues.

Other than the involvement of BCD in the workings of the government, the civil society movement or disability movement in particular as regards disability issues in Botswana, is generally weak. This has in turn hindered the development of proper advocacy strategies for the rights of PWDs in Botswana. The civil society movement at present is not properly coordinated as the BCD is not made up of all organisations that seek to address issues relating to the rights of PWDs.

Establishing close links or working relationships with NGOs and the larger network of civil society is important as these groups are involved directly and indirectly in the promotion and protection of human rights.[64] NGOs may be involved in the implementation of various programmes and activities that could be important to PWDs, by bringing the expertise and ensuring an effective strategic alliance for the benefit of all parties.[65] Further, NGOs initiate national legislative policies and usually have the means to sponsor workshops or roundtable discussions on matters relating to such law reforms. It would thus be strategic for BCD to work closely with NGOs on various projects as it is usually resource constrained. Partnerships with NGOs are thus capable of closing human rights implementation gaps.

Charting the way forward: the rights of PWDs in modern day Botswana

Before the advent of the CRPD, various international instruments, to the exclusion of UN Convention on the Rights of the Child, did not make any reference to disability in their various documents. As a result of this seemingly deliberate policy to neglect the issues surrounding disability, PWDs continue to live in abject poverty, are continuously discriminated against or confronted with certain cultural barriers and social exclusions. It has also been noted that even though the various international instruments apply to persons with disabilities, they were rarely used to promote or protect the rights of PWDs. Most importantly, it has since transpired that the various treaties did not address the social, cultural, economic and legal barriers that prevented PWDs from participating in their communities.

[64] UN Human Rights Office of the High Commission for Human Rights *Professional Training Series No.12: Economic, social and cultural rights: A handbook for national human rights institutions* (2005) 38; also UN Human Rights Office of the High Commission for Human Rights *Monitoring the Convention on the Rights of Persons with Disabilities Guidance for human rights monitors Professional training series* No. 17 (2010)

[65] 'Working with the office of the United Nations High Commissioner for Human Rights, A handbook for NGOs', 20. 'Although many are fiercely independent and often irresponsible, NGOs provide vital early warning and conflict prevention or resolution functions within states that may be at risk. As their involvement has expanded and deepened, particularly in complex humanitarian emergencies, they have acquired more diverse functions, helping to provide security and informal backing for peace processes, facilitating reconciliation and reconstruction, and democracy building ... many NGOs are exploring ways to help prevent deadly conflicts and to work with members of societies who are at risk who are still committed to the protection of human rights, ...' J Stremlau 'African renaissance and international relations' (1999) 6 *South African Journal of International Affairs* 75.

The adoption of the CPRD presented, worldwide, a paradigm shift in so far as disability rights are concerned. Even though Botswana is not party to the Convention, it appears to have recognised this shift and is attempting to move – through its Revised National Disability Policy – towards this rights-based approach. The reality of the situation in Botswana is that the archaic 1996 National Policy is still applicable and all indications point out to the fact that it will still be applicable until the 2010 Draft Policy is adopted. The overall situation of PWDs in Botswana is that they are largely dependent on the government welfare system and do not have well-tailored programmes that could better address their low literacy levels, reduce poverty levels and empower them as well.

It appears that there are no deliberate efforts on the part of the government to ensure that the CRPD is ratified and domesticated. This is evidenced by the revision of the disability policy and the continued indications that it will take some time before Botswana enacts disability legislation. Tellingly, the effects of disability in Botswana are visible hence the ratification and domestication of the CRPD will go a long way in ensuring that the rights of PWDs are properly promoted and protected. It is beyond doubt that the main flaw in so far as the protection of the rights of PWDs is concerned is the absence of specific disability legislation. It is acknowledged that Botswana has made some significant strides in so far as breaking down the cultural barriers is concerned but there is indeed ample room for improvement. The existing government policy does not have specific rehabilitation and community integration programmes for PWDs. In addition, there are no practical guidelines for the easy implementation of the policy. The existing policy has attracted a lot of criticism. Firstly the policy does not adequately mainstream disability into resource allocation tools, National Development Plans and the budget. Secondly, there is a need for the mainstreaming of disability issues into all relevant areas such as all HIV and AIDS policy interventions.

At the moment, there is a discord between the disability policy and the HIV and AIDS policy. It appears that PWDs were not taken into account when the HIV and AIDS policy and programmes were formulated. Increased attention should be focused on PWDs because they are more vulnerable to the disease. They need education on HIV prevention because they face the same challenges that other people face and they are more disadvantaged. The erroneous underlying assumption by policy makers that persons with disabilities are incapable of maintaining sexual relationship has, for example, led to the exclusion of PWDs in most of the government's HIV and AIDS policy interventions. There is also need to mainstream issues of PWDs in other areas such as health, education and transport.

Conclusion

Government's support towards PWDs is commendable and cannot be ignored. It appears that positive measures are being undertaken to ensure that PWDs do not remain marginalised forever. However, there are many implementation gaps necessitating that the government take concerted efforts to ensure that the rights of PWDs are protected. It is therefore safe to conclude that Botswana is behind in terms of achieving the standards that are set by the CRPD or most of the objectives of the CRPD. This is mainly due to the absence of disability legislation in Botswana and as such, PWDs in Botswana continue to be marginalised on many fronts.[66] Given that Botswana's national policy is deficient and that Botswana does not have any disability specific legislation at all, this chapter proposes the revision of the policy and its harmonisation with other policies. Furthermore, it proposes that there should be a disability specific legislation which includes both specific rights and an institutional framework for the monitoring and compliance with the act and to enable its enforcement.

[66] 'Disabled people closed out of HIV-Aids programs – complaint' *Sunday Standard* 22 November 2009 http://www.sundaystandard.info/article.php?NewsID=6341&GroupID=1 (accessed 20 December 2010).

3

Protecting the disabled in Botswana: An anomalous case of legislative neglect

Jimcall Pfumorodze & Charles Manga Fombad

Introduction

Unlike many African countries, Botswana has had a stable economy which has experienced a positive growth for a long period of time. In addition, the country has experienced relative peace and tranquillity and there has not been any conflict or civil strife. However, in spite of all this, not enough attention has been paid to the marginalised in society. The gap between the rich and the poor is wide and widening each day. Although the social welfare system in the country is probably one of the best in Africa, persons with disabilities (PWDs) are almost forgotten. This chapter examines the legal framework for the protection of PWDs in the country. It will start with a brief background and an overview of the position of PWDs and is followed by an assessment of the legal framework for their protection. The next section will consider the prospects for the future and in its concluding remarks consider what needs to be done to improve the situation of PWDs in the country.

The backgound and context

Botswana (formerly Bechuanaland) was a British Protectorate until it gained independence in 1966. At the time of independence, Botswana was one of the poorest countries in Africa with a poorly developed economic, structural and educational infrastructure. However, soon after independence, huge diamond deposits were discovered and the wealth from these diamonds drove growth rates up and Botswana was one of the countries with the highest growth rates in the world during the late 1970s to mid 1990s. Since then, there was a massive expansion in health, education and general infrastructure. Today, Botswana is regarded as one of the economically stable countries in Africa and has enjoyed relative peace, stability and democratic governance since its independence in 1966.

The present population of Botswana is estimated to be around 1,8 million.[1] The 2001 Population Census shows that the population was around 1, 7 million. Of this population, 58 976 were people living with disabilities and this constituted 3,5 % of the entire population.[2] This census also shows that 66 % of PWDs are found in rural areas. Currently, PWDs are facing numerous challenges and these include, inaccessibility to public buildings; lack of financial assistance; lack of materials, for example, aids like walking sticks and wheelchairs and lack of education for affected children most of whom do not attend school; lack of equal participation in socio-economic activities, lack of adequate healthcare, especially for HIV and AIDS, and absence of disability specific legislation. The situation is sometimes exacerbated by stigmatisation and certain superstitious beliefs that regard certain forms of disability as a bad omen. Their situation has been described thus:

> Many disabled people live in isolation and shame behind closed doors because of their condition. Some are suffering additional emotional pains arising from embarrassment due to the inability to accept their conditions ... Many people link disability with superstition and revenge for the commission of crimes. The resultant attitudes then force the disabled to hide and shy away from seeking help even when it is available.[3]

Botswana started providing for welfare and other services to the disabled from independence in 1966.[4] In the early 1970s, the government com-

[1] Central Statistics Office, Botswana available at www.cso.gov.bw (accessed 19 August 2010).

[2] Central Statistics Office, Botswana (n 1 above).

[3] Integrated Regional Information Networks (IRIN) Botswana: Disabled policy under review 1 November 2006, available at http://www.irinnews.org/report.asp?ReportID=56144&SelectRegion=Southern_Africa&SelectCountry=BOTSWANA (accessed 20 August 2010).

[4] HA Furguson-Brown 'The Origins of the welfare and community development programmes in Botswana' (1996) 10 (3) *Pula Botswana Journal of African Studies* 66.

missioned a study on different disabilities that were in the country to enable it to establish an accurate and timely response.[5] This study revealed both the need for rehabilitation services and special education for people with disabilities. Consequently, in 1975, the Ministry of Health introduced the Special Services Unit for the Handicapped (SSUH). Currently, this unit has been developed into a full fledged Rehabilitation Services Division under the Department of Public Health in the Ministry of Health. Furthermore, the Ministry of Education has since 1977 developed the Special Education Division, with a mandate to plan and oversee education of people with special needs. In addition, the then Ministry of Local Government, Land and Housing established the Department of Social Welfare and Community Development in the early 1970s. The services of this department were broadly aimed at providing welfare services to the disadvantaged in society and in some instances the disabled also got assistance from this unit. This department has now been upgraded and transformed into the Department of Social Services.

The numerous welfare programmes under different government ministries mentioned above were complemented by non-governmental organisations (NGOs) which were involved and are still involved in providing various services to individuals and groups of PWDs in Botswana. There are also community-based organisations which were formed by individual communities which work with and for the people with disabilities. In 1980, the Botswana Council for the Disabled (BCD), an umbrella organisation for people with disabilities, was formed. It coordinates the operation of member NGOs which are involved in the rehabilitation, education, vocational and skills training for people with disabilities. It is also involved in advocacy work and has been very vocal in agitating for both a revised national policy on people with disabilities and in demanding specific legislation to deal with PWDs.

In 1996, Botswana adopted and approved a National Policy on Care for People with Disabilities[6]. It noted that disability related institutions and organisations operate in an uncoordinated manner. It therefore adopted a multisectoral national approach based on certain principles. Different ministries and offices were given various responsibilities. It called for co-ordination of multisectoral activities concerning care for PWDs.

5 HA Furguson-Brown (n 4 above).

6 This was adopted and approved through a presidential directive CAR: 5/96 dated February 1996.

The current policy has been much criticised and is under review. Perhaps the strongest criticism of this policy has been made by the Global Consult (2008) which describes it '[as] outdated and out of sync with global trends on disability issues.'[7] It feels that the fundamental flaw of this policy is that it fails to define 'disability.' As a result of this, the scope and coverage of the policy is uncertain. There is no laid down criteria and no uniformity in determining who is disabled and who is not. This uncertainty undermines its understanding by stakeholders and the society at large. The title of the policy is unfortunate. The title suggests that the policy is meant to guide the provision of "care" to those with disabilities. This reduces PWDs into objects of pity and recipients of charity and thus differs from modern approaches to disability which focus more on the rights of PWDs and not discretionary welfare grants. Even the terminology used in the policy is also outdated. It refers to 'disabled persons' yet the modern notion is 'people with disabilities.' The other criticism is that the structures for coordinating the implementation of the policy are very weak and their role and functions are not clearly spelt out. As indicated above, the government is in the process of formulating a new policy. It is hoped that this new policy will address the weaknesses of the present policy. Nevertheless, our main concern in this chapter is with the legal framework.

The legal framework for protecting PWDs in Botswana

To fully appreciate the present legal framework in Botswana, it is necessary to briefly review some of the important international instruments that protect PWDs and see to what extent Botswana's domestic position has been influenced by these.

Botswana's position with respect to international instruments protecting PWDs

The starting point is to note that all international human rights instruments also apply and attempt in various ways to protect PWDs. This is premised on the principles of universality, equality and non-discrimination which are embodied in these human rights instruments. However, there are some

[7] Global Consult (2008) 'National Disability Strategy (Multisectoral Strategic Plan)' 14. Global Consult is a consultancy company which was tasked by the Government of Botswana to look into the issues pertaining to PWDs.

international human rights instruments which specifically protect or have provisions that target PWDs.[8]

The United Nations (UN) system has a plethora of legal instruments protecting human rights. Some of these instruments are non-binding and some are only binding for those states that ratify or accede to them. These instruments can be categorised into two groups. The first category consists of instruments which are regarded as constituting the international bill of human rights. These are:

i) Universal Declaration of Human Rights 1948;
ii) International Covenant on Economic, Social and Cultural Rights (CESCR) 1966;
iii) International Covenant on Civil and Political Rights (ICCPR) 1966;
iv) Optional Protocol to the International Covenant on Civil and Political Rights;
v) Second Optional Protocol to the International Covenant on Civil and Political Rights, aiming at the death penalty.

The second category consists of instruments which are regarded as core international human rights instruments and their monitoring bodies.[9] Some

[8] Examples are UN Standard Rules on the Equalisation of Opportunities of Persons with Disabilities, 1993; Universal Declaration on Human Rights, 1948; Declaration on the Rights of Mentally Retarded Persons, 1971; Declaration on the Rights of Disabled Persons, 1975; Convention on the Rights of the Child, 1989; African Charter on Human and People's Rights, 1981 and Convention on the Rights of Persons with Disabilities and Optional Protocol, 2008. See also, I Brownlie and GS Goodwin-Gill *Basic Documents on Human Rights* (2006).

[9] These include:
i) International Convention on the Elimination of All Forms of Racial Discrimination 1965;
ii) International Covenant on Civil and Political Rights 1966;
iii) International Covenant on Economic, Social and Cultural Rights 1966;
iv) Convention on the Elimination of All Forms of Discrimination Against Women 1979;
v) Convention against Torture and Other Cruel, Inhuman or Degrading Treatment or Punishment 1984;
vi) Convention on the Rights of the Child 1989;
vii) International Convention on the Protection of the Rights of All Migrant Workers and Members of their Families 1990;
viii) International Convention for the Protection of All Persons from Enforced Disappearance;
ix) Convention on the Rights of Persons with Disabilities.

of these treaties have optional protocols which address specific issues.[10] Apart from the UN instruments, there are also African Union (AU) instruments which deal with human rights issues at regional level. These include:

(i) African [Banjul] Charter on Human and Peoples' Rights;
(ii) Protocol to the African Charter on Human and Peoples' Rights, on the establishment of an African Court on Human and Peoples' Rights;
(iii) Protocol to the African Charter on Human and Peoples' Rights on the Rights of Women in Africa;
(iv) African Charter on the Rights and Welfare of the Child.

A number of international instruments is also applicable to PWDs, however the UN's CRPD is the first international instrument which deals exclusively with PWDs. It is not the first human rights instrument to deal with disability concerns. However, unlike its predecessors, it offers persons with disabilities an unprecedented level of protection. The convention details the rights that all persons with disabilities should enjoy, and the obligations of states and other actors to ensure they are respected.

It is the first human rights convention to be concluded in the 21st century. It was adopted by the UN General Assembly on 13 December 2006 and was opened for signature and ratification on 30 March 2007. At the time of writing this chapter, there were at least 147 signatories to this convention and it has 99 ratifications. Furthermore, at the time of writing this chapter, the Optional Protocol to this convention has 89 signatories and 54 ratifications. Although it does not create new rights, the convention promotes and protects the full and equal enjoyment of human rights for PWDs. It contains a mix of both civil and political rights (for example, the right to

[10] These include:
i) Optional Protocol to the International Covenant on Civil and Political Rights 1966;
ii) Second Optional Protocol to the International Covenant on Civil and Political Rights, aiming at the abolition of the death penalty 1989;
iii) Optional Protocol to the Convention on the Elimination of Discrimination Against Women 1999;
iv) Optional Protocol to the Convention on the Rights of the Child on the involvement of children in armed conflict 2000;
v) Optional Protocol to the Convention on the Rights of the Child on the sale of children, child prostitution and child pornography 2000;
vi) Optional Protocol to the Convention against Torture and Other Cruel,Inhuman, or Degrading Treatment or Punishment 2002 and the
vii) Optional Protocol to the Convention on the Rights of Persons with Disabilities.

liberty) as well as economic, social and cultural rights (for example education). Article 4 (2) is to the effect that with respect to economic, social and cultural rights, states would only be expected to 'progressively realise' these rights.[11]

Article 3 sets out the general principles of the convention. These include dignity, autonomy and the freedom to make one's own choice, full and effective participation, respect for differences, equality of opportunity and accessibility.

Article 4 contains general obligations of the state parties above and beyond the more specific obligations contained in the individual articles. It requires that legislation should be adopted when needed, inconsistent legislation should be repealed, disability should be mainstreamed into policy formulation and active consultation should take place with PWDs and their representatives' organisations on all relevant matters. In short, article 4 converts the convention into a trigger for worldwide disability law reform.[12]

The convention has a separate protocol which is attached to the treaty enabling a committee to entertain individual complains and inquiries of systematic abuses. This protocol has to be ratified separately. A new committee on the rights of persons with disabilities will be the treaty's monitoring body.[13]

The convention provides a minimum framework of principles to guide states in developing more effective disability laws and policies. As pointed out earlier, the goal of the convention is not to create new rights, but to ensure, through the use of non-discrimination principles, that all existing rights are made effective for PWDs.

At the international level, the convention established the UN Committee on the Rights of Persons. This committee assesses state performance by reviewing periodic state reports. It entertains individuals or group complaints and also clarifies the norms of the convention. The committee will also provide authoritative interpretations of the convention. A Conference of State parties has also been established at international level with an extremely wide discretion to exchange policy perspective.

[11] See in general UN enable available at http://www.un.org/disabilities/default.asp?id=33 (accessed 25 August 2010).

[12] J TenBroek 'Future of disability rights advocacy and "the right to live in the world"' (2009) *Texas Journal on Civil Liberties & Civil Rights* 1.

[13] Art 1 of the Optional Protocol to the Convention on the Rights of Persons with Disabilities.

At the national level, article 4 of the convention requires that in making policies or laws and in improving them, there should be active consultation between governments and PWDs. A domestic institutional architecture for change is enshrined in Article 33. This article attempts to put in place a system of change at the national level that can transform the disability lawmaking processes. Article 33(1) demands the existence of a 'focal point' as well as co-ordination mechanism within government. Most governments in the world disperse responsibility for disability across many departments. Article 33 requires government departments to consult actively with persons with disabilities. The framers of the convention also require states to designate an independent body or set of bodies to 'promote, protect and monitor' progress in implementing the convention. Human rights commissions, civil rights commissions and national disability bodies such as the National Council on Disability will be at the forefront of such implementing bodies.

Although Botswana is a party to many AU instruments, insofar as the international bill of rights is concerned, it has only signed and ratified the ICCPR. Botswana has not signed and ratified the UN Convention on the Rights of People with Disabilities and its Optional protocol. Thus, it can be concluded that Botswana has not ratified many of these conventions which have a bearing on PWDs. Furthermore, even those it has ratified, it has not domesticated them and so generally speaking, they are not part of the law of Botswana.

The constitutional context

The 1966 Constitution of Botswana contains a bill of rights which covers civil and political rights. This constitution is now fairly old and in many respects outdated. Unlike most modern African constitutions, the Botswana constitution does not specifically prohibit discrimination on the grounds of disability. Modern African constitutions have anti-discrimination provisions which expressly deal with the issues of disability. Examples of these are the constitutions of Gambia, Ghana, Malawi, South Africa and Uganda. These provisions generally prohibit discrimination against PWDs without defining what exactly constitutes discrimination. The constitutions of Ghana, Malawi South Africa and Uganda require the legislature to take affirmative action to combat any discrimination against PWDs. This point must be expressed in a nuanced way to avoid misrepresentation. In the case of the South African Constitution, for example, though section 9(2) mandates affirmative action, it does not explicitly list the beneficiaries of affirmative action except to allude to their membership of a group that is disadvantaged. It is left to the legislature to identity the specific groups. In this connection, the Employment Equity Act has specified the groups as black people, women and people with disabilities.[14]

In Botswana, the constitutional anti-discrimination clause is found in section 3 as read with section 15 of the Constitution.[15] Section 3 is couched in broad terms and states:

> Whereas every person in Botswana is entitled to the fundamental rights and freedoms of the individual, that is to say, the right, whatever his race, place of origin, political opinions, colour, creed or sex, but subject to …

Section 15 specifically prohibits the making of discriminatory laws.[16] In addition, it prohibits public officers acting in their official capacity from treating any person in a discriminatory manner. Section 15 (3) defines discrimination to mean:

> affording different treatment to different persons, attributable wholly or mainly to their respective descriptions by race, tribe, place of origin, political opinions, colour or creed whereby persons of one such description are subjected to disabilities or restrictions to which persons of another such description are not made subject or are accorded privileges or advantages which are not accorded to persons of another such description.

According to this section, discrimination is forbidden only in respect of groups that are defined by race, tribe, and place of origin, political opinion, colour or creed. *Prima facie*, it would thus not be unconstitutional to treat differently persons who are not covered in the above categories. Section 15(3) of constitution does not specifically and categorically mention disability as one of the prohibited grounds of discrimination.

Although there has not been any constitutional challenge of legislation on the grounds that it allows for discrimination against the persons with disability, the courts have had the occasion to make pronouncements on other grounds of discrimination which are germane here. In the case of *Attorney-General v Unity Dow*[17] the respondent argued that certain provisions

[14] Section 1 of the Employment Equity Act.

[15] For a detailed discussion on constitutional anti-discrimination in Botswana see CM Fombad 'The constitutional protection against discrimination in Botswana' (2004) 53 *The International and Comparative Law Quarterly* 139.

[16] See Fombad (as above); DD Ntanda Nsereko *Constitutional Law in Botswana* (2004).

[17] *Attorney-General v Unity Dow* 1992 BLR 119.

of the Citizenship Act[18] were unconstitutional because they discriminated against her on the grounds of sex. It should be noted that section 15 (3) of the constitution did not specifically mention sex as one of the prohibited grounds for discrimination. The court nevertheless struck down that part of the Citizenship Act which allowed Botswana male citizens to pass on their Botswana citizenship to their children born of foreign women while it denied that same right to Botswana female citizens with children fathered by foreign men. It should be noted that this ground was not specifically listed in the Constitution. The court said that the grounds in section 15 (3) are merely indicative and not exhaustive. Amissah JP, said:

> I do not think that the framers of the Constitution intended to declare in 1966 that all potentially vulnerable groups or classes who would be affected for all time by discriminatory treatment have been identified and mentioned in the definition in section 15 (3). I do not think that they intended to declare that the categories mentioned in that definition were forever closed. In the nature of things, as far-sighted people trying to look into the future, they would have contemplated that with the passage of time not only the groups or classes which had caused concern at the time of writing the Constitution but other groups or classes needing protection would arise. The categories might grow or change. In that sense, the classes or groups itemised in the definition would be, and in my opinion, are by way of example of what the framers of the Constitution thought worth mentioning as potentially some of the most likely areas of possible discrimination.
>
> I am fortified in this view by the fact that other classes or groups with respect to which discrimination would be unjust and inhuman and which, therefore, should have been included in the definition were not. ***A typical example is the disabled***. *Discrimination wholly or mainly attributable to them as a group as such would, in my view, offend as much against section 15 as discrimination against any group or class.*[19]

A fairly recent case which, it is submitted, clarifies the position of PWDs a little bit further is *Makuto v The State.*[20] In this case, the Court of Appeal had another occasion to interpret the constitutional anti-discrimination provisions. The court set a precedent where HIV status could be implicitly understood as

[18] Citizenship Act (Cap 01:01).

[19] *Attorney-General v Unity Dow* BLR 119, 146–147. Our emphasis.

[20] *Makuto v The State* 2000 2 BLR 131 (CA).

being on the list of protected grounds from discrimination despite no specific mention of this in the Constitution. The Court had this to say:

> An identifiable group or class of persons who suffer discrimination as such group or class for no other reason than the fact of their membership of the group or class is entitled to challenge that law in court as invalid under the Constitution. If an extreme example may be given today to illustrate the point, I do not think that just because there is, as in this case, no mention of health or physical disability in section 15(3), legislation which provides that no physically disabled person shall be eligible for appointment in the public services can avoid a successful challenge for constitutional validity.[21]

Although the Court of Appeal in the passages quoted above specifically mentioned physical disability as forming a group or class of persons where discrimination is prohibited, these were only *obiter dicta*. Nevertheless, these provide a strong basis for arguing that discrimination on grounds of disability is prohibited by section 15 of the Botswana constitution.

The position under other pieces of legislation

There is no specific legislation or provision in any existing legislation which is designed to protect PWDs in Botswana. This is in stark contrast to some African countries where PWDs are given legislative protection. Examples include Ethiopia[22], Mauritius[23], South Africa[24], Zambia[25] and Zimbabwe[26]. However, the most comprehensive disability anti-discrimination laws are found in Australia[27], Canada[28], Hong Kong[29], Malta[30], the Philippines[31], the United Kingdom[32] and the United States.[33]

[21] *Makuto v The State* 2000 2 BLR 131 (CA) 134.

[22] The Rights of Disabled Persons Act to Employment, Proclamation 101 of 1994.

[23] Training and Development of Disabled Persons Act 9 of 1996.

[24] Employment Equity Act, 1998.

[25] Persons with Disabilities Act 33 of 1996.

[26] Disabled Persons Act, 1992.

[27] Disability Discrimination Act, 1992.

[28] Canadian Human Rights Act, RSC 1985.

[29] Disability Discrimination Ordinance, 1990.

[30] Equal Opportunities (Persons with Disabilities) Act, 2000.

[31] Magna Carta for Disabled Persons, 1992.

[32] Disability Discrimination Act, 1995 and Disability Rights Commission Act, 1999.

[33] Americans with Disabilities Act, 1990.

In spite of the anti-disability legislation deficit in Botswana, there are certain provisions in at least three pieces of legislation that could be interpreted in a manner that will protect PWDs. These are the Employment Act[34], the Workers' Compensation Act[35] and the Children's Act.[36] The relevant sections in these pieces of legislation will be briefly discussed hereunder.

Employment Act

No specific legislation presently exists for the protection of employees with disabilities against discriminatory practices or unfair dismissal from the workplace. The Employment Act is meant to provide for the terms and conditions, rights and obligations of the employers and employees. It also provides for specific rules pertaining to the employment of children, young persons and females.

This act is silent on the rights of people with disabilities. There is only one section where people with disabilities are mentioned. This is section 120, in Part XIII of the Act which is entitled 'Employment of the infirm and handicapped' which provides as follows:

> Where he considers it necessary or expedient in the interests of Botswana to do so, the Minister may make regulations in relation to the employment of persons affected by infirmity or physical handicap and, without prejudice to the generality of the foregoing, such regulations may regulate the conditions under which such persons are employed for the purpose of safeguarding their interests.

So far, the responsible minister has not yet made any such regulations. The focus of the act is primarily on the conditions of employment and this does not seem to cater for the pre-employment discrimination. Hence, it can be argued that even if these regulations were to be enacted by the minister, they would not adequately cover the issue of discrimination at the workplace.

Worker's Compensation Act

This act provides for compensation of workers for injuries suffered or occupational diseases contracted in the course of their employment or for death resulting from such injuries or diseases. According to section 11, an employer is liable to pay compensation for death or incapacity of the

[34] Employment Act (Cap 47:01).

[35] Workers' Compensation Act (Cap 47:03).

[36] Children's Act (Cap 28:04).

employee. The employer whose worker also suffers personal injury or occupational disease arising out of and in the course of the worker's employment shall be liable to pay compensation in accordance with the provisions of the Act. The Act creates three instances where a worker may be compensated due to incapacity. First, there is partial incapacity. This refers to incapacity of a temporary nature caused by injury or occupational diseases contracted, which reduces the earning capacity of a worker in every employment in which he or she was engaged at the time of the accident. Second, there is permanent partial incapacity. This means incapacity of a permanent nature caused by injury or occupational diseases contracted, which reduces the earning capacity of a worker in every employment in which he or she was engaged at the time of the accident. Third, there is total incapacity. This means such incapacity, caused by injury or occupational disease which prevents the worker from getting any employment he or she was capable of before the injury or disease.

In order to ensure that the funds for compensation are available, the employer is required to either have a compulsory insurance for this liability or deposit security with the Commissioner for Worker's Compensation. The determination concerning any payment of compensation is done by the Commissioner with the assistance of the Medical Board. Thus, the act provides some monetary relief for a person whose disability resulted from an injury or occupational disease at the workplace.

Prospects for the future

Without disability specific legislation in place, the ability of the government to protect PWDs is quite limited. It will continue to depend on the goodwill of the government of the day and the ability and willingness of public officers to implement government policies. The prospects for the future depend on two important factors. First, the ability of civil society to vigorously campaign for the enactment of disability legislation. Second, the willingness of the judiciary to be sensitive, bold and creative when dealing with PWDs cases.

A resolute civil society and legal change

The prospects of having disability specific legislation in Botswana in the near future are not good. There is therefore a need for those who are interested in the realisation of disability rights to campaign vigorously in order to convince the government to seriously take this on board. The Botswana civil society can play a crucial part in this regard. The role of the Botswana Council for the Disabled (BCD) which is an umbrella organisation with 30 organisations dealing with issues pertaining to PWDs will be crucial. This organisation was set up in1980 and its main role is to coordinate the activities of all NGOs providing rehabilitation services to PWDs as well as the promotion of organisations and associations for PWDs and monitoring their activities. The mandate of BCD includes representation, coordination, advice and support to its NGO members and advocacy for the rights of people with disabilities in Botswana. The BCD is recognised by the government of Botswana as the official representative body for the NGO disability movement and for disability issues generally. Thus, due to its representative nature, this organisation can play an important role and is a very critical voice in advocating for the rights of PWDs. In doing so, the role of this organisation is to gather views from the entirety of its diverse membership in trying to lobby the government and other stakeholders. In addition to this mother body, PWDs organisations themselves also have a role to play since any policy and legislative measures undertaken by the government have a direct bearing on them. They should get their members more actively involved in the design of programmes that both empowers them as well as promotes their welfare and dignity.

The BCD has been very active in the drafting of the new national disability policy and it has made written submissions some of which were taken on board. In addition, this organisation is also part of the national steering committee for the implementation of the disability policy. However, it faces several challenges. These include lack of information and new technologies in the disability field, inadequate communication between members and inadequate networking with stakeholders. The most serious challenge is that this organisation is funded by the government and has no alternative sources of funding. In addition, it currently has no fundraising projects other than those funded by government funds.

Apart from the BCD, there are also other human rights organisations. These include Ditshwanelo–Botswana Centre for Human Rights and the University of Botswana Legal Aid Clinic. The most active NGO in the country has been the Ditshwanelo–Botswana Centre for Human Rights, an advocacy organisation that was founded in 1993 and has as its mission, to educate, research, counsel and mediate human rights issues, with particular reference to people who are marginalised and disempowered.[37] It has been at the forefront of the campaign to abolish the death penalty in Botswana.[38] It can use its experience and share it with other organisations in promoting the rights of PWDs.

Another institution worth mentioning is the Legal Clinic operated by the staff and students of the Law Department of the University of Botswana, which provides some free legal advice service. The Clinic provides the only social service of its kind in Botswana. It tries to cater for those who cannot afford the services of a lawyer and uses a means test to decide whether a person qualifies for assistance. Although the Legal Clinic tries to advise indigent clients on all problems, it does not usually accept criminal matters and concentrates on issues such as divorce, maintenance and other family problems, housing problems, hire purchase, employment, including worker's compensation, motor vehicle insurance claims, debt collection and attachment and insurance. It therefore plays a very limited role in dealing with human rights issues. The Legal Aid can also play its part by representing PWDs and giving them legal advice.

In addition to advocacy and lobbying, the civil society can also engage in public interest litigation on issues affecting PWDs. Sometimes, in the absence of legislation dealing with PWDs, the courts can advance the rights of PWDs through judicial activism. However, the courts can make such progressive decisions only if proper cases are brought before them. Public interest litigation can play at least two important roles. First, if the plaintiff's claim succeeds, this advances the recognition of the rights and protection of PWDs. Second, whether the case succeeds or not, a public interest case carries with it a lot of publicity which can be used in the advocacy and lobbying. This has also an effect of changing the public awareness and attitude towards PWDs. This may add momentum to the enactment of a disability specific legislation.

Civil society can also campaign vigorously for the signing, ratification and domestication of international human rights instruments which deal with PWDs. This would enhance the rights of PWDs in Botswana. Zander underlined the importance of putting pressure on the government in the following words:

[37] For more on the Ditshwanelo–Botswana Centre for Human Rights, see the website at http://www.ditshwanelo.org.bw/ (accessed 6 September 2011).

[38] For more on the Ditshwanelo–Botswana Centre for Human Rights' activities related to the death penalty, see http://www.ditshwanelo.org.bw/index/Current_Issues/Death_Penalty.htm (accessed 15 March 2011).

> ... the vested interests of all governments is to preserve the normal ways of doing things and to resist pressure for change. Government, of whatever political complexion, is usually moved to change things only when the pressure to do so becomes greater than the convenience of leaving things as they are.[39]

The judicial role

There are two challenges which the judiciary can try to resolve. The first one is the absence of any disability specific legislation and the second one is the non-ratification or non-domestication of important conventions which may improve the situation of PWDs. As the *Unity Dow* case has shown, the judiciary can still intervene in an activist manner that will help PWDs.

There are a number of ways in which human rights instruments can impact positively on the quality of human rights protection in Botswana.[40] This section will discuss how these international human rights instruments can be useful in adjudication before the courts. An international human rights instrument which has been signed, whether or not it has been ratified or domesticated, can be used as an aid to statutory interpretation. In the *Unity Dow* case, Amissah JP cited with approval the following passage from the trial judge in the same case:

> I bear in mind that signing the Convention [the OAU Convention] does not give it the power of law in Botswana but the effect of the adherence by Botswana to the Convention must show that a construction of the section which does not do violence to the language but is consistent with and in harmony with the Convention must be preferable to a 'narrow construction' which results in a finding that section 15 of the Constitution permits discrimination on the basis of sex.[41]

In relation to the significance of international human rights instruments, Fombad has made the following two pertinent observations:

> Firstly, the mere fact that a human rights instrument has not been incorporated through an Act of Parliament does not mean that courts in Botswana should pay no regard to it. Courts must consider them seriously

[39] M Zander *A bill of rights?* (1997) 65.

[40] International human rights instruments may be relevant as an integral part of the domestic law upon incorporation into national law; or as an aid to statutory interpretation; or as part of common law of Botswana; or in the activities of human rights institutions.

[41] *Unity Down* Case 1992 BLR 119 (n 17 above) 154.

when interpreting statutory language and wherever possible reach a conclusion that is consistent with Botswana's international obligations, unless of course, it is absolutely clear that Parliament wanted to disregard or break these treaty obligations. Secondly, one could go further to posit that the importance of international human rights instruments is such that courts should not only consider their provisions but should also take account of their philosophy and the practice that has emerged, as the Court of Appeal did in the *Dow* case. Unforeseen situations could thus be resolved in an imaginative and creative manner by the judges without waiting for Parliament to enact implementing legislation and in this manner the courts can reflect the changing perceptions when dealing with an old Constitution like Botswana's.[42]

Proposals for change

There are three main approaches to legislation on PWDs namely criminal law approach, constitutional law approach and civil rights approach.[43] Botswana's constitution does not specifically mention discrimination on the grounds of disability. This can only be inferred as was discussed above. There is a need for the constitution to be reviewed so that it can specifically prohibit any discrimination based on grounds of disability.

It is recommended that Botswana should have specific legislation dealing with PWDs. This legislation should be modelled along the CRPD with some modifications to meet local circumstances. Five important issues need to be addressed by any future piece of disability legislation.

The first issue concerns the definition of disability and people with disabilities. The two concepts of disability and PWDs are very central to any disability legislation. They determine who has rights and expectations under such legislation.[44] Only someone who comes within the definition can enjoy the protection of such a law. Before advocating for specific rights of

42 CM Fombad 'The Protection of human rights in Botswana: An overview of the regulatory framework' in Fombad, CM (ed) *Essays on the Law of Botswana* (2007) 11–12.

43 For details on these three approaches see T Degener 'Disability discrimination law: A global comparative approach' in L Anna & G Caroline (eds) *Disability rights in Europe: From theory to practice* (2005).

44 BJ Doyle *Disability discrimination: The new law* (1996) 13; WD Goren *Understanding the American Disabilities Act* (2006) 2.

people with disabilities, there is a need for a clear definition of the scope and coverage of the term disability. Traditionally, the term disability referred to the notion of a 'handicapped person'. This notion has been replaced with the concept of a 'person with disability' to correct the inherently socially constructed attitude that some members of society are 'disabled'. Thus, there is a need for a definition which is broad and also which reflects the modern trends of a human rights approach to disability.

The second issue concerns the employment of PWDs. Any future legislation must address the issue of equal access to opportunities for employment. Currently, the legislation does not make any special provision for employment or management of people with disabilities at the workplace. Any new disability legislation should cover discrimination of applicants with disabilities in the recruitment and selection process, as well as discrimination against PWDs while in an employer's employment. The law should use broad and comprehensive general wording to cover all aspects of recruitment process and the employment relationship. Certain employment opportunities such as promotions, transfer, training or receipt of benefits, must be taken into account. In line with the principle of reasonable accommodation, any proposed disability legislation should place a duty on employers to make reasonable adjustments.[45] Furthermore, discrimination against contract workers should also be prohibited. In addition, many employers do not have policies guiding the employment of people with disabilities. Thus, there is a need for legislation to address these discrepancies. There is also a need for the legislation to provide incentives to companies in the private sector who employ PWDs as this may encourage others to do so.

The third issue concerns the problem of access to facilities and amenities by PWDs. In Botswana, most public and private buildings do not provide easy access to PWDs. In addition, roads and parking facilities also seriously limit the access of PWDs. For instance, many workplaces are not easily accessible to PWDs and this contributes to the exclusion from the employment of this group. There is thus a need to provide both for the policy and legislative framework to enable easy access to public buildings by people with disabilities.[46]

[45] For instance, sec 6 of the English Disability Discrimination Act 1995 provides that where any physical feature of premises occupied by trade an employer place a disabled person at a substantial disadvantage in comparison with non-disabled persons, it is the duty of the employer to take reasonable steps to mitigate the effects of such a physical feature.

[46] As above.

Fourthly, there is a need for a national policy framework and legislation which provides for welfare benefits for PWDs and even for their caregivers. These benefits may take the form of disability grants which are given to PWDs who are unemployed. Grants may also be given to parents of minor children with disabilities to assist them with the upbringing of the child. There is also a need for microfinancing for PWDs so that they can start their own income generating projects.

Finally, there is need for an all inclusive system of education to be introduced. Although Botswana has a national policy on education which provides for special education, there is no legislation that gives effect to this. Thus, there is a need to deal with the issue of education by law rather than merely through policy prescriptions which may or may not be followed. With respect to childhood education, there is a need to incorporate the concept of inclusive education.[47] Inclusive education implies an environment in which a child will be able to learn in his or her own way, differently from other children, and still belong in the mainstream setting. Inclusive schools with no enrolment criteria are ideal because it is assumed that everyone can be taught in the same environment, according to their needs.

Education is key to emancipating and empowering PWDs. Although special education was introduced in Botswana in the 1970s, the availability of such facilities are limited especially in rural areas. Furthermore, no legislation compels a parent of a child with disabilities to send that child to school. A study carried out by Global Consult (2008)[48] revealed that educational and training facilities do not cater for people with disabilities and that if people with disabilities are enrolled, they face many barriers of access to the same quality of education as non-disabled people. These barriers include physical ones and others emanating from learning materials designed for non-disabled persons. It was also noted that most teachers and other employees of educational and training institutions are not trained to deal with people with impairment. Given the crucial role which education plays in the employability of people with disabilities, this matter needs to be taken seriously if there are to be equal opportunities for employment of people with disabilities.

[47] For a discussion on inclusive education see J Schoonheim and D Ruebain 'Reflections on inclusion and accommodation in childhood education: From international standard setting to national implementation in A Lawson & C Gooding (eds) *Disability rights in Europe: From theory to practice* (2005) 163.

[48] Global Consult (2008) (n 7 above).

Conclusion

This chapter tried to review the legal framework within which PWDs are protected in Botswana and the attempts taken by the government since independence to alleviate the plight of these people. It shows that on the ground, there are welfare services going on either from the government or from some NGOs. There is no legislation specifically designed to protect PWDs. The current efforts by the government to review the national policy is welcome since there is a possibility that the policy once approved, will be followed by a legislation which creates enforceable rights for people with disabilities. All these are positive steps.

However, given the level of economic development, the political stability and an advanced social security system in the country, the level at which the plight of people with disabilities have not been given adequate attention and support is appalling. The process for revising the national policy and the enactment of disability legislation is taking too long. The prospects for the future are not bright given that Botswana has not even signed the UN Convention on the Rights of People with Disabilities to indicate its willingness to be bound by it. Thus, there is a need for intense advocacy and lobbying if the rights of people with disabilities are to be secured under the law in Botswana.

4

The right to equality in the workplace for persons with physical disabilities in Malawi: Does the convention on the rights of persons with disabilities offer any hope?

Victor Jere

Introduction

> Throughout the ages, the treatment of people with disabilities has brought out some of the worst aspects of human nature. Too often, those living with disabilities have been seen as objects of embarrassment, and at best, of condescending pity and charity.[1]

People with disabilities (PWDs) in Malawi are among the poorest and most disadvantaged.[2] Only 20% of PWDs have access to schools and only 26% to workplace, with welfare and vocational training available to only 5% of those who need it.[3] PWDs have historically endured exclusion and marginalisation and have frequently been excluded from jobs and denied access to opportunities for social interaction.[4]

In 1994, Malawi adopted a new constitution which amongst others, is premised on the recognition of the inherent dignity and worth of each human being,[5] non-discrimination and equality before the law.[6] Furthermore, section

[1] The then United Nations Secretary-General, Kofi Annan, welcoming the adoption of the Convention of the Rights of Persons with Disabilities, 13 December 2006.

[2] International Labour Organisation 'Promoting the employability and employment of people with disabilities through effective legislation in Southern Africa' ILO Malawi country report (2006) 8.

[3] 'Living conditions of people with activity limitations in Malawi: A national representative study' Stiftelsen for industriell og teknisk forskning (SINTEF) Health research report (2004) 17 and 111, available at http://www.sintef.no/helse (accessed 20 August 2010).

[4] *Eldridge v British Columbia (Attorney General)* 1977 151 DLR (4 th) 577, 612 (SCC).

[5] Sec 12(iv) of the Constitution.

[6] Sec 20 of the Constitution; Sec 31(3) also guarantees to every person the right to fair wages and equal remuneration for work of equal value without distinction or discrimination of any kind, in particular on basis of gender, disability or race.

29 of the constitution guarantees to every person the right to work, engage in economic activity and pursue a livelihood anywhere in Malawi. With particular reference to PWDs, section 13(g) of the constitution calls upon the state to support PWDs through greater access to public places, fair opportunities in employment and the fullest possible participation in all spheres of Malawian society.

Other than the constitution, and a cursory provision in the Technical, Entrepreneurial and Vocational Education and Training Authority Act (TEVETA) of 1999 and the Employment Act of 2000,[7] the Handicapped Act of 1971 is the only law that attempts to deal specifically with the issue of PWDs though the Act uses the term 'handicapped persons.' The Act establishes the Malawi Council for the Handicapped (MACOHA) whose responsibility is to promote the welfare of PWDs by amongst others, advising the minister on matters relating to PWDs and administering vocational schools, special training and rehabilitation centres for PWDs.

In 1998, Malawi launched a policy known as Vision 2020 which set out the development progress which is to be achieved by the year 2020. One of the challenges Vision 2020 highlights is the issue of PWDs for which the policy recommends the enactment of a Disability Act, a policy for empowering PWDs and a review of the institutional framework. In the same year, the Ministry for Social Development and Persons with Disabilities[8] was established with a mission amongst others, of formulating and providing policy direction aimed at ensuring that PWDs have equal access to essentials of life and to participate fully in all areas of socio-economic development so as to make Malawi an inclusive society for all. Subsequent thereto, a National Policy on Equalisation of Opportunities for Persons with Disabilities was adopted.[9] Its main objective was to integrate fully PWDs in all aspects of life, thereby equalising their opportunities and enhancing their dignity and well being.

An Equalisation of Opportunities for Persons with Disabilities Bill has been drafted by the government[10] with a view of replacing the Handicapped Act of 1971 which is clearly outdated.[11] It is aimed at better protecting the

[7] Sec 5.

[8] Established in May 1998.

[9] Launched in March 2006.

[10] Originally drafted in March 2008 though it has over time been revised.

[11] According to the Ministry of Justice, the bill has been submitted to cabinet for its consideration before it is taken to parliament for debate and passing into law.

rights of PWDs by, amongst others, eliminating discrimination and better promoting the rights of PWDs especially in the workplace. It widens the scope of discrimination in that discrimination now includes the failure to make reasonable accommodation to the known physical or mental limitations of an otherwise qualified individual with a disability.[12] As the 2006 International Labour Organisation (ILO) country profile of Malawi[13] notes, Malawi is moving towards a right-based approach to disability and anti-discrimination legislation.

On 13 December 2006, the United Nations General Assembly adopted the Convention on the Rights of Persons with Disabilities (CRPD) which was opened for signature on 30 March 2007. Malawi signed the CRPD on 27 September 2007.[14] On 3 April 2008, the CRPD received its twentieth ratification, triggering its entry into force 30 days later.[15] It marks a paradigm shift in attitudes and approaches to PWDs. It takes to a new height the movement from viewing PWDs as 'objects' of charity, medical treatment and social protection towards viewing them as 'subjects' with rights, who are capable of claiming those rights and making decisions for their lives based on their free and informed consent as well as being active members of society. The main purpose of the CRPD is to promote, protect and ensure the full and equal enjoyment of all human rights and fundamental freedoms by PWDs and to promote respect for their inherent dignity.[16] In its preamble, the CRPD recognises that disability is an evolving concept and that it results from the interaction between persons with impairments, attitudinal and environmental barriers that hinder their full and effective participation in society on an equal basis with others.

The CRPD is intended as a human rights instrument with an explicit, social development dimension.[17] The CRPD aims at filling the gap that was there in other human rights instruments which despite their existence PWDs continue to face barriers in their participation as equal members of society. It adopts a broad categorisation of PWDs and reaffirms that all persons with all types of disabilities must enjoy all human rights and fundamental

[12] Sec 30(2)(d).

[13] ILO Malawi country report (n 2 above) 20.

[14] Malawi ratified the CRPD on 27 August 2009.

[15] Art 45(1) provides that the Convention is to enter into force after the thirtieth day of the deposit of the twentieth instrument of its ratification or accession.

[16] CRPD, art 1.

[17] CRPD, Preamble, para (y).

freedoms. It clarifies and qualifies how all categories of rights apply to PWDs and identifies areas where adaptations have to be made for PWDs to effectively exercise their rights and areas where their rights have been violated, and where protection of rights must be reinforced.

This chapter analyses the current legal framework in so far as the right to equality and non-discrimination in relation to the workplace and the right to work for PWDs is concerned. Firstly, it defines disability before looking at what the right to work entails. Then it looks at the CRPD in so far as the right to equality and the right to work for PWDs are concerned. The chapter then analyses Malawi's current constitutional, legislative and policy protection of rights of PWDs in so far as the right to equality in the workplace is concerned. The chapter argues that the current constitutional and legal framework in Malawi does not effectively protect the right to equality and non-discrimination in the workplace for PWDs and as such is not in conformity with international standards. Further, the chapter argues that no meaningful progress in implementing the CRPD has been achieved so far. The chapter concludes by offering some suggestions on how the Malawian legal framework can be reformed to comply with international standards, especially the CRPD. In this chapter, the term PWDs refers to persons whose disability arises due to impairment of the limbs.

Disability defined

What disability is and who may or may not be a person with disability are fairly contested matters, as there is no universally accepted definition of disability.[18] This arises from the fact that PWDs do not form a homogeneous group, and there are different kinds of barriers, which have to be overcome in different ways.[19] Thus, disability is a concept that is not susceptible to a rigid, incontestable definition, and much depends on the context. It is capable of a very fluid and encompassing construction so as to include virtually everyone at some stage in their lives.[20] According to Shearer, 'each and every one of us knows moments of inability, moments when the body and

[18] BM Altman 'Disability definitions, models, classification schemes and applications' in GL Albrecht, KD Seelman & M Bury (eds) *Handbook of disability studies* (2001); S Briesenden 'Independent living and the medical model of disability' (1986) 1 *Disability, Handicap and Society* 173.

[19] World Programme of Action (WPA) para 22, adopted by the Vienna World Conference on Human Rights A/CONF.157/23 12 July 1993.

[20] S Wendell *The rejected body: Feminist philosophical reflections on disability* (1996) 13.

mind that we take for granted let us down, refused to work for us.'[21] The line between these moments of inability and finding ourselves categorised as disabled is only one of degree, a matter which is as dependent upon the demands which society makes upon us as is the inherent quality of our inability.[22] However, most times, society only recognises certain obvious deviations from what is regarded as normal as disability. According to the Kenya National Commission on Human Rights, unlike other social distinctions like gender, age or colour, disability has no singularly overarching trait which is obvious in all people who either are categorised or regard themselves as disabled.[23]

The World Health Organisation (WHO)'s International Classification of Impairments, Disabilities and Handicaps of 1980, defined disability as a term which, in relation to an individual, describes a functional limitation (for performing tasks, skills and behaviour) which he or she may have arising from physical, intellectual or sensory impairment, medical conditions or mental illness. Such impairments, conditions or illnesses may be permanent or transitory in nature. This definition is founded on the 'medical' model of disability which is preoccupied with the medical aspects of disability. Crossley describes the medical model in the following terms:

> The defining characteristic of the medical model is its view of disability as a personal trait of the person in whom it inheres. The individual is the locus of the disability and, thus, the individual is properly understood as needing aid and assistance in remedying the disability. Under this view, while the cause of impairments may vary, the disabled individual is viewed as innately, biologically different and inferior. The physical difference of the individual is often apparent, and the nondisabled see the individual's inferiority and resulting social disadvantage as flowing from that physical difference. Thus, according to the medical model of disability, the disabled individual's problem lies in her impairment.[24]

The medical model has been criticised for accentuating the stigma attached to disability because of its binary divide between normality and abnormality

[21] A Shearer *Disability: Whose handicap?* (1981) 1.

[22] Shearer (n 21 above) ix.

[23] 'Objects of pity or individuals with rights: The right to education for children with disabilities' (2007) 7, report by the Kenya National Human Rights Commission, 7.

[24] M Crossley 'The disability kaleidoscope' (1999) 74 *Notre Dame Law Review* 621,649–650; NB Miller *Everybody's different: Understanding and changing our reactions to disabilities* (1999) 34.

with no continuum of human abilities representing human diversity.[25] Failure to conform to the norm, results in one being labelled as a deviant both in a biological and social sense.

On the other hand, the social model conceives disability in a more holistic manner that takes into account extrinsic factors in the creation of disability. It seeks to rebut the assumption of organic inferiority so as to affirm the equal worth and human dignity of PWDs and implicate society in the creation of disability.[26] The social model involves a switch away from focusing on physical limitations of particular individuals to the way physical and social environments impose limitations upon certain groups or categories of people.[27]

Subsequently, the WHO's International Classification of Functioning adopted the social model and defined disability as follows:

> A disability is the *social* outcome of a physical or mental *impairment*. Impairment only becomes a handicap in the context of a given society, often because this society does not respect the needs and the rights of its citizens living with impairment. Disability, therefore, is not a natural, but a social fact. Furthermore, disability is not only an individual destiny, but also the outcome of situations and decisions for which the disabled person is no more responsible than any other citizen, like bad sanitary and health conditions, war, etc. The disabled person carries the consequences of collective situations and decisions. Society, in turn, has a special collective responsibility to eliminate the exclusions that turn impairment into a disability.[28]

The CRPD states that PWDs include those who have long-term physical, mental, intellectual or sensory impairments which in interaction with various barriers may hinder their full and effective participation in society on an equal basis with others.[29] This reflects the 'social model of disability,' and leaves room for those interpreting and implementing the CRPD to utilise

[25] C Ngwena 'Deconstructing the definition of disability under the Employment Equity Act: Social deconstruction' (2006) 22 *South African Journal of Human Rights* 626.

[26] H Hahn 'Accommodation and the ADA: Unreasonable bias or biased reasoning' (2000) 21 *Berkeley Journal of Employment and Labour Law* 171.

[27] M Oliver *Social work with disabled people* (1983) 23.

[28] World Health Organisation *International classification of functioning, disability and health* assembly (2001).

[29] Art 1.

differing conceptualisations of disability as they evolve over time. The social model of disability understands disability as a social construct, not as an inherent characteristic. Rather than seeking to change or alter the person with disabilities, the social model instead emphasises the removal of societal barriers that exclude people with disabilities, including environmental, institutional and attitudinal barriers. Furthermore, the preamble recognises the 'diversity of persons with disabilities', thus reminding those implementing the CRPD that persons with disabilities are a heterogeneous group encompassing people with a range of impairments and functional capacities from a wide variety of social, ethnic and religious contexts.

Nowadays as demonstrated by the CRPD, a human rights model towards issues of disability has been adopted. At the core of this model is the notion that all human beings regardless of their disabilities are equal and have rights that are inalienable. Firstly, it focuses on the inherent dignity of human beings and, after that if necessary, on the person's medical impairments. The practical consideration for policy makers arising from this perspective is the imperative of focusing on a person's abilities rather than his or her disability. Secondly, it places the individual at the centre of all decisions affecting that person. Finally, it locates the problem of disability in society rather than inside the person. This last aspect of the 'human rights' model of disability traces the 'problem' of disability to the absence of action by state and non-state actors for mitigating the difference represented by disability. These institutions have responsibilities for tackling socially created obstacles to ensure full respect of the dignity and equal rights of all persons.[30]

The right to work

According to the Kenyan National Human Rights Commission, the poverty levels which PWDs face are far higher in relation to the rest of society. The opportunities for livelihood available to PWDs are less obvious since disability undermines the actual or perceived ability of a person to interact in educational, economic, social or indeed political arenas. Poverty itself breeds disability and disability is a harbinger for more poverty.[31] The breaking of this poverty trap calls for a conscious and concerted effort by society to ensure the rights

[30] Oliver (n 27 above).

[31] Report of the Kenya National Human Rights Commission (n 23 above).

of PWDs.[32] PWDs are human beings, endowed with human rights and should be guaranteed equal opportunity through the elimination of all socially determined barriers which exclude or restrict full participation in society.[33]

Recognition of the inherent dignity and of the equal and inalienable rights of all human beings is the foundation of freedom, justice and peace in the world.[34] The Universal Declaration of Human Rights (UDHR) guarantees to every person the right to work, to free choice of employment, to just and favourable conditions of work and to protection against unemployment.[35] Furthermore, the UDHR guarantees to every individual the right to a standard of living adequate for the health and well-being of himself and of his family.[36] All human beings are entitled to the enjoyment of the rights in the UDHR without any limitations or qualifications.[37]

It also provides for the right to work under equitable and satisfactory conditions as well as guarantees the right to dignity and the enjoyment of the rights and freedoms recognised in the UDHR without distinction of any kind.[38] Similar guarantees are also provided for in the International Covenant for Economic, Social and Cultural Rights (CESCR).[39]

The right to work is essential for the realisation of all other human rights and forms an inseparable and inherent part of human dignity.[40] All human beings, including PWDs, have the right to be able to work and thereby live in dignity. The right to work contributes to the survival of the individual and to that of his or her family and also to the individual's development and recognition within the community, especially when work is freely chosen or accepted.[41] Work is a defining feature of human existence, a means of sustaining life and of meeting basic needs.[42] PWDs generally experience

[32] 'Achieving equal employment opportunities for persons with disabilities through legislation' http://www.ilo.org/public/english/employment/skills/disability/index (accessed 18 August 2010).

[33] Vienna Declaration and Programme of Action adopted by the World Conference on Human Rights of 1993, para 64.

[34] UDHR 1948, Preamble para 1.

[35] Art 23(1).

[36] Art 25(1).

[37] Art 2.

[38] UDHR, arts 2, 5 & 15.

[39] Preamble, para 1; arts 2, 6, 7 & 11.

[40] General Comment No 18 of the Committee on Economic, Social and Cultural Rights, para 1.

[41] (n 39 above); The preamble to the International Labour Organisation Convention No 168 of 1988.

[42] KQ Hall 'Feminism, disability and embodiment' (2002) 14 *National Women's Studies Association Journal* (vii).

problems and difficulties in carrying out their daily activities and in their ability to fully participate in society. They experience physical and social barriers in the form of reduced accessibility to local services such as schools, hospitals and the workplace, discrimination and negative attitudes in society at large.[43] PWDs are often marginalised and belong to the poorest segments of society.[44] Unemployment in Malawi is generally high with the percentage of PWDs unemployed being higher than that of non-disabled people. According to the Stiftelsen for industriell og teknisk forskning (SINTEF) 2004 report, 58% of disabled people are unemployed as compared to 53% of non-disabled people.[45] The ILO 2006 country report for Malawi stated that only 26% of PWDs have access to the work place.[46] The major contributing factor to this is the failure to adopt positive measures that would allow PWDs to achieve a level playing field with non-disabled people.

The Convention on the Rights of Persons with Disabilities and its implications on PWDs and the right to work

Even though an extensive body of non-binding international documents addressing PWDs was already in existence when the CRPD was being contemplated, the philosophical approach of many of these documents was inconsistent with the principle of equality and full societal inclusion of PWDs. Furthermore, the non-binding nature of these international documents meant that they were infrequently implemented by governments. There was also a lack of a monitoring mechanism to gauge the implementation of these documents with only the United Nations Standard Rules on the Equalisation of Opportunities for PWDs having a Special Rapporteur to monitor its implementation.[47] Furthermore, despite the fact that binding international law has always been equally applicable to PWDs, governments and treaty

[43] Stiftelsen for industriell og teknisk forskning (SINTEF) Health research report (n 3 above) 4.

[44] Vienna Declaration and Programme of Action (n 33 above) para 46.

[45] Stiftelsen for industriell og teknisk forskning (SINTEF) Health research report (n 3 above).

[46] ILO Malawi country report (n 2 above).

[47] K Guernsey *et al Convention on the Rights of persons with Disabilities: Its implementation and relevance for the World Bank* (2007) 3, discussion paper no 0712 available at http:// www. worldbank.org/sp (accessed 1 August 2010)

monitoring bodies have not historically been attentive to the situation of PWDs and the barriers they face to fully enjoy their human rights. This was clearly revealed by an in-depth study commissioned by the Office of the High Commissioner for Human Rights, which concluded that PWDs had been "invisible" in, for example, the international human rights system.[48] The report recommended the adoption of a specific Convention dealing with PWDs which would, amongst others, encourage mainstreaming of disability throughout international law. Many developing countries realised that they would not be able to reach their Millennium Development Goals as long as PWDs continued to be discriminated against and marginalised from society. Thus, the international community came to see a convention such as the CRPD as an important tool to utilise in both ensuring full equality and inclusion of PWDs, and in achieving a wide variety of development goals.[49]

The CRPD does not seek to create new rights for PWDs, but rather elaborates and clarifies existing obligations for countries within the disability context. It establishes a committee of experts to monitor its implementation at the international level, and it also provides for the operation of independent national level monitoring mechanisms.[50] The CRPD also has an Optional Protocol that recognises the competence of the Committee on the Rights of PWDs to receive and consider communications from or on behalf of individuals or groups of individuals subject to its jurisdiction who claim to be victims of a violation by that State Party of the provisions of the Convention.[51] The CRPD is therefore comprehensive both in terms of its substantive content, monitoring and implementation mechanism.

The Convention is the first comprehensive international legal instrument specifically dealing with PWDs, and whose provisions reflect global consensus and are an authoritative commentary on the manner in which countries should fulfil their obligations towards PWDs.[52] In his official statement on the adoption of the CRPD, the then Secretary-General, Kofi Annan, noted that 'we have already learnt from experience, in countries that

[48] See generally G Quinn & T Degener *et al* 'Human rights and disability: A study on the current use and future potential of the United Nations human rights instruments in the context of disability' (2002) (study commissioned by the OHCHR), available at http://www.ohchr.org/english/issues/disability/study.htm (accessed 13 July 2010).

[49] Quinn & Degener *et al* (n 48 above).

[50] The CRPD, arts 33 & 34.

[51] Optional Protocol to the Convention on the Rights of Persons with Disabilities, art 1(1)

[52] Quinn & Degener *et al* (n 48 above).

have implemented legislation related to disability, that change comes more rapidly when laws are in place.'[53] It is therefore anticipated that the CRPD will both prompt as well as guide the passage and reform of domestic legislation ensuring substantive equality and non-discrimination for PWDs.

Equality and the right to work under the CRPD

Non-discrimination, equality of opportunity and accessibility are some of the general principles of the CRPD.[54] Article 5 calls upon state parties to recognise the equality of all persons before and under the law and that they are entitled without any discrimination to the equal protection and equal benefit of the law. Furthermore, state parties are to prohibit all discrimination on the basis of disability and guarantee to persons with disabilities equal and effective legal protection against discrimination on all grounds. In this regard, article 5(3) calls upon states to take all appropriate steps to ensure that reasonable accommodation is provided in order to promote equality and eliminate discrimination.

Article 27 of the CRPD obliges states to recognise the right of PWDs to work, on an equal basis with others and that this right includes the right to the opportunity to gain a living by work freely chosen or accepted in a labour market and work environment that is open, inclusive and accessible to PWDs. States are to safeguard and promote the realisation of the right to work by taking appropriate steps, including through legislation to, *inter alia,* prohibit discrimination on the basis of disability in all matters of employment, including conditions of recruitment, hiring and employment, continuance of employment, career advancement, safe and healthy working conditions. Article 27 further obliges state parties to ensure that reasonable accommodation is provided to PWDs in the workplace.

Article 2 defines reasonable accommodation as necessary and appropriate modification and adjustments not imposing a disproportionate or undue burden, where needed in a particular case, to ensure to persons with disabilities the enjoyment or exercise on an equal basis with others of all human rights and fundamental freedoms.

[53] 'Secretary-General Hails Adoption of Landmark Convention on Rights of People with Disabilities,' Official Statement of the UN Secretary General, SG/SM/10797, 13 December 2006. Available at http://www.un.org/News/Press/docs/2006/sgsm 10797. doc.htm (accessed 1 August 2010).

[54] Art 3.

Malawi's Constitutional and legal framework

According to the World Bank Social development notes: Community driven development, No 100/May 2005, the lack of a comprehensive legislation on disability, unclear sector agendas and weak coordination between civil society, local and national government have posed particular challenges in ensuring an enabling environment for the inclusion of people with disabilities.[55] As already noted, history has shown that positive change regarding the rights of PWDs occurs more rapidly in countries that have implemented disability related legislation.[56] This part analyses Malawi's legal framework relating to equality in the workplace for PWDs as against the CRPD.

Constitutional framework

The constitution of Malawi, which amongst others, seeks to guarantee the welfare and development of all Malawians[57] is premised on the principle of equality and non-discrimination. Section 20 of the constitution provides that discrimination of persons in any form is prohibited and all persons are, under any law, guaranteed equal and effective protection against discrimination on grounds of race, colour, sex, language, religion, political or other opinion, nationality, ethnic or social origin, disability, property, birth or other status.

Section 29 guarantees to every person the right to freely engage in economic activity, to work and pursue a livelihood anywhere in Malawi. Furthermore, the rights to fair and safe labour practices, fair remuneration and equal remuneration for equal work are provided for in section 31. Recognising the vulnerable position of PWDs, section 13(g) (i) calls upon the state to actively promote the welfare and development of PWDs by adopting and implementing policies and legislation aimed at ensuring that PWDs have fair employment opportunities and the fullest possible participation in all spheres of the Malawian society. Section 30 guarantees to every person the right to development and as such to the enjoyment of economic, social, cultural and political development. Section 30(1) specifically states that PWDs are to be given special consideration in the application of this right

55 World Bank 'Examining inclusion: Disability and community driven development' World Bank social development notes 33013, No 100/May 2005, 3.

56 As above.

57 Preamble to the constitution.

and in this regard, Section 30(2) calls upon the state to take all necessary measures to ensure the realisation of this right. Such measures are to include equality of opportunity for all in their access to basic resources, education, health services, food, shelter, employment and infrastructure. Section 30(3) further calls upon the state to take measures to introduce reforms aimed at eradicating social injustices and inequalities.

Legislation

5.2.1 The Handicapped Persons Act of 1971

This is the main piece of legislation specifically dealing with issues of PWDs in Malawi. The Handicapped Persons Act was intended to make provision for the improvement of the care, assistance and education of the handicapped persons.[58] The term handicapped is one which is no longer considered appropriate in referring to PWDs as it is one of those that are ascribed to them, and locates disability in the person as a way of social labelling which connotes a negative status. This is in contrast to the recently used terms which tend to be self-descriptions by PWDs themselves.

Even the objectives of the Act reveal an outdated approach of treating PWDs as objects of charity and social protection as opposed to the recent trend of viewing them as 'subjects' with rights. For instance, as already noted, the main objective of the recently adopted CRPD is to promote, protect and ensure the full and equal enjoyment of all human rights and fundamental freedoms by PWDs and to promote respect for their inherent dignity. Section 2 of the Act defines a handicapped person as one who by reason of any defect or impairment of the mind, senses or body, congenital or acquired, is unable to take part in normal education, occupation and recreation, or who by reason of any such defect or impairment, requires special assistance or training to enable him to take part in normal education, occupation or recreation. This definition espouses the medical model of disability which as we have already seen, views disability as a personal trait lying in the individual who by virtue of the disability is regarded as in need of assistance to remedy the disability.

However, nowadays the social model of disability is preferred over the medical model. The social model conceptualises disability in a holistic manner that takes into account extrinsic factors such as social and environmental factors in the creation of disability. This social model is

[58] The Handicapped Persons Act, Preamble.

reflected in the definition of disability adopted by the CRPD which defines PWDs as including those who have long-term physical, mental, intellectual or sensory impairments which in interaction with various barriers may hinder their full and effective participation in society on an equal basis with others.[59]

The Act contains no substantive provision regarding the rights of PWDs. The main thing it does is to establish MACOHA which is to act as an agent of the government in promoting the welfare of the handicapped.[60] MACOHA's core functions are to: (i) advise the Minister in regard to all matters affecting the welfare, education, training and employment of the handicapped; (ii) promote public interest in the welfare and care of the handicapped; (iii) administer vocational and special training centres for the handicapped; (iv) administer rehabilitation service for the handicapped; and to raise and receive funds and donations for the welfare of the handicapped.[61]

The Employment Act No 6 of 2000

The Employment Act touches on the issue of disability in its provisions which deal with the prohibition of discrimination. Section 5 provides that no person shall discriminate against any employee or prospective employee on the grounds of race, colour, sex, language, religion, political or other opinion, nationality, ethnic or social origin, disability, property, birth, marital or other status or family responsibilities in respect of recruitment, training, promotion, terms and conditions of employment, termination of employment or other matters arising out of the employment relationship.

According to section 5(2), subsection (1) does not preclude any provision, programme or activity that has as its object the improvement of conditions of disadvantaged persons, including those who are disadvantaged on the grounds enumerated in subsection (1). Furthermore, section 5(3) stipulates that any person who contravenes this action shall be guilty of an offence and liable to a fine of K10 000 and to imprisonment for two years.

Other than the above provision, it is only section 6(1) which also mentions the issue of disability. It provides that every employer shall pay employees equal remuneration for work of equal value without distinction or discrimination of any kind, in particular, on basis of race, colour, sex language,

[59] The Handicapped Persons Act, art 1.

[60] As above, secs 3 & 10.

[61] As above, sec 10.

religion, political or other opinion, nationality, ethnic or social origin, disability, property, birth marital or other status or family responsibilities.

This Act simply concentrates on formal equality in total disregard of the fact that equal application of needs or rules or policies without considering their differing effect on certain individuals or groups may result in discrimination against them and perpetuate inequality. The act should have had provisions dealing with reasonable accommodation for PWDs, as this is indispensable for the achievement of equality in the workplace.

Technical, Entrepreneurial and Vocational Education and Training Authority Act of 1999

This Act establishes the Technical, Entrepreneurial and Vocational Education and Training Authority (TEVETA) as well as its board whose composition, according to section 6 (i), must include one member representing PWDs. That is the only mention of PWDs in the entire Act as the Act does not have a single provision dealing substantively with PWDs. This is a major shortfall in the Act, considering the fact that its main function is to provide for training of employees. It was essential for the Act to have substantive provisions on employees with disabilities.

Policy

5.3.1 National policy on equalisation of opportunities for PWDs

In June 2006, Malawi developed a comprehensive National Policy on Equalisation of Opportunities for Persons with Disabilities that notably deals with employment and education. This policy was developed in order to promote the rights of PWDs by providing them equal opportunities, adapting the environment to their needs and encouraging society to positively change its attitude towards PWDs and assist them in assuming full responsibility as active members of society.[62] The policy aims at ensuring that concrete steps are taken for PWDs to access the same fundamental rights and responsibilities as any other Malawian.[63]

The policy came about after the realisation that PWDs in Malawi face numerous challenges that have resulted in their exclusion from mainstream

[62] 'Malawi Government National policy on equalisation of opportunities for persons with disabilities' (2006) (iv) & (v).

[63] As above. On page 7, the policy affirms that PWDs are entitled to the same human rights as all other citizens as enshrined in the UDHR, the Malawi constitution and other international instruments.

society, making it difficult for them to access their fundamental social, political and economic rights.[64] The challenges include environmental barriers such as inaccessible public and private buildings; institutional barriers such as expulsion, exclusion and segregation from key social institutions; attitudinal barriers ranging from various kinds of prejudices and economic barriers such as access to credit facilities and employment. In so far as employment is concerned, PWDs have restricted employment opportunities mainly due to discrimination, inadequate education or training, job and experience. This has resulted in high rates of poverty among PWDs as many of them depend on welfare or beg for a living. Whereas poverty in Malawi is widespread, there is a close link between poverty and disability with poverty often causing disability and disability increasing poverty.[65]

The policy identifies the failure to adopt international commitments in national policies and law as one of the challenges to the successful implementation of the policy. It notes that despite Malawi being a signatory to a number of international instruments dealing with PWDs, these instruments are meaningless unless the principles enshrined in these instruments are reflected in domestic law.[66] In many respects, the policy is in line with current international approach towards disability. It correctly identifies the reasons why PWDs have been excluded and marginalised in every aspect of the Malawian society and the steps that need to be taken to ensure that their rights to equality and dignity are respected. It marks a shift away from the approach of regarding PWDs as objects of charity and pity in favour of a holistic human rights based approach.

Equalisation of Opportunities for Persons with Disabilities Bill 2008

The Equalisation of Opportunities for Persons with Disabilities Bill (the Bill) is an offspring of the National Policy on the Equalisation of Opportunities for Persons with Disabilities which was adopted with a view of ensuring that concrete steps are taken to ensure promotion of the rights of PWDs as equal members of the society. The Malawi Law Commission noted in its Constitutional Review Report of 2007 that although it had received valid submissions relating to the protection and promotion of the rights of PWDs, the issues could better be addressed in an Act of Parliament which the

[64] Malawi Government National policy on equalisation of opportunities for persons with disabilities' (n 62 above) 1.

[65] As above, 4.

[66] As above, 25.

Ministry of Justice had already been approached to draft so as to replace the Handicapped Persons Act.[67] Considering the fact that the Policy recognises the failure to implement the principles enshrined in the various international instruments dealing with disability to which Malawi is a party as one of the major challenges of its successful implementation, at the very least one would expect the Bill to embody the principles enunciated in the recently adopted CRPD.

The Bill proposes to enact new legislation to promote the rights of PWDs to enable them to play a full and participatory role in society. It provides for equalisation of opportunities which it defines as a process by which the various systems of society are made available and accessible to all, including PWDs.[68] It recognises the cross-cutting nature of disability and the need to mainstream disability in all policies, plans, programmes and services of all public, private and civil society organisations.[69] Furthermore, it obliges government to adopt policies on equalisation of opportunities for PWDs whose aim shall be to fully integrate PWDs in all aspects of life in order to enhance their dignity and well-being so that they have essentials of life. In this regard, the government is to ensure the attainment of a barrier-free environment that will enable PWDs to have access into public and private buildings and establishments as well as make guidelines for the provision of architectural facilities or structural features for PWDs to be enforced in public buildings and facilities.[70] This also includes access to public transport facilities.[71] This in a way echoes the CRPD which aims at promoting and protecting the human rights of all PWDs by removing the various barriers that they face in their participation as equal members of their society. For instance, in terms of article 9(2)(a) of the CRPD, the government is to take appropriate measures to develop, promulgate and monitor the implementation of minimum standards and guidelines for the accessibility of facilities and services open or provided to the public.

According to section 2 of the Bill, a person with disability is defined as any person who, by reason of any impairment of the mind, senses or body, congenital or acquired, is unable to participate fully in regular education, occupation and recreation, or who, by reason of such impairment, requires

[67] Malawi Law Commission 'Constitutional review final report' (2007) 44.

[68] The Equalisation of Opportunities for Persons with Disabilities Bill 2008, sec 2.

[69] As above, sec 34.

[70] As above, sec 26.

[71] As above, sec 27.

special assistance or training to enable him to participate in regular, mainstream or inclusive education, occupation or recreation and other spheres of life.[72] The Bill seems to draw a distinction between disability, handicap and impairment. Section 2 of the Bill defines disability as any restriction or lack, resulting from impairment, of ability to perform an activity in the manner or within the range considered normal for a human being. On the other hand, it defines handicap as a disadvantage in a given individual resulting from an impairment or disability that limits or prevents the fulfilment of a role that is normal depending on age, sex, social and cultural factors for that individual. Whilst impairment is defined as any loss or limitations of psychological, physiological or anatomical structure or function.

The distinction sought to be made by the Bill between disability, handicap and impairment is nowadays illusory. The definition of disability suggests that that disability amongst others, results from impairment and at the same time the definition of handicap suggests that handicap may result from an impairment or disability. On the other hand, impairment may well encompass disability and handicap. It would appear that it is just a matter of semantics as what one may refer to as a handicap may well be referred to as a disability or impairment. Of course in the past, others would define impairment as an individual limitation and disability as a socially imposed restriction.[73] If anything, the term handicapped is one of the terms that was used to refer to PWDs but which is no longer deemed appropriate for being demeaning and tantamount to negative social labelling.

Furthermore, the definitions of disability and handicap, just like the definition of a disabled person are inadequate as they all seem to locate the disability in the individual and disregard the role of the environment or society in the creation of disability. In a way, it can be said that the Bill sticks to the outdated medical model of disability instead of the conventional human rights approach. The inadequacy of the above definitions is apparent when you consider them in light of the CRPD which under article 1 states that PWDs should include those who have long-term physical, mental, intellectual or sensory impairments which in interaction with various barriers may hinder their full and effective participation in society on an equal basis with others.

[72] As above, sec 2.

[73] S French 'Disability, impairment or something in between?' in J Swain *et al* (eds) *Disabling barriers-enabling environments* (1993) 17.

One of the significant developments the Bill brings about is the concept of reasonable accommodation. Whilst it does not define the term reasonable accommodation, section 2 of the Bill stipulates that reasonable accommodation includes amongst others, making existing facilities used by employees readily accessible to and usable by individuals with disabilities. In appropriate cases, it will entail acquisition or modification of equipment or devices, making appropriate adjustments or modifications for PWDs. According to section 30 of the Bill failure to reasonably accommodate the needs of PWDs without a proper justification would be tantamount to discrimination which is prohibited both under the Bill and the constitution. According to section 30 (2) (d) of the Bill, failure by any person or employer to provide reasonable accommodation to a physical or mental disabled is an offence (discrimination). Nevertheless, there is no offence if it can be demonstrated that the accommodation would impose an undue hardship on the operation of the business of the person or employer. Section 2 of the Bill defines undue hardship as an action requiring significant difficulty or expense, when considered in light of; (a) the nature and cost of the accommodation needed under this Act; (b) the overall financial resources of the facility or facilities involved in the provision of the reasonable accommodation; (c) the overall financial resources of the covered entity; and (d) the type of operation or operations of the covered entity including the composition, structure and functions of the workforce of such entity.

The requirement of reasonable accommodation is complemented by section 30(8)(a) which calls upon the government to formulate schemes for the employment of PWDs, which should ensure the creation of a non-handicapping environment in the workplace for PWDs. Furthermore, section 35 obliges government to endeavour to ensure economic empowerment for PWDs.

The requirement of reasonable accommodation in the workplace is a huge step in the right direction if true equality is ever to be achieved in the Malawian employment sector because past experiences have shown that equal application of rules or policies without considering their differing effect on certain individuals or groups may result in discrimination against them, which accounts for the high rate of unemployment amongst the population of PWDs in Malawi. However, whilst provisions on reasonable accommodation in the Bill should be commended, it may have been prudent for the Bill to include a definition of what reasonable accommodation is just as the CRPD does. As matters currently stand, one cannot be faulted for getting the impression that reasonable accommodation is a phenomenon for the workplace only. Hopefully, a definition will clarify the fact that reasonable accommodation covers all spheres of life.

Apart from the above substantive provisions, the Bill establishes a National Coordinating Committee on Disability issues whose main task amongst others, is to advise government on formulation of policies, programmes, legislation and projects with respect to disability.[74] However, the Bill does not have a single provision specifically dealing with women with disabilities. Whereas it is generally accepted that PWDs face various challenges and barriers to access the workplace, it has also been noted that the situation is even worse for women with disabilities.

While men with disabilities have serious employment problems, women with disabilities are significantly worse off and this seems to be true for all types and levels of disabilities. Men with disabilities are almost twice as likely to have jobs as women with disabilities. Furthermore, women with disabilities are also significantly poorer than men with disabilities, partly due to the fact that they are more likely to be unemployed and partly due to the fact that when they work they receive considerably lower wages than men with disabilities.[75]

Probably, it is in recognition of this fact that the CRPD calls upon states to recognise that women and girls with disabilities are subject to multiple discrimination, and in this regard to take measures to ensure the full and equal enjoyment by them of all human rights and fundamental freedoms.[76]

Conclusion and recommendations

Conclusion

Whilst the constitution guarantees the right to equality and non-discrimination as well as the right to work to all individuals, the reality is that these rights are more of chapter rights than real rights for PWDs. These rights have not yet translated into reality in society. One of the major reasons is that apart from the constitutional guarantee to equality, there is no legislative framework that gives effect to this constitutional guarantee of equality. The effectiveness and adequacy of laws promoting the rights and welfare of PWDs

[74] The Equalisation of Opportunities for Persons with Disabilities Bill 2008 (n 68 above), sec 6.

[75] F Bowe *Disabled women in America: A statistical report drawn from census data* (1984) 40.

[76] CRPD, art 6(1).

in general is essential for the achievement of true equality in the workplace for PWDs. Strict equal or even-handed application of rules or policies without due regard to their effects on certain individuals or groups causes or perpetrates discrimination instead of ensuring equality of opportunity.[77] 'The accommodation of differences is the essence of true equality'[78] as formal equality serves merely to maintain the status *quo* and perpetuate structural inequality.

Malawi's approach to issues concerning PWDs, just like all other issues concerning PWDs, has been needs-based instead of rights-based. The approach has been aimed at addressing short-term needs of PWDs instead of addressing the vast array of limitations created and imposed by unemployment, discrimination, exclusion, and ignorance.[79] This has resulted in the further marginalisation of PWDs.

The Equalisation of Opportunities for Persons with Disabilities Bill that is awaiting parliamentary approval comes at a time when the CRPD, a comprehensive and integral international convention to promote and protect the rights and dignity of PWDs, has been adopted and entered into force. However, the Bill fails in some material respects to comply with the current international standards as espoused by the CRPD as evidenced by the use of outdated terms such as handicapped, inadequate definition of disability, failure to define reasonable accommodation and absence of any provision dealing with women with disabilities.

The right to work for PWDs goes hand in hand with their right to equality and dignity. At the same time, true equality can only be achieved by recognising their differences and providing them with reasonable accommodation. If PWDs are to enjoy full equality in the workplace and fully realise their right to work, the legal and policy framework must set an enabling environment, reflecting the social model of disability in which the barriers to participation are recognised to lie in the social and physical environment.[80]

77 C Ngwena 'Interpreting aspects of the intersection between disability, discrimination and equality: Lessons for the Employment Equity Act from comparative law' (2005) *Stellenbosch Law Review* 547.

78 P McIntyre & J Lamer in *Andrews v Law Society* (1989) 1SCR 143, 169.

79 RL Metts, 'Disability issues, trends and recommendations for the World Bank,' Discussion paper No. 0007 (2000) 29, available at http://siteresources.worldbank.org/DISABILITY/Resources/280658l172606907476/DisabilityIssuesMetts.pdf (accessed 7 September 2011).

80 ILO 'People with disabilities: Pathways to decent work' ILO tripartite workshop report, Malawi (2006) 9. Available at http://www.ilo.org/wcmsp5/groups/public/-ed_emp/-ifp_skills/documents/publication/wcms_107785.pdf (accessed 7 September 2011).

Recommendations

The Equalisation of Opportunities for Persons with Disabilities Bill should define disability in terms which take into account how the CRPD views disability, which is based on the social model. It would also be beneficial if the Malawian government was to ensure that it submits its periodic reports to the various treaty bodies to which it is under an obligation to do so, especially the Committee on the Rights of Persons with Disabilities from the interaction with these treaty bodies Malawi stands to gain a lot on how it can improve its disability legislation and keep it up to date.[81]

The issue of protecting and promoting the rights of PWDs needs to be mainstreamed. However, this task should not only be left to the ministry responsible for PWDs, rather it should be a multisectoral approach involving all ministries and government departments. A lot of sensitisation on the need for equalisation of opportunities also needs to be done as part of combating stereotypes and prejudices attached to PWDs.[82] On this aspect, the focus should not be on disability awareness but rather on diversity awareness since disability differences are just part of the wide array of human differences such as ethnicity, race, age, culture and religion.

As one way of accelerating the inclusion of PWDs in the workplace whereby their equality is guaranteed by means of an enabling environmental which reasonably accommodates their means, government should provide incentives to employers who employ a certain percentage of PWDs.

At the end of the day, it mainly comes down to political will. Good legislation on disability does not necessarily translate to better protection and promotion of the rights of PWDs on the ground if the legislation is not implemented and enforced. It is only through effective implementation of the law that societal attitudes can be positively influenced to enhance the promotion and protection of the rights and welfare of PWDs in general.

[81] Article 35 of the CRPD obliges every state party to submit a comprehensive report on measures taken to give effect to its obligations under the present Convention and on the progress made in that regard, within two years after the entry into force of the present Convention for the State Party concerned. Thereafter reports are to be submitted after every four years.

[82] For instance, it will be easier for society, for example in the workplace to accept and strive for the inclusion of PWDs if this inclusion starts right from the education sector.

5

Human rights and humanitarian assistance for refugees and internally displaced persons with disabilities in Africa

Michael Ashley Stein & Janet E. Lord

The authors thank Andrew Solomon for thoughtful comments on this chapter; Amanda DeBerry, Kelli Falgout and Nicole Sonia for research assistance and staff at the United Nations Office of the High Commissioner for Refugees for background materials.

Introduction

Of the estimated six hundred and fifty million persons with disabilities (PWDs) worldwide, some three to four million are refugees or internally displaced within their own countries.[1] Already among the most marginalised members of their communities prior to forced migration, they experience heightened risk during and following flight. Recent humanitarian crises suggest that assistance operations nonetheless fail either to anticipate or adequately respond to the needs of disabled beneficiaries.[2] The 2006 adoption of the United Nations Convention on the Rights of Persons with Disabilities (CRPD)[3] has helped to highlight disability-inclusion as a rights issue in these circumstances.[4] Indeed, the preamble of the CRPD recognises that 'the

1 See U Janz 'Report by Udo Janz, Director of UNHCR New York Office: Conference of the States Parties to the Convention on the Rights of Persons with Disabilities' (3 September 2010). Comprehensively addressing the needs of refugees and internally displaced persons requires considering the different legal frameworks and state obligations that apply in respect of these distinct groups. Nonetheless, because our focus is on equal access to various services and processes by persons with disabilities, we are comfortable conflating these two categories for the purposes of this discussion.

2 See generally JE Lord *et al* 'Disability inclusive development and natural disasters' in RP Malloy (ed) *Law and Recovery from Disaster: Hurricane Katrina* (2008) 71.

3 Convention on the Rights of Persons with Disabilities, GA Res 61/106, UN Doc A/RES/61/106 (13 December 2006) (CRPD).

observance of applicable human rights instruments are indispensable for the full protection of persons with disabilities, in particular during armed conflicts and foreign occupation'.[5] Ensuring the protection of persons with disabilities in humanitarian response, however, requires concrete and implemented programming guidance that moves beyond rhetoric.[6]

The challenge of human rights-based protection for refugees and internally displaced persons (IDPs) with disabilities is of acute interest to Africa. Forced migration from and within conflict affected countries – such as Congo, Liberia, Rwanda, Sierra Leone, and Sudan – highlights the extremely precarious position of individuals with disabilities even amongst this already vulnerable population. Nonetheless, research on refugees and IDPs with disabilities has been scanty.[7] Buoyed by the advent of the CRPD, some recent studies have focused on the ramifications to disabled populations affected by the highly publicised natural disasters of the 2007 Asian Tsunami[8] and the 2010 Haitian earthquake.[9] Yet almost no attention has been paid to the situation that prevails for persons with disabilities in post-conflict Africa. This is especially true for women with disabilities who experience an added layer of discrimination due to social stigma and culturally construed duties.[10] The dearth of Africa-focused analyses is particularly ironic given the strong support by African delegations for affirming state obligations under the CRPD to protect persons with disabilities in situations of risk.[11]

4 See eg CRPD (n 3 above), art 11 (addressing situations of risk).

5 CRPD (n 3 above) Preamble (u).

6 See generally JE Lord & MA Stein 'Ensuring respect for the rights of people with disabilities' VO Pang *et al* (eds) *The human impact of natural disasters: Issues for the inquiry-based classroom* (2010).

7 Among the rare exceptions are Women's Commission for Refugee Women and Children 'Disabilities among refugees and conflict-affected populations' (June 2008); Women's Commission for Refugee Women and Children, 'Disabilities among refugees and conflict-affected populations: Resource kit for field workers' (June 2008). While lauding the existence of this work, we also note that it does not consistently adhere to disability rights-based notions or terminology.

8 See eg International Disability Rights Monitor 'Disability and tsunami relief efforts in India, Indonesia and Thailand' (2005).

9 See eg S Eitel 'Haitians cope with disabilities, before and after Quake'. USAID Front-Lines. September 2010. Available at http://www.usaid.gov/press/frontlines/fl_sep10/p05_haiti100910.html. (Accessed 5 September 2011).

10 See generally Human Rights Watch 'As if we weren't human' 26 August 2010 http://www.hrw.org/en/reports/2010/08/26/if-we-werent-human (accessed 21 December 2010).

11 See eg S Matsebula, Office on the Status of Disabled Persons in the Presidency of South Africa 'Statement of the second session of the *ad hoc* committee on a comprehensive

This chapter proceeds as follows: Part two provides an initial assessment of the impact that forced migration has upon persons with disabilities, with special emphasis on the African context. Next, part three delineates the CRPD's vision for incorporating refugees and IDPs with disabilities in humanitarian activities, and in particular ensuring those individuals are able to access human rights-based response services. Part four reviews existing protective frameworks for refugees and IDPs, and assesses their adequacy for meeting the needs of persons with disabilities. Finally, part five charts out a research agenda for designing more inclusive strategies for refugees and IDPs with disabilities in situations of risk in Africa. Part six is the concluding section of the chapter.

The impact of forced migration on persons with disabilities

There are numerous adverse effects of forced migration on persons with disabilities. The circumstances surrounding involuntary movement are often disabling and can create secondary impairments for individuals with existing disabilities. Flight is typically marked by chaos, with the displacement process breaking up networks of family, friends and community who provide assistance and support for disabled persons. Thus, even when people with disabilities are not abandoned, they still may be separated from their caregivers on whom they rely. Assistive devices such as crutches, wheelchairs and canes, along with necessary medications, may be lost or left behind.

The destruction of health, rehabilitation and transportation infrastructure during conflict or other emergency likewise has serious consequences. The devastating impact of flight on the psychosocial well-being of the affected population is also a major risk factor. And lack of adequate general medical care can increase the likelihood of disablement in the midst of these crises. In order to understand the strategies for effective disability-inclusion in the African context, it is essential to appreciate the specific needs of refugees and IDPs with disabilities.

and integral international convention on protection and promotion of the rights of persons with disabilities' 16–27 June 2003 ('The impact of dual or multiple discrimination faced by individuals such as, women, children, refugees, minorities or persons with multiple and or severe disabilities or other status should also be included.').

Physical insecurity and access barriers

Refugee and IDP camps are never ideal locations, but for individuals with disabilities, they teem with risk. Physical insecurity is heightened for PWDs who are socially construed to be weak and vulnerable, hence prime targets for exploitation. Sexual violence, which is a major problem for displaced women and girls generally, may well be more of a threat for disabled women and girls due to the overall insecurity of camps for the displaced.[12] A Human Rights Watch Report on persons with disabilities in Northern Uganda documented physical and sexual violence against women refugees with disabilities and pointed to one case where a husband of a refugee with a disability explained:

> I can't stay away from home. I heard there was food at another camp … I went there, but that place was far, and I stayed for a night. [My] neighbor came back [before me] and raped my wife.[13]

In addition, the physical layout and infrastructure of camps for the displaced are often difficult to traverse, especially for persons who use wheelchairs or crutches, or for individuals with brain injuries whose balance is compromised. In the refugee settlement areas in Dadaab, Kenya, for example, the placement of the camp in a sandy river delta presented considerable mobility challenges for many disabled people.[14] As a result, one of the humanitarian assistance organisations with expertise in designing and distributing assistive devices introduced specially designed wheelchairs with tires capable of transiting across sandy ground.[15] Too often, however, humanitarian operators on the ground have little or no disability expertise with which to respond to such environmental challenges.

Urban communities where refugees and IDPs seek refuge may be even less welcoming for persons with disabilities because of their inaccessibly built environments. Trenchantly, studies indicate that the number of refugees and IDPs moving to urban areas is on the rise and that protection standards in urban areas are not necessarily better than those in camps or rural areas.[16]

12 N Groce 'HIV and disability: Capturing hidden voices' (2004) 10.9 Available at http://site resources. worldbank.org/DISABILITY/Resources/Health-and-Wellness/HIV AIDS.pdf (accessed 5 September 2011).

13 Human Rights Watch (n 10 above) 34.

14 Women's Commission (n 7 above) 17.

15 Women's Commission (n 7 above) 17.

16 See E Coker *et al* 'Health education for urban refugees in Cairo: A pilot project with young men from Sierra Leone and Liberia' (January 2003) 4. Available at http://www.

Due to lack of historical awareness, urban infrastructure across Africa often excludes and isolates persons with disabilities, in turn limiting their ability to attain services.

Loss of family and caregiver supports

Refugees and IDPs with disabilities commonly lose their support systems during flight, as families are broken up and disabled persons (and others, such as children and the elderly) are separated from their caregivers. Achieving reunion at borders and at refugee and IDP camps with family members and friends is even more difficult for persons with mobility and visual disabilities due to physical barriers. Likewise, communication barriers make it more difficult for deaf persons or individuals with intellectual disabilities to effectively make their needs known when locating lost relatives and caregivers. And persons with psychosocial disabilities may manifest symptoms due to heightened stress or lack of medication; with the result that social stigma precludes their receiving the assistance they require. Humanitarian workers are generally not trained or prepared to help beneficiaries with disabilities, and so focus on a vague and aggregate assemblage of 'the most vulnerable'.[17] In practice, this means that women, children and elderly persons are the primary focus, while persons with disabilities are neglected.

Barriers to healthcare and rehabilitation services

Persons with disabilities face myriad obstacles in accessing health and rehabilitation services, situations which are aggravated for disabled refugees and IDPs. Stairs or other physical barriers to treatment facilities bar the way of wheelchair and cane users and lack of sign language interpreters can prevent deaf persons from receiving services, public health educational campaigns in camps often are visual and therefore not useful to blind persons, and radio campaigns do not reach deaf persons.[18]

aucegypt.edu/GAPP/cmrs/reports/Documents/Andrea.pdf (accessed 5 September 2011); see also N Obi & J Crisp 'Evaluation and the implementation of UNHCR's policy on refugees in urban areas' (2002) 3–4. Available at http://www.unhcr.org/ (accessed 5 September 2011).

17 See Lord *et al* 'Disability inclusive development and natural disasters' in RP Malloy (n 2 above).

18 KL Kirschner & RH Curry 'Educating health care professionals to care for patients with disabilities' (2009) 302 *Journal of the American Medical Association* 1334–1335.

Addressing the specific health and rehabilitation needs of refugees and IDPs with disabilities is especially challenging if providers are not sufficiently equipped to accommodate their needs. Too often, humanitarian organisations focusing on health access are not disability-inclusive in their approach.[19] A case in point is a health education project for urban refugees from Liberia and Sierra Leone in Cairo, Egypt. The project indicated that the refugees faced a number of barriers to health maintenance 'relating to the specific situation of the refugee population in question, including gender, age, religion, educational level, knowledge of the host-country language, the loss of important social supports and many more'.[20] Remarkably, the project paid no attention to the particular barriers experienced by disabled refugees in this population and thus resulted in no disability-specific solutions to improve access. This was notwithstanding the fact that the project recognised the relevance of mental health concerns based on the trauma experienced by these refugees in the context of civil war in their own countries.[21]

Along similar lines, research undertaken in the area of HIV and AIDS and disability suggests that persons with disabilities are often incorrectly assumed to be sexually inactive, or unlikely to use drugs, or to be at small risk for sexual abuse[22] despite contrary empirical evidence.[23] In consequence, unfounded notions have led public sexual and reproductive health programmes for refugees and IDPs to overlook persons with disabilities, and this exclusion has had a particularly severe impact on women and adolescent girls with disabilities.[24]

In urban environments, similar challenges exist for refugees with disabilities. Difficulties in accessing health services for refugees and IDPs without disabilities have been well documented. For instance, one study noted myriad obstacles encountered by African refugees, but did not take

[19] See MA Stein *et al* 'Equal access to health care under the UN Disability Rights Convention' in R Rhodes *et al* (eds) *Medicine and social justice: Essays on distribution and care'* (2011) (forthcoming).

[20] Coker *et al* (n 16 above) 5.

[21] For a contrasting approach, see RF Mollica 'Healing invisible wounds: Paths to hope and recovery in a violent world' (2008).

[22] See generally Groce (n 12 above); NE Groce & R Trasi, 'Rape of individuals with disability: AIDS and the folk belief of virgin cleansing' (2004) 363 *The Lancet* 1663–1664.

[23] Groce (n 12 above).

[24] K Fleming *et al Vulnerability for households with persons with disabilities and HIV/AIDS in Chongwe, Zambia* (2010) 6–7.

into account the mental health needs of that population, including rehabilitation services, psycho-social supports, and other health care concerns.[25]

Lack of access to basic needs

Humanitarian aid packages historically have not considered the needs of disabled persons and so historically, inadequate support has been provided to enable meaningful access to relief aid, cash assistance and health care. Findings from field studies confirm, in uniform fashion, that refugees with disabilities do not receive priority or specific accommodations in terms of food distribution needs in refugee camps. According to the Women's Commission Report:

> In all the refugee camps, participants in the field studies pointed out that the food distribution systems were not suited to refugees with disabilities. Food distribution points were frequently far from refugees' homes and they had to line up for long periods, or try to push their way through large crowds, to receive their food – which was difficult for many.[26]

Distribution processes typically are not modified to meet the needs of persons with disabilities and so fail to meet standards of equality by not providing individual accommodations that ensure equitable access to food, water and other necessities. Not only may persons with mobility impairments be forced to wait in long lines, but also water distribution points may be erected with physical obstacles such as platforms or steps. Fighting through crowds and going a long way to obtain necessities can be daunting or impossible, especially when persons with disabilities are separated from their family and peer support. An added barrier is the need for assistance in food preparation for persons with disabilities who are unable to do so. Each of these obstacles is compounded for women with disabilities because of culturally gendered expectations that they feed and care for their families.

Accommodation in the realm of access to food and nutrition could also entail extra or special rations, as in the case of some children with disabilities. In Nepal, for example, special rations of vitamin-enriched milk were distributed to disability centers at refugee camps resulting in marked health

[25] See Coker *et al* (n 16 above) 4; see also F Baingana *et al* 'Mental health and conflicts: Conceptual framework and approaches in health' (February 2005). Available at http://hpod.pmhclients.com/pdf/baingana-mental-health.pdf (accessed 5 September 2011)

[26] See Women's Commission (n 7 above) 18.

improvements for children with disabilities.[27] In Kenya, the United Nations High Commission for Refugees (UNHCR) facilitated an arrangement with the World Food Programme that prioritised distribution to persons with disabilities to facilitate and enhance access to food. Another modification involved using mobile units to distribute food to persons who were unable to collect food rations, thereby responding to transport and other barriers.[28]

Lack of access to clean water and sanitation

In many countries, clean water and sanitation may be generally accessible to the public, but inaccessible to persons with disabilities.[29] Going to a latrine or simply trying to get water from a well is either impossible or nearly so due to physical barriers. This situation has a disparate impact on disabled refugees and IDPs. Obstacles preventing access to clean water and safe sanitation are many and varied. Natural physical barriers include placement of camp latrines at considerable distance from living space, requiring persons to travel a long way or across rough terrain. Locations of latrines can mean the difference between safety and sexual violence for women and girls with disabilities due to their remoteness within the camp setting and lack of lighting. Likewise, the positioning of clean water distribution centres impacts women and girls with disabilities who are expected to carry water on behalf of their family units. Other physical barriers pertaining to infrastructure design include narrow entrances and lack of space inside latrines, steps and slippery floors, no grab bars to assist with balance, among others.

Moreover, institutional obstacles stand in the way of inclusion, as water and sanitation projects in refugee camps do not harness the expertise of persons with disabilities through consultation processes or the hiring of disability experts.[30] Given the dearth of information about accessible design options and lack of staff understanding and awareness about disability, it is

[27] Women's Commission (n 7 above) 18.

[28] Women's Commission (n 7 above) 18.

[29] See generally HE Jones & RA Reed 'Water and sanitation for disabled people and other vulnerable groups: designing services to improve accessibility' (2005); see also WELL 'Why should the water and sanitation sector consider disabled people?' Briefing note n 12 (2005); WaterAid Mali 'All people, one goal, all access: Water and sanitation access for people with disabilities' Briefing note (2007); M Tesfu & P Magrath 'Equal access for all – 2: Water and sanitation access for people with motor disabilities' Briefing note n 9 (2006); M Tesfu & P Magrath 'Water and sanitation access for people with motor disabilities' Main research report (2007).

[30] Jones & Reed (n 29 above) 5.

unlikely that obstacles in the natural and built physical environment will be ameliorated even though small and low cost changes could remediate most of them. Experience in West Africa demonstrates that enhancing accessibility to sanitation facilities for persons with disabilities is indeed possible with some amount of awareness and training.[31]

Barriers to education

Persons with disabilities in many countries have difficulty accessing education. Many are illiterate and unable to read. Studies suggest that the global literacy rate for persons with disabilities is as low as three percent, and for disabled women as low as one percent.[32] Because humanitarian relief programmes focus first on feeding and watering a population, and next providing health care, education takes a distant third place as a priority. As refugees or IDPs, this lack of access does not improve for persons with disabilities.

Notwithstanding problems around the globe in rendering educational systems accessible to children with disabilities, recent examination indicates that there are some positive models from which to draw in the refugee context. According to one study, refugee camps in Kenya, Thailand, and Nepal all disclosed positive examples of inclusion with common denominators being well-trained inclusive education staff, teacher training and supports to accommodate children with disabilities.[33]

Inaccessible employment programmes and microfinance initiatives

Finding meaningful and non-exploitative work is a challenge for persons with disabilities the world over and is particularly difficult when they also are refugees and IDPs. Employment programmes are frequently inaccessible,

[31] For a relevant study in Ethiopia, see Tesfu & Magrath, 2006 (n 29 above). On a project in Mali in which latrines were adapted to facilitate use by blind persons, see WaterAid Mali (n 29 above).

[32] Groce (n 12 above) 10.

[33] A Leymat 'Inclusive microfinance: Reaching disabled people through partnership development' http://www.gre.ac.uk/__data/assets/pdf_file/0005/451976/6_Leymat_FullPaper.pdf (accessed 21 December 2010).
Women's Commission Report (n 7 above) 23–26.

and microfinance initiatives historically have neglected persons with disabilities as potential participants.[34]

Pilot projects point to the utility of inclusion in microfinance, as disclosed by schemes run in Ethiopia and Kenya. In both instances, disabled peoples organisations – the Ethiopian Federation of Disabled Persons and the National Union of Disabled Persons in Uganda – worked with mainstream microfinance institutions to enhance access to services otherwise not reaching disabled beneficiaries.[35] In the Ugandan example, a partnership between the Association of Microfinance Institutions in Uganda with the National Union concluded that inclusion, as opposed to special products or conditions, was a successful strategy, combined with targeted efforts to reach disabled beneficiaries and to make facilities and services accessible to them. Working with disabled peoples organisations was central to their inclusion.[36]

Barriers to resettlement and inability to prove refugee status

UNHCR's guidelines on resettlement of refugees have tended, inexplicably, to disfavor refugees with disabilities. In the 1996 manual, 'UNHCR Community Service Guidelines on Assisting Disabled Refugees: A Community-Based Approach',[37] UNHCR cautioned against resettlement for disabled refugees, instead offering without elaboration that 'it is more advisable to help integration of the disabled in their own communities.'[38] UNHCR has embraced policies and guidelines that appear to be more accommodating to various categories of vulnerable populations, yet disability still is not prioritised in

[34] See generally H Bernard *et al* 'Good practices for Economic Inclusion of People with Disabilities' (August 2006) http://www.handicap international.org/uploads/media/goodpractices GB 2coul.PDF. (Accessed 21 December 2010); S Dyer, 'The Inclusion of Disabled People in Mainstream Micro Finance Programmes', paper presented at the 'Staying Poor: Chronic Poverty and Development Policy Conference' (7–9 April 2003); J Goldstein 'A new financial access frontier: People with disabilities.'Concept paper (June 2010); C Lewis 'Microfinance from the point of view of women with disabilities: lessons from Zambia and Zimbabwe' (2004) 12 *Gender and Development.*

[35] A Leymat 'Inclusive microfinance: reaching disabled people through partnership development' (undated) http://www.gre.ac.uk/__data/assets/pdf_file/0005/451976/6_Leymat_FullPaper.pdf (accessed 21 December 2010).

[36] R Mersland *et al* 'Access to mainstream microfinance services for persons with disabilities: Lessons learned from Uganda' (2009) 29 *Disability Studies Quarterly* http://www.dsq-sds.org/issue/view/8 (accessed 21 December 2010).

[37] See UNHCR 'Community service guidelines on assisting disabled refugees: A community-based approach' (1996) http://www.unhcr.org/refworld/docid/49997ae41f.html (accessed 21 December 2010).

[38] UNHCR (n 37 above) 16.

the context of resettlement.[39] Still, positive change may be in the offing. In 2005, UNHCR applied its group resettlement procedure, designed to streamline and render more efficient the relocation of minority refugee groups, to a group of disabled refugees in a Kenyan camp.[40] That process facilitated the resettlement of some 2 000 refugees with disabilities and their families.

An additional barrier to resettlement concerns access to documentation needed to facilitate determination of refugee status. Lack of documentation often prevents refugees and IDPs from receiving humanitarian assistance, accessing government services, such as healthcare and education, and also finding employment. Many refugees and IDPs require assistance in obtaining documentation because records are lost or abandoned during flight. For persons with disabilities, discrimination often results in refusal to provide documentation. They may never have had such documentation in the first place due to poverty, illiteracy, or social stigma that result either in not being registered at birth or being denied documentation later on in life. This can significantly impact the ability of persons with disabilities to make a successful claim of refugee status, access humanitarian assistance and certain government services, and also realise other fundamental human rights such as the right to participate in political affairs (for example, the right to vote). Proving status can be difficult for any refugee and IDP, and those with disabilities are at a particular disadvantage. Absent appropriate accommodations, such barriers will prove insurmountable for many persons with disabilities.

The CRPD and situations of risk

The CRPD was adopted by the UN General Assembly on 13 December 2006, following some five years of work by an Ad Hoc Committee that was tasked with first considering the need for, and then drafting, the treaty.[41] It

[39] A 2008 handbook published by UNHCR concerning women and girls shows some progress insofar as it reflects a more rights-oriented approach to disability and provides better coverage of the needs of women and girls refugees with disabilities. 'UNHCR Handbook for the Protection of Women and Girls' (2008) http://www.unhcr.org/refworld/pdfid/49997ae41f.pdf (accessed 21 December 2010).

[40] Women's Commission (n 7 above) 35.

[41] United Nations Ad Hoc Committee on a Comprehensive and Integral International Convention on Protection and Promotion of the Rights and Dignity of Persons with Disabilities, G.A. Res. 168, U.N GAOR, 56th Sess., Supp. No. 168, U.N. Doc. A/RES/56/168 (2001).

entered into force on 3 May 2008. The CRPD negotiation process was driven by a participatory dynamic that involved state representatives, people with disabilities and disabled persons organisations, and an array of non-governmental organisations.[42] African delegations played a prominent role in the drafting of the instrument – especially South Africa, Uganda, Kenya, and Sierra Leone[43] – and African States were amongst the CRPD's first signatories.[44]

The CRPD embraces a social model of disability that recognises persons with disabilities as active agents and equal holders of rights. This rights-based approach affirms that all people with all types of disabilities must enjoy all human rights and fundamental freedoms, irrespective of their social or economic status.[45] At the same time, the CRPD defines disability 'as an evolving concept' that 'results from the interaction between persons with impairments and attitudinal and environmental barriers that hinders their full and effective participation in society on an equal basis with others' and not as an inherent characteristic.[46] This reorients disability issues away from paternalistic and overly protective models that cast persons with disabilities as passive and helpless victims in need of charitable benevolence.[47]

Significantly, the CRPD creates an additional mandate for the UN, including the United Nations High Commisioner for Human Rights (UNHCHR), and the application of its provisions to UN programming is

[42] See MA Stein & JE Lord 'The Law and Politics of US Participation in the UN Convention on the Rights of Persons with Disabilities' in S Hertel & K Libal (eds), 2011 *Human Rights in the United States: Beyond Exceptionalism*, 199.

[43] An archive of the CRPD negotiaions is maintained at the United Nations Enable website, available at http://www.un.org/disabilities/default.asp?id=1423 (accessed 21 December 2010).

[44] For instance, the following African States signed on March 30 2007, the first day the CRPD opened for signature: Algeria, Cape Verde, Congo, Ethiopia, Gabon, Ghana, Kenya, Morroco, Niger, Nigeria, Sierra leone, South Africa, Sudan, Tunisia, Uganda, and Tanzania. See http://www.un.org/disabilities/countries.asp?id=166 (accessed 22 December 2010).

[45] For an overview of the CRPD and its reflection of the social model of disability, see R Kayess & P French 'Out of darkness into light? Introducing the Convention on the Rights of Persons with Disabilities' (2008) 8 *Human Rights Law Review* 1–27.

[46] See CRPD (n 2 above) Preamblular para (e).

[47] See O Lewis 'The Expressive, educational and proactive roles of human rights: An analysis of the United Nations Convention on the Rights of Persons with Disabilities' in B McSherry & P Weller (eds) *Rethinking rights-based mental health laws* (2010).

being facilitated and coordinated through an Inter-Agency Group.[48]

A core mandate of the CRPD is to clarify and make applicable existing general human rights obligations to the context of the lived experiences of persons with disabilities.[49] This remit motivated the drafting of a disability-specific treaty and arose due to the absence of disability rights, explicitly or programmatically, from the protection accorded all persons under the existing international human rights system and indeed international refugee law as well as international humanitarian law.[50] All of these systems, while in theory applicable to persons with disabilities, render disabled persons largely invisible or aggregated amongst a broader group of 'vulnerable' or 'other' persons in need of protection.[51]

A central theme emerging from the CRPD and specifically reflected in its obligations is the need to ensure the full participation of people with disabilities in all spheres of life, including the development of national and international laws, policies and programs.[52] This includes ensuring the meaningful inclusion of persons with disabilities and their representative organisations in the planning, design, implementation and evaluation of each country's development programmes in order to ensure a full success in the implementation of humanitarian and other economic and social development strategies.[53] Participation in decision-making is thus a core element of the rights protection framework of the CRPD and is a vital

[48] The Group is charged with coordinating the work of the United Nations system in support of the promotion and implementation of the Convention which includes the development of a draft strategy and plan of action to mainstream the CRPD throughout the work of the UN system. For a summary of the work of the Inter-Agency Support Group, see Report of the Secretary-General, Status of the Convention on the Rights of Persons with Disabilities (7 July 2009) UN Doc. A/64/128 http://daccessdds.un.org/doc/UNDOC/GEN/N09/393/77/PDF/N0939377.pdf?OpenElement (accessed 22 December 2010) (CRPD Status).

[49] JE Lord & MA Stein 'The domestic incorporation of human rights law and the United Nations Convention on the Rights of Persons with Disabilities' (2008) 83 *Washington Law Review* 456 (noting that the 'Convention sets forth a host of general obligations familiar to human rights treaties').

[50] In their report, Degener and Quinn argue that the lack of any binding human rights law for disabled persons helped provoke a move towards an international treaty on disability. T Degener & G Quinn 'A survey of international, comparative and regional disability law reform' (2002) part I, B, 3 http://www.nhri.net/pdf/disability.pdf (accessed 22 December 2010).

[51] MA Stein 'Disability human rights' (2007) 95 *California Law Review* 83.

[52] See CRPD (n 3 above) art 4(3).

[53] See CRPD (n 3 above) art 32.

precondition for inclusive programming in the refugee protection context. This mandate is reinforced through the inclusion of participation as a general principle within Article 3, a state obligation in Article 4, and as a specific substantive right in Article 29 on participation in political and public life.[54] Because the CRPD is a holistic human rights treaty whose obligations must be understood to run horizontally across the instrument,[55] a convincing argument can be made for any individual Article being related to persons with disabilities when they are also refugees or IDPs.[56]

Failures in ensuring that humanitarian response and assistance to refugees and IDPs take the needs of disabled persons into account prompted the drafters of the CRPD to include a specific provision on protection in times of risk, including armed conflict and natural disasters. This provision was heavily supported by the African Group.[57] During the Second Ad Hoc Session, Disabled Peoples International contended that refugees and internationally displaced persons are a category amongst persons with disabilities whose rights must be further elaborated if a convention was to adequately cover the full spectrum of human rights.[58] In consequence, Article 11 provides that:

> States Parties shall take, in accordance with their obligations under international law, including international humanitarian law and international human rights law, all necessary measures to ensure the protection and

[54] See CRPD (n 3 above) arts 3, 29.

[55] JE Lord & MA Stein 'Social rights and the relational value of the rights to participate in sport, recreation and play' (2009) 27 *Boston University International Law Journal* 281 ('The application of a holistic and integrated human rights approach as set forth in the CRPD recognises the importance of a comprehensive rights framework, inclusive of social rights').

[56] See generally Vienna Declaration and Programme of Action, World Conference on Human Rights (14–25 June 1993) U.N. Doc. A/CONF.157/24 63 (human rights are 'indivisible, interrelated and interconnected').

[57] For an updated list of States Parties, see the United Nations Enable website, available at http://www.un.org/esa/socdev/enable/rights/convtexte.htm (accessed 22 December 2010).

[58] See Disabled Persons' International 'DPI position paper regarding a new international human rights convention for disabled people, February 2003' in Views submitted by governments, intergovernmental organisations and United Nations bodies concerning a comprehensive and integral international convention on the protection and promotion of the rights and dignity of persons with disabilities U.N. Doc. A/AC.265/2003/4+A/AC.265/2003/4/Corr.1 (June 16–27, 2003). In addition, the Economic Commission for Latin America and the Caribbean asked that consideration be given to people with disabilities when they experience additional discrimination as refugees and displaced persons. See C Arigas 'Response submitted by the ECLAC to the Second Session' http://www.un.org/esa/socdev/enable/rights/uncontrib-eclac.htm (accessed 2 December 2010).

> safety of persons with disabilities in situations of risk, including situations of armed conflict, humanitarian emergencies and the occurrence of natural disasters.[59]

Article 11 thus requires positive measures of protection and safety by state parties for people with disabilities affected by situations of humanitarian emergencies and risk, including efforts directed at assisting refugees and IDPs.[60] The necessity of such provision also is recognised overtly in the CRPD's preamble,[61] and was suggested at an African regional workshop.[62]

Notable among the nine core United Nations human rights treaties, the CRPD also includes an inclusive development provision.[63] Specifically, Article 32 governs the activities of states parties in cooperative efforts with each other, international and regional organisations, and civil society, especially disabled persons organisations.[64] Among the enumerated appropriate measures is a directive for state parties engaging in international cooperation efforts to ensure that these schemes, 'including international development programmes, is inclusive of and accessible to persons with disabilities'.[65] This clearly applies to humanitarian emergency programmes designed to reach refugees and IDPs. In addition, Article 32 calls upon states parties to facilitate and support capacity-building activities such as training programmes, and sharing information and best practices; facilitate cooperative research and access to technical and scientific information; and the appropriate provision of economic and technical assistance, and the sharing and transfer of technologies.[66]

[59] CRPD (n 3 above) art 11.

[60] CRPD (n 3 above) art 11.

[61] CRPD (n 3 above) Preamble (u) (underscoring that 'the observance of applicable human rights instruments are indispensable for the full protection of persons with disabilities, in particular during armed conflicts and foreign occupation').

[62] Regional Workshop On Promoting the Rights of Persons with Disabilities: Towards a New UN Convention Final Declaration, Munyonyo – Kampala, Uganda (5–6 June 2003) 21 ('A Preamble to the Convention should: ... recognise the impact of dual or multiple discrimination faced by individuals such as ... refugees, minorities or persons with multiple disabilities or other status').

[63] MA Stein *et al* 'Disability Rights, the MDGs and Inclusive Development' in M Langford *et al* (eds) *Millennium Development Goals and Human Rights: Past, Present and Future*, 2011 (forthcoming).

[64] See CRPD (n 3 above) art 32.

[65] CRPD (n 3 above) art 32(1)(a).

[66] CRPD (n 3 above) art 32(1)(a)–(d).

Other articles implicitly reference the right of persons with disabilities to be included in humanitarian efforts by state parties and accord protection rights applicable to disabled refugees and IDPs. Article 10, for example, recognises the inherent right to life for people with disabilities and requires state parties to 'take all necessary measures' to ensure the enjoyment of that right by disabled people, on an equal basis with others.[67] Article 16 of the CRPD requires state parties to accord protection to persons with disabilities from exploitation, violence and abuse and to provide rehabilitation, reintegration and protection for survivors of violence and other forms of abuse.[68] Article 18 recognises the rights of persons with disabilities to liberty of movement, freedom to choose their residence, and to a nationality. It further specifies, among other things, that persons with disabilities must not be deprived, on the basis of disability, of their ability to obtain, possess and utilise documentation of their nationality or other documentation of identification, or to utilise relevant processes such as immigration proceedings.[69] These are clearly important protections for refugees and IDPs.

Article 28 compels state parties to ensure an adequate standard of living and social protection, including equal access to 'clean water services' and 'public housing programmes'.[70] Similarly, Article 25 requires equal access to health care,[71] while Article 26 makes certain the provision of habilitation and rehabilitation.[72] Article 20 facilitates access to mobility aids and training.[73] And Article 31 requires states to collect disaggregated statistical data on disability and to observe human rights and fundamental freedoms within the framework of data collection and use.[74]

The CRPD also emphasises the importance of accessibility in order to facilitate the right of persons with disabilities to 'live independently and participate fully in all aspects of life'.[75] Article 9 specifically requires States Parties to undertake appropriate accessibility measures in order to ensure that persons with disabilities have equal access to the physical environment,

[67] CRPD (n 3 above) art 10.

[68] CRPD (n 3 above) art 16.

[69] CRPD (n 3 above) art 18.

[70] CRPD (n 3 above) art 28, 28(2)(a), 28(2)(d).

[71] CRPD (n 3 above) art 25.

[72] CRPD (n 3 above) art 26.

[73] CRPD (n 3 above) art 20.

[74] CRPD (n 3 above) art 31.

[75] CRPD (n 3 above) art 9.

transportation, information and communications as well as to other facilities and services in both urban and rural areas.[76] In this regard, States are required to identify and then remove obstacles and barriers to accessibility, including in buildings, roads, transportation, schools, housing, medical facilities, information, communication and other services. This provision has application to refugee camps as well as urban settlements and States have a responsibility to effectively monitor the implementation of accessibility measures in these contexts. Articles 6 and 7 compel, respectively, that women and children with disabilities enjoy the full spectrum of human rights.[77]

Previously, humanitarian assistance organisations have rarely had disability inclusion policies or guidelines to assist in the design and implementation of their work, nor included training that addresses the specific needs of disabled refugees and IDPs.[78] Nonetheless, and as will be discussed in the next part, the ratification of the CRPD by nearly one hundred states has served as an impetus for the development of disability inclusive policies by a number of major bilateral and multilateral donors.[79] This, in turn, should compel similarly inclusive policy turns by implementers of humanitarian assistance programmes serving refugees and IDPs. The obligations set out in the CRPD provide a model for ensuring that such policies are put into place and that governments are carefully monitoring the policies and practices of emergency responders.

Disability inclusion in the protection framework

An understanding of how disability is relevant to refugee law and policy is largely absent in both theory and practice. The refugee law framework, and the emerging protection framework for IDPs, renders the experience of disabled refugees largely invisible. Nonetheless, the mandate created by the CRPD is serving as an impetus for the United Nations as well as for other organisations to focus on disability inclusion.

[76] CRPD (n 3 above) art 9.

[77] CRPD (n 3 above) arts 6, 7.

[78] See M Kett & J Twigg 'Disability and disasters: Towards an inclusive approach' in Y Klynman *et al World disasters report 2007* (2007) 89; Stein *et al* (n 63 above).

[79] See generally JE Lord *et al* 'Disability and International Cooperation and Development: A review of Policies and Practices'. A discussion paper no 1003 (May 2010) http://siteresources.worldbank.org/DISABILITY/Resources/Publications-Reports/Disability_and_Intl_Cooperation.pdf (accessed 22 December 2010).

The Refugee Convention sets out the rights which individuals are entitled to once they have been recognised as refugees. The 1951 Refugee Convention, however, only references disability in the context of a provision on labor legislation and social security and simply affirms that refugees are entitled to the same social security rights as citizens of the country.[80] The ability of refugees with disabilities to realise these rights is seriously undermined in view of the fact that the vast majority of countries in the world, including most African countries, have under-developed disability rights law and policy frameworks. The 1951 Convention provides that all refugees must be granted identity papers and travel documents that allow them to travel outside the country, a right that may be compromised for refugees with disabilities because they may have no birth registration or other documentation to bring with or because they are denied the right to obtain travel documentation on account of their disability. While the Convention requires that refugees must receive the same treatment as nationals of the receiving country with regard to a range of rights, such as free access to the courts, including legal assistance and access to elementary education, and access to public relief and assistance, in practice, multiple barriers prevent persons with disabilities access to these rights generally, irrespective of their immigration status.

Disability is not an explicitly recognised ground of persecution in the 1951 Convention. Under the existing definition, a person with a disability could claim refugee status by falling within the category of "social group." Grounding a successful claim therefore hinges on an understanding of the socially constructed nature of disability, a perspective that does not always obtain among immigration officials and judges, nor within refugee assistance agencies. While the refugee definition can and should encompass disability-based claims of persecution, greater awareness is required of how disability can influence the type of persecution or harm experienced and the reasons for this treatment. Clearly, a precondition to improving refugee and IDP response for persons with disabilities in Africa is enhancing disability awareness and the specific needs of disabled refugees and IDPs.

Likewise, the emerging protection regime for IDPs, including the Guiding Principles on Internal Displacement,[81] is not particularly disability-inclusive,

[80] Office of the United Nations High Commissioner for Human Rights 'United Nations Conference of Plenipotentiaries on the Status of Refugees and Stateless Persons: Convention relating to the Status of Refugees' (14 December 1950) art 24 http://go. micro soft.com/fwlink/?LinkId=68925 (accessed 22 December 2010).

[81] See generally UNHCR 'Guiding principles on internal displacement' 1 September 2004 http://www.idpguidingprinciples.org/ (accessed 22 December 2010).

however, there are signs of hopeful progress. The Guiding Principles do recognise that persons with disabilities are entitled to protection and assistance.[82] Article 9 of the African Union Convention for the Protection and Assistance of Internally Displaced Persons in Africa likewise calls on state parties to accord special protection to internally displaced persons who are persons with disabilities.[83] Other components of the evolving protection framework for IDPs also make reference to persons with disabilities, including the revised Framework for Durable Solutions[84] and the Inter-Agency Standing Committee's Operational Guidelines on Human Rights and Natural Disasters.[85] These highly influential documents emphasise the principle of non-discrimination in relation to persons with disabilities, for example. Other instruments negotiated within the framework of the African Union are beginning to pay closer attention to disability inclusion and many of these are relevant for all persons, including refugees and IDPs. Thus, for example, the African Charter on Elections, Democracy and Governance calls on States to adopt measures to guarantee the rights of, among others, persons with disabilities, refugees and IDPs.[86]

It remains the case however, that the protection framework has not adequately facilitated disability inclusion in practice, on the ground, whether in Africa or elsewhere.

Charting a research agenda for Africa

Ensuring the adequate protection of people with disabilities in humanitarian crises ultimately requires a better integrated and implemented policy approach to drive field-based solutions. Policymakers can only properly target priorities and develop appropriate responses if they first acknowledge

[82] UNHCR (n 81 above) principle 4(1) (2).

[83] African Union Convention for the Protection and Assistance of Internally Displaced Persons in Africa (Kampala Convention) (23 October 2009) art. 9 http://www.unhcr.org/4b7eb01c6.html (accessed 22 December 2010).

[84] See Report of the Representative of the Secretary-General on the human rights of internally displaced persons, Walter Kälin, Addendum, 'Framework on durable solutions for internally displaced persons,' 29 Dec. 2009, A/HRC/13/21/Add.4.

[85] See Inter-Agency Standing Committee's Operational Guidelines on Human Rights and Natural Disasters, Brookings Bern Project (June 2006).

[86] See African Charter on Democracy, Elections and Governance (30 January 2007), art. 8(2), http://www.un.org/democracyfund/Docs/AfricanCharterDemocracy.pdf (accessed 19 February 2011).

the life experience and concerns of persons with disabilities. Ensuring that responses are appropriately contextualised and are designed to meet the real needs of persons with disabilities on the ground can be fostered through disability-specific field assessments undertaken by researchers with disability expertise, together with persons with disabilities' organisations working on the ground. Charting out a research agenda is part and parcel of developing inclusive policies and strategies that will shape humanitarian response on the ground. Worldwide, including Africa, relatively little examination has been undertaken on the needs of refugees and IDPs with disabilities. In order to build the evidence base required to design and operationalise inclusive programming, this area requires promotion and funding. The following research agenda seeks to help formulate specific strategies to enhance inclusion in refugee response in the African context.

Engage in participatory action research to enhance disability need assessments

Participatory action research undertaken to determine refugee and IDP needs in specific African contexts must include the participation of disabled refugees and IDPs, including in the design and implementation of the research. Research design should be directed at identifying the specific needs of persons with disabilities and formulating strategies to ensure their participation in decision-making, including in refugee camp leadership, on disability watch teams to enhance protection and security for disabled refugees in camps and in relation to specific decision-making such as procedures to ensure direct distribution of food to persons with disabilities.

Research accessible designs for refugee and IDP camps

Such research should be targeted towards promoting greater access and enhance security according to the needs of persons with disabilities, including ensuring that shelters and latrines are accessible, providing better lighting, and developing disability assistance teams who can provide support needs indicated by refugees and IDPs with disabilities.

Research disability inclusion in training programmes

In order to foster inclusion for refugees and IDPs with disabilities, it is essential that disability awareness training be provided for aid personnel, border guards, police, military units and peacekeeping forces, asylum officers and others who come into contact with disabled refugees and IDPs. Research into existing programming can identify opportunities for integrating disability-specific information, such as material written by and with disabled refugees themselves. Research can also disclose good practices, such as the placement of staff with disability awareness training in reception centers at refugee and IDP camps and settlements and in border areas where refugee crossings occur.

Assess strategies for prioritising the needs of disabled refugees in the resettlement process

Resettlement policy and process in the context of persons with disabilities requires review and analysis against the CRPD's human rights framework. Such research should be directed at reviewing UNHCHR and country resettlement policies for persons with disabilities, including prioritisation programmes, as well as reviewing procedures by which disabled refugees receive appropriate disability accommodations at all stages of the resettlement process.

Analyse the disability inclusive components of refugee and IDP access to microfinance programmes, employment, and other reintegration activities

Persons with disabilities are too often left out of development activities, and this is also the case for refugees and IDPs with disabilities seeking access to microfinance programmes, employment and income generating activities as well as education and training. Research agendas designed to address the inclusion of refugees and IDPs with disabilities should ensure that persons with disabilities are part of the research project and are appropriately disaggregated as opposed to subsumed under the 'most vulnerable' category. Such inclusion should be directed at identifying barriers to inclusion and facilitating concrete strategies of inclusion.

Conclusion

The invisibility of a disability rights narrative in both refugee and IDP law and policy has contributed to a singular lack of accessible programming in responses to displacement, not only in Africa, but worldwide. The ratification of the CRPD in countries across the African continent and corresponding law and policy should, it is hoped, trigger the broadening and deepening of refugee and IDP protection for beneficiaries with disabilities. Looking forward, disability-specific research in the area of refugee and IDP protection should help prompt thoughtful, disability-specific planning in the humanitarian assistance realm, both as a matter of humanitarian policy as well as field implementation. Recognition of people with disabilities in refugee and IDP humanitarian circumstances has an added benefit of raising the awareness of public education officials about the disability population. Ultimately, taking specific steps to ensure the inclusion of persons with disabilities in humanitarian response avoids future human harm and reduces redevelopment costs.

The CRPD, as one of the most rapidly ratified human rights treaties ever, is serving as a major impetus for disability inclusion in emergency response. The CRPD provides a useful template for the formulation of research agendas that can help drive thoughtful and effective inclusive responses in Africa and elsewhere. A handful of humanitarian assistance donor agencies have committed themselves to disability inclusive schemes, including the US Agency for International Development and the Australian Agency for International Development.[87] The United Nations Development Programme and other UN agencies and programmes are likewise reconsidering their mandates in the light of the CRPD.[88]

Persons with disabilities and their representative organisations must be recognised as resources essential to the development process and, in particular, as agents in the building of inclusive societies in which rights flourish. Emergency preparedness, whether responding to refugee or IDPs flows during situations of risk such as armed conflict or as a result of natural disaster or other emergency, must include the participation of persons with disabilities themselves. Any research agenda focused on disability inclusion in the context of African refugee and IDP populations must, accordingly, include the participation of the disability community.

87 USAID 'Disability and development' http://www.usaid.gov/about_usaid/disability/ (accessed 1 December 2010); see also AusAID 'Disability in Australia's aid program' http://www.ausaid.gov.au/keyaid/disability.cfm (accessed 19 July 2010).

88 See generally Lord (n 79 above).

6

Domesticating international standards of education for children with intellectual disabilities: A case study of Kenya and South Africa

Lorenzo Wakefield & Nkatha L. Murungi

Introduction

The right to education for persons with disabilities is established in various international law instruments. It is also trite that the right to education for children, including children with disabilities, is universally acknowledged. This is evidenced by the near universal ratification of the Convention on the Rights of the Child (CRC), as well as the African Charter on the Rights and Welfare of the Child (ACRWC), which both provide for a right to education for all children without discrimination on any ground, including disability. The Convention on the Rights of Persons with Disabilities (CRPD), which is the latest addition to the list of human rights conventions relative to persons with disabilities, also addresses the rights of children with disabilities to education.

Notably however, international law approaches the right to education for children with disabilities in a rather generic way. This means that the rights of children with intellectual disabilities have to be gleaned from the general provisions of the conventions. In view of the centrality of intellectual capacity in the context of education, it is imperative to decipher the import of the right to education for children with intellectual disabilities. For this purpose, this chapter explores the content of international law on the right to education of children with intellectual disabilities. It uses two case studies to assess the approach of African states to the domestication of the obligations in this regard. Kenya and South Africa have both ratified the CRC, ACRWC and the CRPD.[1] Further, Kenya has ratified and South Africa signed the International Covenant on Economic, Social and Cultural Rights (CESCR).

The definition of intellectual disability

In conceptualising disability, two important models have been developed to express a lens through which disability is viewed. These two are the social and medical models of disability. The medical model aims to 'conceptualise disability as a physical or mental condition that inheres in the body of the disabled person'.[2] As can be deduced from its name and this basic conceptualisation of this model, it can be determined that this model focuses solely on disability as a medical 'condition' for which a medical answer is needed. On the other hand, the social model defines 'disability as resulting from an interaction between a person's physical or mental characteristic and an inaccessible or inhospitable physical or social environment'.[3] In this way, the model locates the problem associated with disability outside the person with disability. The social model of disability places a focus on using legislative solutions to remedy the inequalities that persons with disabilities face each day. In other words, it philosophically views persons with disabilities as different, and not incapable.

The CRPD provides an inclusive definition of disability, which aims to cover all the different types of disabilities. In terms of article 1, a 'person with a disability' includes:

> Those who have long-term physical, mental, intellectual or sensory impairments which in interaction with various barriers may hinder their full and effective participation in society on an equal basis with others.

On the other hand, the definition of a person with a disability is not always static and changes depending on the context of the laws that covers such areas. It will therefore not be incorrect to argue that the definition of what constitutes a person with a disability does not come without its fair amount

[1] The CRPD was adopted by the UN General Assembly on 13 December 2006 and entered into force on 3 May 2008. South Africa ratified the CRPD on 30 November 2007, Kenya ratified on 19 May 2008.

[2] J Cantor 'Defining disabled: Exporting the ADA to Europe and the social model of disability' (2008–2009) 24 *Connecticut Journal of International Law* 403.

[3] Cantor (n 2 above) 404.

of complication, as this definition changes depending on which treaty or legislation it is contained within.[4]

Unlike the definition of what constitutes a person with a disability, defining what constitutes a person with an intellectual disability is not as problematic. Nevertheless, the explanation of what constitutes a person with an intellectual disability needs some explaining. A person with intellectual disability is commonly understood as someone with 'a diminished ability to adapt to the daily demands of the normal social environment'.[5] Intellectual disability can be categorised into four levels; mild, moderate, severe and profound. Persons are diagnosed with mild intellectual disabilities when their intellectual quotient (IQ) levels fall between 50 and 69. Those with moderate intellectual disabilities would normally have an IQ between 35 and 49, while persons with severe intellectual disabilities would have an IQ between 20 and 34. Profound intellectual disabilities are diagnosed on people with an IQ below 20.[6]

The World Health Organisation describes intellectual disability to include what is commonly termed as 'mental retardation', 'mental handicapped' and 'learning disabilities'.[7] The same report goes further to explain that all of these situations have two 'significant limitations' in common, being 'intellectual functioning and adaptive behaviour', as well as the 'manifestation of these symptoms before adulthood'.[8] The use of adjectives like 'significant limitations' implies a level of severity of the intellectual disability. It is thus arguable that the World Health Organisation definition does not include cases of persons with mild or moderate intellectual disabilities.

For purposes of this chapter, the following explanation of a person with an intellectual disability is adopted. It is drawn from the inclusive definitions

[4] H Combrinck 'The hidden ones: Children with disabilities in Africa and the right to education' in J Sloth-Nielsen (ed) *Children's rights in Africa: A legal perspective* (2008) 303.

[5] H Combrinck 'Sexual offences against persons who are mentally disabled' in D Smythe & B Pithey (eds) *Sexual Offences Commentary: Act 32 of 2007* (2011) 14–3.

[6] Western Cape Forum for Intellectual Disabilities 'Discussion document for the education of learners with severe and profound intellectual disabilities' (2000) 5. (On file with the authors). See also P Mittler 'Meeting the needs of people with an intellectual disability: International perspectives' in S Herr *et al* (eds) *The human rights of persons with intellectual disabilities: Different but equal* (2003) 29–30 for an explanation of the levels of intellectual disability.

[7] World Health Organisation 'Atlas: Global resources for persons with intellectual disabilities' (2007) 19.

[8] As above.

of disability in both the CRPD and the CRC:

> Persons with intellectual disabilities are those who have long-term intellectual impairments which in interaction with various barriers may hinder their full and effective participation in society on an equal basis with others.

This inclusive definition of a person with an intellectual disability is preferred, as it covers the essential elements of disability in general, while placing a focus on long-term intellectual impairments, which speaks to the specificity of an intellectual disability.

International standards of education for children with intellectual disability

General provisions

A general right to education in international law was first recognised in the Universal Declaration of Human Rights (UDHR).[9] However, the first internationally binding agreement on the right to education was the CESCR. Article 13 thereof establishes the right 'of everyone' to education directed at the full development of the human personality and the sense of its dignity. This has been interpreted to mean that 'education must make the individual aware of his own worth and of the human rights which accrue to him on this basis'.[10] Article 13(2) further sets out a range of duties for state parties to ensure that these objectives are met. Article 14 sets out the duty of state parties to deliver free and compulsory primary education. Where this standard is not yet established as at the time of ratification of CESCR, then the state party is to adopt progressive measures to achieve free compulsory education within a 'reasonable number of years'.

The CRC establishes the right of children to education and the duty of the state 'to make primary education compulsory and available free for all'.[11] The article obliges states to encourage the development of different forms of secondary education including general and vocational education. The education of a child is directed, *inter alia*, to the development of a child's

[9] Art 26.

[10] KD Beiter *The protection of the right to education in international law* (2006) 96.

[11] The CRC, art 28.

personality, talents and mental and physical abilities to their fullest potential.[12] It has been argued that in comparison to articles 13 and 14 of CESCR, the right to education in the CRC is couched in weaker terms.[13]

The ACRWC stipulates that 'every child has a right to an education' directed *inter alia* to the promotion and development of their personality, talents and mental and physical abilities to their fullest potential.[14] State parties to the ACRWC are to provide 'free and compulsory basic education' and to take special measures in respect of 'disadvantaged children' to ensure equal access to education for all sections of the community.[15] The duty to provide 'free and compulsory basic education' as stipulated in this article is an immediate obligation of state parties as distinct from that under the CRC which allows for progressive realisation.

The right to education for children with disabilities

Article 23(3) of the CRC obliges state parties to ensure that children with disabilities have effective access to education and training. In addition, article 2(1) of the CRC requires state parties to ensure the realisation of rights under the CRC to every child in their jurisdiction without discrimination on any grounds including disability. Hence whereas articles 28 and 29 of the CRC do not mention children with disabilities, application of article 2 precludes their discrimination in accessing education. The CRC Committee in General Comment Number 1[16] helped to identify the relevance and significance of articles 28 and 29 of the CRC to children with disabilities.[17]

Article 23(2) of the CRC recognises the special needs of children with disabilities and obliges state parties to encourage and ensure assistance to the child or those caring for the child upon application and subject to the availability of resources. However, the preconditions for eligibility to the assistance render this right very weak.[18] Hence, some commentators argue

[12] As above, art 29(a).

[13] Beiter (n 10 above) 116.

[14] Art 11(1).

[15] As above art 11(3).

[16] Committee on the Rights of the Child, General Comment No 1 'The aims of education' U.N. Doc. CRC/GC/2001/1 (2001).

[17] U Kilkelly 'Disability and children: The Convention on the Rights of the Child (CRC)' in G Quinn & T Degener (eds) *Human rights and Disability: The current use and future potential of United Nations human rights instruments in the context of disability* (2002) 199.

[18] Combrinck (n 4 above) 307.

that the other provisions of the CRC such as article 2 provide a higher standard of education for children with disabilities.[19]

Article 13 of ACRWC recognises the right of children with disabilities to special measures of protection in keeping with their 'physical and moral needs and under conditions which ensure [their] dignity, promote [their] self-reliance and active participation in the community'. The article also recognises the need for support in qualified circumstances. Notably however, it does not point out areas of assistance such as education as does article 23(3) of the CRC. Even though education is catered for under article 11 of the ACRWC, the education needs of children with disabilities are different from those of their peers without disabilities.[20] Therefore, the failure to explicitly mention education, coupled with the limitations to accessing assistance, undermines the fulfilment of the rights of children with disabilities in the ACRWC.

The CRPD is the first legally binding international instrument to deal exclusively with the rights of persons with disabilities.[21] In article 7, the CRPD obliges state parties to take all necessary measures to ensure the full enjoyment of the rights and fundamental freedoms of children with disabilities on an equal basis with other children. Article 24 requires state parties to ensure an inclusive education system at all levels.[22] It prohibits the exclusion of children with disabilities 'from the general education system on the basis of disability' or denial of 'access to an inclusive, quality and free primary education and secondary education on an equal basis with others in the community in which they live'.[23] State parties are to ensure that reasonable accommodation of an individual's requirements is provided, and that children with disabilities receive the support required, within the general education system, to facilitate their effective education.[24]

It is apparent that international children's rights law recognises the right to education for children with disabilities, and in as far as possible, their right to be educated within the general education system. It further recognises their entitlement to education on an equal basis with other children and to be provided with assistance where necessary to achieve this right.

[19] Kilkelly (n 17 above) 199.

[20] M Gose *The African Charter on the Rights and Welfare of the Child* (2002) 91.

[21] Combrinck (n 4 above) 309.

[22] Art 24(1).

[23] Art 24(2)(a) & (b).

[24] Art 24(2)(c)–(d).

Interpretation of the states' obligations

In General Comment No 1, the CRC Committee stated that the aims of education are to promote, support and protect the core values of the CRC. These are human dignity innate in every child, and his or her equal and inalienable rights. The Committee further stated that education is directly linked to the realisation of the child's human dignity and rights[25] and must be provided in a manner that respects such inherent dignity.[26] Education must recognise that every child has unique characteristics, interests, abilities and learning needs. The curriculum must be tailored to the different needs of different children in order to equip them with the necessary skills to face the challenges that confront them in life.[27] The text of the General Comment No 1 reiterates the need to respect the dignity of a child in education, which is fundamental to the realisation of the right to education for children with disabilities in general and those with intellectual disabilities in particular. The failure of General Comment No 1 to infer a right to an effective or inclusive education under articles 28 and 29 of the CRC has been criticised as missing an opportunity to satisfactorily address the right of children with disabilities to education.[28]

In General Comment No 9,[29] the CRC Committee, drawing from goal number 2 of the Millennium Development Goals, stated that 'children with disabilities have the same right to education as all other children and shall enjoy [that] right without any discrimination and on the basis of equal opportunity as stipulated in the Convention'.[30] The Committee further noted that the core message of article 23 of the CRC is that children with disabilities should be included in society and that measures taken for the implementation of the CRC should explicitly aim at their maximum inclusion.[31] In recognition of the diverse needs of children with disabilities, the Committee expressed need for individualised attention to help them develop their skills.[32]

[25] General Comment No 1, para 1.

[26] General Comment No 1, para 8.

[27] General Comment No 1 para 9.

[28] Kilkelly (n 17 above) 200.

[29] Committee on the Rights of the Child, General Comment No 9 (2006) 'The rights of children with disabilities, CRC/C/GC/9 27 February 2007.

[30] General Comment No 9 (as above), para 62.

[31] General Comment No 9 (as above), para 11–13.

[32] General Comment No 9 (as above), para 63.

In General Comment No 5,[33] the Committee on Economic, Social and Cultural rights (CESR) reiterated and supported the view that persons with disabilities are best educated in the general education systems.[34] State parties are thus bound to ensure that teachers are trained to educate children with disabilities within regular schools and to provide the necessary equipment and support to bring children with disabilities to the same level of education as their peers without disability.[35]

It is apparent thus far that the right to education for persons with disabilities as defined in international law does not take into account the various types of disability. This approach subtly presumes similarity of education needs for all types of disability. Even the CRPD, the only international instrument that recognises a category of persons with intellectual disability, addresses the rights of persons with disability in generic terms. This is problematic in view of the fact that in the context of education, cognitive ability, which often underlies intellectual disability, is the fundamental element. The generic approach is also evident in the proposed approach to education, particularly in the advocacy for an inclusive education system.

Approaches to education of children with intellectual disability

Generally, the right to education is founded upon four essential features set out by the UN Committee on Economic, Social and Cultural Rights (Committee on ESCR)[36] as the minimum standard for all forms and levels of education. These are availability, accessibility, acceptability and adaptability of education.[37] Availability refers to the presence of context appropriate and functional educational institutions and programmes. Accessibility requires that all people should be able to access institutions and programmes without discrimination in law and in fact, within physical and economic reach.

33 Committee on Economic, Social and Cultural Rights, General Comment No 5 'Persons with disabilities' (eleventh session, 1994), U.N. Doc E/1995/22 at 19 (1995), U.N. Doc. HRI/GEN/1/Rev.6 at 24 (2003).

34 The Committee on ESCR was quoting from Rule 6 of the Standard Rules on the Equalisation of Opportunities for Persons with Disabilities, annexed to General Assembly resolution 48/96 of 20 December 1993.

35 General Comment No 5, para 35. The Committee on ESCR reiterated this position in its General Comment No 13 on the right to education in article 13 of CESCR.

36 Committee on Economic, Social and Cultural Rights, General Comment No 13 on the right to education (Art. 13) E/C.12/1999/10 (1999)

37 As above, para 6.

Notably, the CESR's conception of accessibility does not seem to give credence to the needs of children with intellectual disabilities, who may be affected by factors other than distance or affordability. Acceptability, on the other hand, relates to the substance and form of education requiring it to be relevant, qualitative and culturally appropriate. Finally, adaptability requires that education is flexible enough to adapt to the needs of students within diverse social and cultural settings. These features address the standards of education in general, but they may, in as far as they apply to children with intellectual disabilities, be used as benchmarks for assessing whether states have complied with the duty to protect their right to education.

Inclusive education

Inclusion is 'the process of addressing and responding to the diversity of needs of all learners through increasing participation in learning, cultures and communities, and reducing exclusion within and from education. It involves changes and modifications in content, approaches, structures and strategies, with a common vision covering all children of the appropriate age range and a conviction that it is the responsibility of the regular system to educate all children ...'[38] Inclusion is concerned with the identification and removal of barriers.[39] Education of children with intellectual disability is therefore but one of the facets of inclusion. However, this broad definition of inclusion informs the understanding of inclusive education.

In General Comment Number 9, the CRC Committee defined inclusive education as 'a set of values, principles and practices that seek meaningful, effective, and quality education for all students, that does justice to the diversity of learning conditions and requirements not only for children with disabilities but for all students.[40] In terms of the Salamanca Declaration,[41] inclusive education requires that education be provided for all within the regular education system.[42] This has also been interpreted to mean that such education should be provided in integrated settings in mainstream educational settings. [43] It is based on the belief that persons with disabilities

[38] UNESCO 'Guidelines for inclusion: Ensuring access to education for all' (2005) 13.

[39] UNESCO (n 38 above) 15.

[40] General Comment No 9, para 67.

[41] Salamanca Statement and Framework for Action on Special Needs Education adopted at the World Conference on Special Needs Education (1994).

[42] M Schulze *Understanding the UN Convention on the Rights of Persons with Disabilities: Handbook on the rights of persons with disabilities* (2009) 121.

[43] Beiter (n 10 above) 507.

have an equal right to share the opportunities of self-fulfilment enjoyed by the unimpaired.[44]

Inclusive education is widely endorsed as the appropriate channel for the education for children with disabilities.[45] Articles 24 and 7 of the CRPD, coupled with General Comments Numbers 1, 9 of the CRC Committee and 5, 13 of the Committee on ESCR, provide a comprehensive framework for the development of inclusive approaches to education of children with disabilities. In the opinion of the CRC Committee, inclusion of children with disabilities in the groups of children in the classroom can show them that they have a recognised identity and belong to the community of learners, peers and citizens.[46] This suggestion presumes peer support that is deemed to enhance the esteem of the child with disabilities. It is anchored in the belief that students in special schools do not enjoy the same range of academic and leisure activities as children in mainstream schools, and that the needs of individual pupils are not met in a comprehensive or dedicated manner.[47]

The CRPD lays down in explicit terms the commitment of states to the goal of inclusive education.[48] Rule 6 of the Standard Rules for the Equalisation of Opportunities for Persons with Disabilities[49] also calls upon State Parties to ensure that the education of persons with disabilities is an integral part of the education system. Rule 6(4) requires that where education is compulsory, it should be provided to children with 'all kinds and all levels of disability including the most severe'. The needs of children with learning disabilities should, as far as possible, be met in mainstream schools with extra support rather than in special schools[50]and free of charge.[51] In effect, schools, teachers, and students have a duty to adapt to learners with divergent needs and abilities.[52] There are also some egalitarian and economic arguments that are advanced to support inclusion and mainstreaming of education for children with disabilities.[53] In practice though, the concept of inclusive education or

[44] J Fortin *Children's rights and the developing law* (2003) 371.

[45] Beiter (n 10 above) 507.

[46] General Comment No 9, para 64.

[47] Kilkelly (n 17 above) 198.

[48] Art 24(2)b.

[49] UN General Assembly Resolution 48/96 of 20 December 1993.

[50] Fortin (n 44 above) 371.

[51] General Comment No 9, para 65.

[52] Beiter (n 10 above) 507.

[53] See generally, Beiter (n 10 above) 135 on the egalitarian arguments.

what it entails is ill understood. Whereas it is widely perceived that inclusive education entails moving children with disabilities from special schools to regular schools, the meaning of inclusive education in fact is teaching the child with disability in an environment that is best suited for learning in view of their disability.[54] In as far as children with intellectual disabilities are concerned, especially in the case of severe and profound disabilities, this may entail teaching such children in special schools. The manner and form of inclusion is to be dictated by the needs of the child, 'since the education of some children with disabilities requires a kind of support which may not really be available in the regular school system'.

There are some limits to inclusiveness. There is no hard and fast criterion for the determination of whether a child with disabilities is eligible for admission to an inclusive school. However, some factors that are particularly relevant to intellectual disability may be instructive; the nature and severity of the disability, advantages and disadvantages of such schooling and the possibility of strain on the human, financial, technical and organisational resources.[55] Children with severe intellectual disabilities often pose special difficulties that ordinary schools are either unable or reluctant to deal with.[56] Besides, even though the theory of inclusive integration is widely and pedagogically supported, it does not guarantee integration of the child with disabilities with their peers. Other realities such as 'the possibility of isolation of children with disabilities by other children or difficulty in making friends with the other learners'[57] exist. It has been shown for instance that despite the integration of pupils into the regular system, attitudes in regular schools are still tinged with prejudice against children with disabilities.[58]

Special education

Special education refers to education of persons with disabilities in separate settings, apart from the regular educational system. With the current emphasis

[54] Kenya National Human Rights Commission (KNHRC) 'Objects of pity or individuals with rights: The Right to education for children with disabilities' (2007) 26, occasional report available at http://www.knchr.org/dmdocuments/Occassional_Paper.pdf (accessed 7 September 2011); South African Department of Education 'White paper 6: Special needs education: Building an inclusive education and training system' (July 2001) 3.

[55] Beiter (n 10 above) 509.

[56] Fortin (n 44 above) 371.

[57] Fortin (n 44 above) 373.

[58] KNHRC (n 54 above) 33.

on inclusive education, special education is increasingly viewed as a means of last resort or a transitive measure to the inclusive system. Hence, it may be considered only where the general school system does not adequately meet the needs of all persons with disability or in preparation of learners to join the general school system.[59] In terms of rule 6 of the Standard Rules for the Equalisation of Opportunities for Persons with Disabilities, special education should be seen as a temporary expedient pending the restructuring of the general school system to adequately meet the needs of children with disabilities.[60] This too connotes a transient role of special education. In general then, it is evident that the role of special education for persons with disabilities is increasingly diminishing. However, in as far as intellectual disabilities are concerned, special education still commands a niche in which regular education is not possible as in the case of severe and profound disability. For this reason, the CRC Committee proposes that 'a continuum of services and programme options in circumstances where fully inclusive education is not feasible in the immediate future' should be maintained.[61] This phraseology implies a need for progressive realisation of inclusive education and the possibility of the existence of circumstances in which inclusive education may not be feasible.

South Africa's compliance with domesticating international standards on the right to education for children with intellectual disabilities

The constitutional right to education

Before the dawn of constitutional democracy in South Africa, racial division existed in the provision of education. This system of segregation also found itself present in education provided to children with disabilities.[62] Thus children with disabilities were not only unfairly discriminated based on race, but also based on their respective disability.

With the dawn of democracy in South Africa, the right to basic education was entrenched in the Constitution.[63] Section 29(1)(a) of the Constitution

[59] Schulze (n 42 above) 124.

[60] Fortin (n 44 above) 371.

[61] General Comment No 9, para 66.

[62] South Africa Department of Education (n 54 above) 9.

[63] Act 108 of 1996.

grants everyone the right to basic education.[64] Woolman and Bishop here correctly argue that the word 'access' is absent in the wording of this right, which means this right is not subject to the general socio-economic rights limitations of 'reasonable legislative measures' and 'availability of resources'.[65] Therefore, it would not be incorrect to argue that the constitutional right to basic education for children with intellectual disabilities is not subject to socio-economic limitations in South Africa and it is to be granted to everyone, which includes children with intellectual disabilities.[66]

This obviously does not mean that such right cannot be subject to general limitation, as per section 36 of the Constitution. Section 36 of the Constitution stipulates that all rights within the Bill of Rights may be subject to reasonable and justifiably limitations, by way of a law of general application. In other words, if any of the legislation, under discussion below, is reasonable and justifiable, it may limit a child with an intellectual disability to the right to basic education. This law of general application only applies to legislation and not policies and programmes.[67]

Legislative and policy analysis of the right to education for children with intellectual disabilities

South Africa has enacted legislation and policy documents to give effect to constitutional principles and international law that it has ratified. These include the National Education Policy Act,[68] the South African Schools Act[69] and more specifically in relation to the right to education for children with disabilities, White Paper 6 on Special Needs Education.

[64] Section 29(1)(a) of the Constitution reads: 'Everyone has the right to a basic education, including adult basic education ...'

[65] S Woolman & M Bishop 'Education' in S Woolman, T Roux & M Bishop *Constitutional law of South Africa* (2009) 57–10.

[66] 'Everyone' in this instance means citizens and persons with permanent residence status as found by the Constitutional Court in the case of *Khosa and Others v Minister of Social Development and Others* 2004 6 BCLR 569 (CC). See also B Bekink & M Bekink 'Children with disabilities and the right to education: A call for action' (2005) 1 *Stellenbosch Law Review* 132.

[67] S Liebenberg *Socio-economic rights: Adjudication under a transformative constitution* (2010) 94.

[68] Act 27 of 1996.

[69] Act 84 of 1996.

The National Education Policy Act

The National Education Policy Act regulates the drafting, monitoring and evaluation of education policies. In terms of section 4(b) of this Act, education policies have to be created to enable 'the education system to contribute to the full personal development of each student, and to the moral, social, cultural, political and economic development of the nation at large, including the advancement of democracy, human rights and the peaceful resolution of disputes'. Bekink and Bekink are of the view that this section indirectly addresses the issue of the right to education for children with intellectual disabilities, as it 'guarantees an education system that enables every student to develop his or her personality to its full potential'.[70] More importantly, section 4(d) of this Act requires the Department of Education to adopt a policy to 'ensure that no person is denied the opportunity to receive an education to the maximum of his or her ability as a result of physical disability'. Even though this section directly speaks to adopting policy based on physical disability, it fails to oblige the Government to adopt any policy on the right to education for children with other forms of disabilities, including those with intellectual disabilities. Thus, it is difficult to agree with Bekink and Bekink who argue that an expansive interpretation of physical disability should be adopted to include other forms of disability, other than physical disability.[71]

The South African Schools Act

The principal piece of legislation governing the right to education in schools in South Africa is the South African Schools Act. In its preamble, the legislation recognises that a new system for schools that has a 'strong foundation for the development of all people's talents and capabilities ... combat racism and sexism and all other forms of unfair discrimination and intolerance ...' is needed to redress the past injustices. It is evident from the preamble that the schooling system provided for in this Act is founded upon the values of non-discrimination and the development of everyone, including children with intellectual disabilities.

The South African Schools Act makes it compulsory for every learner to attend school up to age of 15 years or ninth grade, whichever comes first.[72]

[70] Bekink & Bekink (n 66 above) 137.

[71] As above.

[72] Sec 3(1).

'Learner' is defined in the Act as 'any person receiving education or obliged to receive education'.[73] Section 29 of the Constitution recognises everyone's right to basic education. As argued above[74], 'everyone' includes children with intellectual disabilities. Therefore 'learner', as defined in the South African Schools Act includes a child with intellectual disability. Section 3(2) of the South African Schools Act sets a different standard for compulsory education for learners at special schools by requiring the Minister of Education to publish in the *Government Gazette* the age of compulsory school attendance. As of yet, no such age has been published. It is presumed that the age stipulated for compulsory school attendance for children without disabilities, would apply to children with disabilities.

Section 5(1) of the South African Schools Act stipulates that 'a public school *must* admit learners and serve their educational requirements without unfairly discriminating in any way'.[75] This provision implies a duty on public schools not to unfairly discriminate against any prospective learner. This could also mean that a school cannot unfairly discriminate against a student with an intellectual disability at the point of admission. Section 5(6) of the Act places a duty on both the head of the education department and the principal of a school to consider the 'fights and wishes' of parents of children with special education needs.

Considering that there are various degrees of intellectual disabilities,[76] it might not be such an obvious argument on what constitutes reasonable accommodation for children with intellectual disabilities in the mainstream public school system. In other words, whether reasonable accommodation in the mainstream public school system could be made for children with mild intellectual disabilities is not the same for children with severe intellectual disabilities. The level of intellectual disability for the latter requires much more care and attention, which could possibly not be provided for within the mainstream public school sector. Another area of confusion would be on whether it would constitute unfair discrimination to not reasonably accommodate a child with a moderate intellectual disability in the mainstream public school system. This brings evidence to light that a peculiar response is needed which would inform the broader notion of inclusive education for children with intellectual disabilities.

[73] Sec 1(ix).

[74] See 4.1 on the constitutional right to education.

[75] Authors' emphasis added.

[76] See point 2 above for an explanation of these levels of intellectual disability.

Where it is unreasonable to accommodate children with intellectual disabilities in the mainstream public school system, the duty is placed on the state to provide alternative schools to cater for their needs. The need for alternative schools for children with disabilities should only be justified by the inaccessibility of mainstream public school system, and the best interest of children with intellectual disabilities. It should also be kept in mind that this should be done within the goal of one uniform system of education, as envisaged by the South African Schools Act.[77]

Education White Paper 6 on Special Needs Education: building an inclusive education and training system

In 2001, the South Africa Department of Education published White Paper 6 (policy document) on Special Needs Education. This document reiterated the government's stance on strengthened special schools for children with disabilities, as part of an inclusive system.[78] The objective of the policy document was to 'extend the policy foundations, frameworks and programmes of existing policy for all bands of education and training so that our education and training system will recognise and accommodate the diverse range of learning needs'.[79] In the introduction, the then Minister of Education, professor Kader Asmal, placed an emphasis on creating improved special schools for children with severe disabilities.[80]

Inclusive education and training in the White Paper are defined fairly broadly and include important tenets such as: acknowledging that all children have the ability to learn; enabling education structures to meet the needs of everyone; and respecting differences in learners, which includes those with intellectual disabilities.[81] The policy also acknowledges that impaired intellectual development would require a curriculum adaptation to suit the needs of learners, which demands accommodation. In order to implement this White Paper, the Department of Education established a directorate for inclusive education.[82]

77 The Preamble to the South African Schools Act; also B Bekink & M Bekink (n 66 above) 139–140.

78 South African Department of Education (n 54 above) 3.

79 South African Department of Education (n 54 above) 24.

80 As above.

81 South African Department of Education (n 54 above) 6–7.

82 Combrinck (n 4 above) 315.

Various parts of the 2001 White Paper at the time of writing are not yet implemented.[83] One such example is the revision of the age grade norms to accommodate children with special learning needs such as children with intellectual disabilities. Apart from it being an obligation in terms of the White Paper,[84] it is also required in terms of the South African Schools Act.[85]

Another unfortunate feature of White Paper 6 is that it is aimed at progressively realising the right to inclusive education for children with disabilities.[86] As mentioned above,[87] the constitutional right to basic education in South Africa is not a socio-economic right and therefore it is not subject to the inherent limitations of such rights. The fact that White Paper 6 is structured around progressively realising the right to inclusive education for children with disabilities is therefore *prima facie* unconstitutional.

Challenge to the education of children with severe and profound intellectual disabilities in South Africa

In a relatively recent (at the time of writing) judgment by the Western Cape High Court, the right to education for children with severe and profound intellectual disabilities was under scrutiny.[88] In their heads of argument, the applicants contended that children with severe and profound intellectual disabilities receive no education at all and that the subsidy provided by the State is 'wholly inadequate' to realise the right to education for such children.[89] In its judgment, the High Court found that no provision for

[83] In a 2010 media report, the current Minister of Basic Education, Angie Motshekga, highlighted the need to implement South Africa's 'progressive policy' on inclusive education. See 'Motshekga highlights rights of disabled to education' *The Citizen* 13 August 2010 at http://www.citizen.co.za/index.php?option=com_content&view=article&id=106221&catid=25:local-news&Itemid=34 (Accessed 26 August 2010).

[84] South African Department of Education (n 54 above) 27.

[85] Section 3(2). The South African Schools Act provision relates to the compulsory enrolment of children with special education needs.

[86] Page 36 of the White Paper reads: 'The policy proposals described in the White Paper are aimed at developing an inclusive education and training system that will ensure that educational provision for learners with special needs is largely integrated over time into what are currently considered to be 'ordinary schools.'

[87] See part 4.1 of this chapter on the Constitutional right to education.

[88] See *Western Cape Forum for Intellectual Disability v Government of the Republic of South Africa and Government of the Province of the Western Cape* Case No: 18678/2007 (unreported judgment of 11 November 2010).

[89] Applicants Heads of Argument *Western Cape Forum for Intellectual Disability v Government of the Republic of South Africa and Government of the Province of the Western Cape* 8–10.

children with severe and profound intellectual disabilities was provided for in relation to attending special schools.[90] The High Court was also of the correct view that the State has a constitutional obligation to realise the right to basic education for everyone, and that mere cooperation with organisations like the applicant does not entirely fulfil this obligation.[91] Finally, the High Court also found that there was no reasonable and justifiable limitation for the infringement of the right to basic education for children with severe and profound intellectual disabilities.[92] The High Court ordered that the State take reasonable measures (which also include interim steps) to realise the right to basic education for children with severe and profound intellectual disabilities.[93]

Therefore, whereas South Africa has attempted to realise the right to education for children with disabilities (in general) through the South African Schools Act and White Paper 6, the Western Cape High Court found that the response to the right to basic education for children with intellectual disabilities is inadequate.

Education for children with intellectual disabilities in Kenya

Legal and policy framework

The new Constitution of Kenya[94]recognises the right of all children, without any discrimination on grounds such as disability, to free and compulsory basic education.[95] While the right to education in general is a socio-economic right in terms of the new Constitution,[96] education for children creates an immediate obligation and is not subject to progressive realisation implicit in socio-economic rights.[97] The Constitution further recognises the right of every person with a disability 'to access educational institutions and facilities for persons with disabilities that are integrated into society to the extent

[90] The *Western Cape Forum for Intellectual Disability* case, para 18.

[91] The *Western Cape Forum for Intellectual Disability* case, para 24.

[92] The *Western Cape Forum for Intellectual Disability* case, para 45.

[93] The *Western Cape Forum for Intellectual Disability* case, para 52.

[94] The Constitution was adopted on 4 August and promulgated on 27 August 2010.

[95] Art 53 as read together with article 27 of the new Constitution.

[96] Art 43 of the Constitution.

[97] Art 53 states that 'Every child has the right ... to free and compulsory basic education'.

compatible with the interests of the person.'[98] The interpretation of this provision is likely to be problematic, because it seems to propagate the idea that the right of persons with disability to access educational facilities is limited to facilities for persons with disability. The meaning of the latter part of the provision is also not clear.

In terms of the Kenyan Children's Act[99] a child may not be discriminated on the basis of disability.[100] The Act establishes the right of all children, including children with disabilities, to free and compulsory basic education in accordance with article 28 of the CRC.[101] However with respect to children with disabilities, the Act stipulates that they are entitled to '... education and training free of charge or at a reduced cost' and to be treated with dignity.[102] This implies that unlike their peers, children with disabilities in Kenya, unlike their peers without disability, may be expected to cover a certain extent of the cost of their education on their own. To that extent, this provision contradicts section 7 of the same Act, and article 53 of the Constitution. It also contradicts article 28 of the CRC which requires state parties to make primary education compulsory and available free for all. Section 12 is also reflective of the other shortcoming of section 7(2), which apportions the responsibility for education on both parents and government. This is contrary to international human rights law which puts the responsibility for primary education solely on the government.[103] It should be noted however that the Act precedes the Constitution the provisions of which prevail.

The Persons with Disability Act[104] defines disability as 'a physical, sensory, mental or other impairment, including any visual, hearing, learning or physical incapability, which impacts adversely on social, economic and environmental participation'.[105] This definition includes persons with intellectual disability. The Act outlaws denial of admission to learning institution on the basis of disabilities if the prospective learner has the capacity to acquire substantial learning in the course.[106] The responsibility for the

[98] Art 54.

[99] Act No 8 of 2001.

[100] Sec 5.

[101] Sec 7(2).

[102] Sec 12.

[103] See part 3:1 above.

[104] Act No 13 of 2003.

[105] Sec 2.

[106] Sec 18(1).

realisation of this right vests on the government to the maximum of its available resources.[107] The Act proscribes denial of admission to any person with disability to any course of study by reason only of such disability, if the person has the ability to acquire substantial learning in that course.[108] This would mean that learners with mild and moderate intellectual disabilities should be accommodated in the regular education system. It embodies the principle of reasonable accommodation established under article 24 of the CRPD.

Education of children with disabilities in Kenya falls under the broader framework of Special Needs Education. It appears that this category of children was initially understood to cover children with sensory, physical and mental disabilities. The group has subsequently been expanded to include children with wide variety of other needs including children with cerebral palsy, 'mental handicaps', down syndrome and autism,[109] some of whom can be regarded as having intellectual disabilities. It is however apparent that the policy neither perceives of a specific category of children with intellectual disabilities nor envisages the internationally accepted levels of intellectual disabilities, that is, mild, moderate, severe and profound. The Special Needs Education policy[110] gives general directives that are intended to apply to all the children within that broad spectrum.

The government of Kenya introduced free primary education (FPE) programme in 2003. Soon thereafter, a task force[111] was established to 'carry out an appraisal exercise on special needs education' so as to enable the government to plan for the provision of education to learners with special needs. The task force observed that many children with disabilities who enrolled in regular schools as a result of the FPE eventually dropped out due to lack of equipment and facilities.[112] The task force also concluded that the

[107] Sec 11 of the Act. The Persons with Disability (Amendment) Bill, 2007 proposed an amendment to this provision to do away with the limitation based on resource availability. In section 6, the Bill proposed a section 11(2) of the Disability Act with specific immediate obligations of the state including 'the full enjoyment by children with disabilities of all human rights and fundamental freedoms.' The Bill is yet to be passed into law. The Bill predates Kenya's ratification of the CRPD but clearly progressively embodies the principles thereof.

[108] Sec 18 of the Act.

[109] Ministry of Education, Science and Technology 'The National Special Needs Education Policy Framework' final draft (July 2009) 17.

[110] Ministry of Education, Science and Technology Policy (n 109 above).

[111] Task Force on Special Needs Education (2003).

[112] KNHRC (n 54 above) 18.

only way that the government would provide special education for all children with disabilities was through inclusive education. It noted that inclusive education was already taking place in some of the schools but that the teachers were not sure of how it was to be implemented. Besides, very few of the teachers had training on special needs education and the physical facilities and learning materials in many schools were not appropriate for children with disabilities.[113]

In Sessional Paper No 1 of 2005, the government outlined its policy on education and training by recommending inclusive education, 'including the removal of barriers to education for children with disabilities and awareness creation to eradicate negative beliefs associated with disability'.[114] While committing itself to the goal of education for all by 2015, the policy failed to prescribe specific measures to address the challenges identified with respect to education for children with intellectual disability. This shortcoming suggests that the education of children with disabilities is not a priority in education planning in Kenya.[115]

It is apparent that even though children with intellectual disability benefit from the entirety of rights of children and persons with disability in Kenya, there is no particular focus on their needs in the context of education. The situation mirrors the international legal framework which also does not address the unique needs of children with intellectual disabilities as a distinct category. The Persons with Disability (Amendment) Bill of 2007, which is yet to be presented to Parliament, establishes a duty of the government to provide services to accommodate students with disabilities.[116]Though this slightly improves on the standard established under the Persons with Disabilities Act of 2003, a lot remains to fully realise the right to education for children with intellectual disabilities in Kenya.

Challenges to the education of children with intellectual disabilities in Kenya

Persons with disabilities in Kenya have immense difficulties exercising the right to education despite the centrality accorded to this right in numerous existing government policy documents as a mechanism for poverty

[113] As above.

[114] As above.

[115] KNHRC (n 54 above) 19.

[116] Sec 10(a).

eradication and development.[117] Approximately 90% of children with disabilities in Kenya are either at home or in regular schools with little or no specialised assistance.[118] Special needs education in Kenya suffers inadequate funding, lack of a clear policy framework, low progress in assessing and placing children with disabilities, few qualified teachers and lack of teaching and learning resources.[119] Lack of clear guidelines on the implementation of inclusive education or reliable data on children 'with special needs' further constrains special needs education in Kenya.[120]

Education for children with disabilities in Kenya is undertaken within segregated, integrated or inclusive educational settings. Despite international pressure to educate children with disabilities in integrated settings, the bulk of children with disabilities in Kenya who are in school are in special schools.[121] Children with intellectual disabilities are particularly vulnerable in the Kenyan education system. There is growing understanding, both internationally and in Kenya, of the diversity intrinsic in this category of disability. [122] However, progress in aligning education services with this knowledge is slow and isolated, and most often not government initiated.[123] This illustrates disconnect between inclusive education as enunciated in government policy and its implementation.

The high number of learner enrolment associated with FPE affects children with intellectual disability disproportionately. Children with severe

[117] See for instance Ministry of Education, Science and Technology 'Development of education in Kenya' (2004) 2. Available at http://chet.org.za/manual/media/files/chet_hernana_docs/Kenya/National/MEST%202004_Development%20of%20education%20in%20Kenya.pdf (accessed 15 October 2010).

[118] As above, also report presented at the 47th Session of the International Conference on Education convened by UNESCO in 2004 available at http://unesdoc.unesco.org/images/0014/001410/141072e.pdf (accessed 7 September 2011).

[119] UNESCO 'Fact book on education for all' (2006) 28–29.

[120] UNESCO (n 119 above) 33 and Ministry of Education, Science & Technology (note 109 above) 7.

[121] KNHCR (n 54 above) 21.

[122] For instance, some groups of children previously regarded as mentally impaired such as those suffering from autism spectrum disorder are now recognised as a distinct group requiring interventions that are best administered separate from other children with intellectual disabilities. See KNHRC (n 54 above) 21.

[123] See the efforts of the Autism Society of Kenya including the establishment of pilot units for children with autism spectrum disorder in some of the Nairobi City primary schools in preparation of the children for integration into the regular school system. The work of the Autism Society of Kenya is donor funded. See www.autismsocietyofkenya.org (accessed 12 October 2010).

or profound intellectual disabilities require specialised and personalised attention which is not feasible in large groups of students. Consequently, parents are increasingly opting for private schools that are adequately resourced to take in learners with disability.[124] Notably also, the FPE programme currently does not apply to early childhood education, the critical point at which the difficulties, if at all, of the child with intellectual disabilities are likely to be identified.[125]

Several reasons account for the failure of the concept of inclusive education to take off with respect to children with intellectual disabilities in Kenya. First is the question of resources ranging from teachers, facilities and learning materials.[126] Secondly, there is a lack of proper involvement of all the stakeholders, particularly the teachers in the formulation of the policy with the effect that teachers do not feel part of the process. In addition, there is lack of awareness on the rights of children with disabilities in education or government policy on the same. In addition, the school curriculum is at variance with the needs of children with disability burdening the teacher to effectively and innovatively interpret it.[127]

Evidently, inclusive education has the potential to achieve effective education of children with intellectual disabilities in Kenya. It is only in this way that education can be made accessible to these children in view of the large number of regular schools across the country. Reviewing the general curriculum will be necessary to accommodate the learners with intellectual disability. The competitive outcome based approach of the current (8–4–4) education system[128] systematically excludes children with intellectual disabilities because schools are more inclined to reject learners whose academic performance is likely to affect their ranking. The general system therefore needs to adapt to the needs of the children with intellectual disability.

[124] KNHRC (n 54 above) 25.

[125] General Comment No 9, para 65.

[126] For instance, while the recommended ratio of student – teacher numbers for children with intellectual disabilities is 6 pupils to 1 teacher, in many special schools that ratio is as high as 1:15 or 20 students, and worse in inclusive settings where some public primary schools have as high as 100 students per class. KNHRC (n 54 above) 29–30.

[127] KNHRC (n 54 above) 28.

[128] See DN Sifuna 'Prevocational subjects in primary schools in the 8–4–4 education system in Kenya' (1992) 12 *International Journal of Educational Development* 133–145 on the origins and operation of the 8–4–4 education system in Kenya.

Conclusion

It is important to highlight that international law does not have a specific focus on children with intellectual disabilities, despite the centrality of intellectual capacity in the context of education. This lack of recognition at the international level is being reflected at the domestic level. Thus, as in the case of Kenya and South Africa, there is no special emphasis on the right to education for children with intellectual disabilities, as a specific category, in the domestic spheres.

Drawing from the foregoing, it is concluded that South Africa has not taken any steps to domesticate article 24 of the CRPD, since the 2001 White Paper has not been reviewed after South Africa ratified this instrument in November 2007. Kenya, on the other hand, has since ratification of the CRPD, drafted an education policy. This policy however does not seem to domesticate article 24 of the CRPD. Therefore, even in the presence of a constitutional framework and policy developments in relation to education for children with disabilities, both countries have not taken any concrete steps to realise the right to education for children with intellectual disabilities.

7

Protection of disabled employees in South Africa: An analysis of the Constitution and Labour Legislation

Ilze Grobbelaar-du Plessis & Stefan van Eck

Introduction

The disability discourse within South Africa is not only influenced by international developments[1] but is also exposed to numerous impulses peculiar to itself. This chapter is focused on the effect which the final Constitution of the Republic of South Africa of 1996[2] as well as labour legislation,[3] is having on the rights of disabled employees in South Africa.

The impact of the South African political history and the effect which the transition to a constitutional democracy in 1994 had on persons with disabilities should not be underestimated. A brief historical overview of the disability discourse which preceded the final Constitution serves as an introduction to this chapter. This is followed by an analysis of the present constitutional provisions, as well as a discussion of the most important labour legislation applicable to disabled employees. South Africa is a ratifying party

[1] The most significant supranational instruments are the World Programme of Action concerning Disabled Persons adopted by the General Assembly (GA) of the United Nations (UN) on 3 December 1982 (resolution 37/52), the International Year of Disabled Persons adopted by the GA of the UN on 16 December 1976 (resolution 31/123), the UN Decade of Disabled Persons adopted by the GA of the UN on 23 November 1984 (resolution 39/260) and the Standard Rules on the Equalisation of Opportunities for Persons with Disabilities adopted by the GA of the UN on 20 December 1993 (resolution 48/96).

[2] The Constitution of the Republic of South Africa, 1996, hereafter the 'Constitution'.

[3] More specifically, the Employment Equity Act 55 of 1998 and the Labour Relations Act 66 of 1995.

to the Convention on the Rights of Persons with Disabilities (CRPD),[4] which endorses the social rather than the medical model of disability. The social model explicitly recognises disability as a human rights issue.[5] This chapter examines whether our constitutional framework and labour legislation endorse the rights of persons with disabilities in the workplace as a human rights issue in line with the social model.[6] Finally, the chapter contains some observations and conclusions pertaining to the position of disabled employees at the workplace.

Medical and social models of disability

To what extent people with disabilities would qualify for protection under any particular jurisdiction depends to a large extent on whether the country concerned follows the medical or the social model of disability. According to the medical model of disability, the question whether a person qualifies for protection has historically mainly been a health and welfare issue. State intervention has traditionally been channelled through welfare institutions, usually controlled by non-disabled people bestowing charity on people with disabilities. Charity so dispensed comprised treatment and other benefits which were provided in an attempt to obviate the disabled persons' need for begging and hiding. The emphasis was on the physical or psychological

4 The CRPD and Optional Protocol adopted by the GA of the UN on 13 December 2006 (resolution A/RES/61/10624). South Africa signed the CRPD and its Optional Protocol on 30 March 2007 and ratified the CRPD and Optional Protocol on 30 November 2007.

5 UN Human Rights Office of the High Commission for Human Rights *Monitoring the Convention on the Rights of Persons with Disabilities – Guidance for human rights monitors Professional training series No 17* (2010) 8.

6 Legislation that *indirectly* refers to people with disabilities and more specifically *indirectly* refers to disabled employees, does not fall within the scope of the discussion in this chapter. The authors' focus will be on legislation that *directly* refers to people with disabilities, and more specifically, disabled employees. The reason for this approach is that legislation, and more specifically, anti-discrimination law which do not expressly mention disability, will probably not be applied to protect people with disabilities specifically. This method was also used by T Degener in 'Disability discrimination law: A global comparative approach' in A Lawson & C Gooding (eds) *Disability rights in Europe* (2005) 87, wherein she states that '[i]n the context of equal rights, disabled people have until recently been a forgotten minority. Consequently, it was assumed (based on experience of German and international law) that an anti-discrimination statute which did not expressly mention disability (or health status) *would probably not, in practice, be applied for the protection of disabled people*' (our emphasis).

nature of the impairment and the dependence of the disabled on the non-disabled. People with disabilities were seldom included as part of the management or the decision-making process of the organisations acting in the interest of the disabled. The view that disability was a health and welfare issue gave rise to a social attitude amongst members of society in terms of which persons with disabilities (and their families) were isolated from mainstream communal activities. Their dependency on state assistance disempowered these people and undermined their self-confidence and capacity to interact on an equal level with colleagues in the working environment, and with other members of society elsewhere.[7]

In terms of the social model, any disability is not primarily due to some or other condition inherent in the particular person with a disability, but to the manner in which the physical and social environment within which such person must operate, has been arranged. This is usually done with a view to the needs and lifestyle of a particular sector of the community, namely the non-disabled majority, and more often than not, obstacles (or barriers) and impediments in the way of the disabled minority are the inevitable result. This model emphasises an understanding of disability as something that stems from environmental and attitudinal barriers. It accentuates barriers as the cause of the abnormality of disability and concentrates on strategies to remove these barriers. Society must therefore be rearranged to accommodate everybody – including persons with disabilities – on an equal footing.

The past three decades have been a period of transition during which the view on disability has worldwide changed from one favouring the medical model, to one favouring the social model of disability. This transition is of particular importance since the two models represent opposing sets of values on the spectrum of protection for people with disabilities.[8]

[7] BA Areheart 'When disability isn't "just right": The entrenchment of the medical model of disability and the *Goldilocks* Dilemma' (2008) 83 *Indiana Law Journal* 6; M Jones & LA Marks 'Law and the social construction of disability" in Jones & Marks (eds) *Disability, divers-ability and legal change* (1999) 5; G Quinn & T Degener *Human rights and disability: The current use and future potential of United Nations human rights instruments in the context of disability* (2002) 10; Integrated National Disability Strategy White Paper, Office of the Deputy President, November 1997 http://www.info.gov.za/white papers/1997/disability.htm (accessed 15 October 2010).

[8] n 7 above.

The position of persons with disabilities before the new constitutional dispensation

Prior to the present constitutional dispensation, many people in South Africa experienced double discrimination based on race and on disability. Black disabled people had to cope on a daily basis with poverty, deprivation of rights and violence emanating from the apartheid system. It is important to note that all disabled people, black and white, experienced discrimination and marginalisation based on disability. Due to their disability, working opportunities, education, and suitable health and social services were limited.[9] Many white disabled people joined the struggle against white minority rule because they could identify with the discrimination experienced by black people. Disabled people were generally regarded as sick and in need of care. On account of their marginalisation, they were not seen as equal to others and as having rights and responsibilities equal to those of other citizens.[10]

Before 1994, legislation relevant to persons with disabilities were fragmented and only dealt in passing with matters pertaining to disabilities. Legislation enacted prior to 1994 – such as the National Welfare Act of 1978 and the Mental Health Act of 1973 – is only of historical interest as they reflected the medical model of disability and are not the focus of this chapter. In 1984, persons with disabilities constituted the first non-racial disabled persons' organisation in South Africa, namely 'Disabled People South Africa' (DPSA).[11] Although black and white persons with disabilities experienced the impact of the apartheid system differently, the establishment of this organisation was a direct consequence of the struggle – as victims of discrimination – against the white minority government.[12] This organisation was the biggest non-racial disability organisation in South Africa which was controlled and managed by persons with disabilities. It played a pivotal role in the struggle that was carried on for more than twenty years on behalf of

[9] C Howell *et al* 'A history of the disability rights movement in South Africa' in B Watermeyer *et al* (eds) *Disability and social change: A South African Agenda* (2006) 48.

[10] C Howell & S Chalken *Disability – Our voices, our rights: The history of disabled people in South Africa and the struggles of the disability rights movement in South Africa (1980–2001)* (2003) 5–8. See also Howell *et al* (n 9 above) 48.

[11] See also F Bhabha 'Disability equality rights in South Africa: Concepts, interpretation and the transformation imperative' (2009) 25(2) *South African Journal on Human Rights* 222.

[12] Howell *et al* (n 9 above) 48.

disabled South Africans.[13] In the early 1990s, DPSA made formal contact with the African National Congress (ANC), which was expected to form the new government.[14] During the course of this contact, the importance of an integrated disability policy was highlighted.[15]

In 1991, the disability unit of Lawyers for Human Rights, in consultation with numerous disability organisations in South Africa, and with the co-operation of DPSA, embarked upon the slow process of compiling a disability rights charter by people with disabilities.[16] In December 1992, the council of DPSA adopted the *Disability Rights Charter of South Africa.* Howell *et al*[17] describe this historical event as follows:

> Few people would disagree that the formulation of the Disability Rights Charter was an extremely important moment, not only providing an opportunity for disabled people throughout the country, both in and outside formal structures, 'to band together', but also providing the movement 'with a weapon ... to get into the new democracy' ... most important because it located disability 'within a human rights approach', and as a 'progressive document' it served as the basis for subsequent discussions with the ANC.

It was important for persons with disabilities to be directly involved in the drafting process of the *Disability Rights Charter of South Africa*. This involvement of the disabilities sector contributed to the fact that the *Charter* was at that stage the embodiment of the most progressive approach towards conceptualising disability. The *Charter,* at long last, expressly rejected the medical model of disability and endorsed the social model of disability.[18] This change in emphasis from the medical to the social model was of great

[13] Howell *et al* (n 9 above) 49–53.

[14] In 1990, subsequent to the release of Nelson Mandela and the unbanning of the ANC and the Pan Africanist Congress, negotiations began with the National Party government with a view to creating a new constitution for the Republic of South Africa.

[15] According to Howell *et al* (n 9 above) 62, it was DPSA's initiatives to integrate disability issues into ANC policy frameworks which 'were followed up by submissions and lobbying at CODESA, with the result that the Constitution recognises the prevention of unfair discrimination on the basis of disability as well as the implementation of measures designed to redress inequalities experienced by disabled people in the past.'

[16] For this purpose, people with disabilities were mobilised throughout South Africa. In this regard, see the 'Disability Rights Charter of South Africa' http://www.dpsa.org.za/documents/disabilityrightscharter.php (accessed on 23 October 2010).

[17] n 9 above 58; and Bhabha (n 11 above) 222.

[18] See para 2; and Bhabha (n 11 above).

importance. This was a clear indication that persons with disabilities in South Africa were – as long ago as the 1990s – understood to have meaning in accordance with the view at international level which reflected the social model of disability. In this period, which preceded the interim Constitution of 1993 (interim Constitution),[19] activists came out in stern support of a basis for the ideological recognition of disability as a human rights and development issue.

Both the involvement of persons with disabilities in the drafting of the *Disability Rights Charter of South Africa,* which endorsed the social model of disability, and the new constitutional framework entailed a significant turning point in the understanding of disability.[20] Labour legislation and constitutional provisions which have a direct bearing on people with disabilities will now be examined in order to determine whether or not the social model of disability is embodied in these provisions.

The 1996 Constitution of the Republic of South Africa

The Bill of Rights

The Bill of Rights is the cornerstone of democracy in South Africa and the rights of all people, including persons with disabilities, are entrenched in the overarching 'democratic values of human dignity, equality and freedom'.[21] An important feature of the Bill of Rights is that it binds all government institutions and the courts,[22] and that it protects all people in South Africa. Furthermore, the provisions of the Bill of Rights are enforceable by the courts.[23]

The word 'everyone' is used in a number of provisions of the Constitution and it includes citizens and non-citizens[24] within the boundaries of the

[19] In terms of sec 8(2) of the interim Constitution of the Republic of South Africa Act, 1993 '[n]o person shall be unfairly discriminated against, directly or indirectly, and, without derogating from the generality of this provision, on one or more of the following grounds in particular: race, gender, sex, ethnic or social origin, colour, sexual orientation, age, disability, religion, conscience, belief, culture or language.'

[20] Degener (n 6 above) 87.

[21] Sec 7(1) of the Constitution.

[22] Sec 8(1) of the Constitution.

[23] Sec 8(3) of the Constitution.

[24] Sec 8(2)–(3) of the Constitution determine that the Constitution is binding and applicable to natural persons; I Currie & J De Waal *The Bill of Rights handbook* (2005) 35; and *Mohammed v President of the Republic of South Africa* 2001 3 SA 893 (CC).

Republic of South Africa. The Constitution further emphasises in section 237 that the state must perform all constitutional obligations diligently and without delay.

The word 'everyone' is sufficiently comprehensive to include persons with disabilities. The Bill of Rights explicitly protects persons with disabilities' right to dignity,[25] right to equality[26] and right to bodily and psychological integrity.[27] Every person with a disability further has a right to privacy[28] and to freedom of expression,[29] association,[30] movement and residence,[31] as well as a right to choose a trade, occupation or profession freely.[32] These persons also have a right to fair labour practices,[33] health care,[34] education[35] and access to courts.[36] Furthermore, children with disabilities have the same rights as non-disabled children.[37] However, the rights contained in the Bill of Rights may be limited in terms of section 36 of the Constitution to the extent that the limitation is reasonable and justifiable in an open and democratic society.

Section 7(2) provides that the state must respect, protect, promote and fulfil the rights in the Bill of Rights. The state's obligation may be positive or negative in nature.[38] It does not only prohibit the state from interfering with the exercise of the said rights, but in other cases, it compels the state to act. The obligation to protect and to promote rights in some instances imposes a positive obligation on the state to introduce, where necessary, appropriate legislative, administrative, financial, judicial or other suitable measures in order to allow the execution of the rights. The state's obligation to promote a right also entails an obligation on the state to inform the entitled person

[25] Sec 10 of the Constitution.

[26] Sec 9 of the Constitution, which will be discussed in more detail in para 4.2.

[27] Sec 12(1) of the Constitution.

[28] Sec 14 of the Constitution.

[29] Sec 16 of the Constitution.

[30] Sec 18 of the Constitution.

[31] Sec 21 of the Constitution.

[32] Sec 22 of the Constitution.

[33] Sec 23 of the Constitution.

[34] Sec 27 of the Constitution.

[35] Sec 29 of the Constitution.

[36] Sec 34 of the Constitution.

[37] Sec 28 of the Constitution.

[38] Currie & De Waal (n 24 above) 13–18.

about the existence of the right, an obligation which could be of particular importance to disabled persons.[39]

It is of significance that the rights contained in the Bill of Rights and their interpretation by the courts, have resulted in the development of a body of constitutional jurisprudence relevant to workers, employers and their representative bodies.[40]

The Constitution, and more specifically the rights contained in the Bill of Rights, could potentially affect labour law in three ways. Firstly, the rights contained in the Bill of Rights could be applied to test the validity of labour legislation aimed at compliance with fundamental rights. Secondly, the rights could be employed to interpret existing labour legislation which has been promulgated in compliance with fundamental rights. And finally, the rights could be used as a tool to develop the common law in those instances where it does not provide sufficient protection.[41] It is however, important to note that it is inappropriate for a litigant to rely on any provision of the Constitution if legislation has already been enacted to give effect to the specific principle provided for in the relevant constitutional provision. So, for example, the Constitutional Court has held that it is not fitting for a trade union to bypass applicable legislation by relying on the right to engage in collective bargaining[42] where specific legislation has already been introduced to give effect to this provision of the Constitution.[43]

In the contribution below, section 9 (the right to equality) and section 23(1) (the right to fair labour practices) of the Bill of Rights and the relevant labour legislation will be evaluated in order to determine whether the fundamental rights of disabled people in the workplace receive sufficient recognition within the existing legal framework as a human rights issue bearing upon the social model of disability.

[39] See S Liebenberg 'The interpretation of socio-economic rights' in Chaskalson *et al Constitutional law of South Africa* (2003) 6. With socio-economic rights, there is an obligation on the state to launch awareness raising – similarly, there is a obligation on the state to raise awareness of the rights of persons with disabilities.

[40] A Van Niekerk *et al Law@work* (2008) 33–53.

[41] Van Niekerk *et al* (n 40 above) 34 gives recognition to H Cheadle in this regard who delivered an address at the annual Butterworths LexisNexis Current Labour Law seminar, 2007.

[42] Sec 23(5) of the Constitution provides that every trade union and employer 'has the right to engage in collective bargaining'.

[43] *SA National Defence Union v Minister of Defence* 2007 9 BLLR 785 (CC) confirmed *NAPTOSA v Minister of Education, Western Cape* 2001 2 SA 112 (C) and *Minister of Health v New Clicks SA (Pty) Ltd* 2006 2 SA 311 (CC) in this regard.

The constitutional right to equality

4.2.1 The concept 'equality'

What does the concept 'equality' mean?[44] Gathered from South African jurisprudence, 'equality' does not seem to be a simple concept.[45] Unlike the American case law on equality where a formal equality concept takes the lead, substantive equality is pursued in South Africa.[46] Dupper explains the difference between formal and substantive equality as follows:[47]

> In short, formal equality means sameness of treatment – the law must treat persons in the same manner regardless of their circumstances. Substantive equality takes the circumstances of people into account and requires the law to ensure equality of outcome. The Constitution, it is then stressed, requires us to look at substance. It requires us to focus on the purpose or effects of rules and conduct and not merely on their form.

Formal equality requires everybody to be equal bearers of rights. However, the real social and economic disparities of individuals or groups such as disabled employees are not taken into account. Formal equality can therefore lead to substantive inequality. On the other hand, substantive equality takes the real social and economic circumstances of groups or individuals into consideration, when determining whether the constitutional commitment to equality was achieved.[48]

[44] F Venter 'Die beperkings van regstellende gelykheid' (2004) *Potchefstroom Electronic Law Journal* 1–2 points out that the term 'equality' is referred to in sec 1 (the founding provisions), several times in the Bill of Rights, and further in secs 185 and 187 in connection with two constitutional commissions (the commission for the promotion and protection of the rights of cultural, religious and linguistic communities and the commission for gender equality).

[45] *Brink v Kitshoff NO* 1996 4 SA 197 (CC) para 40; and I Currie & J De Waal (n 24 above) 231.

[46] Venter (n 44 above) 5.

[47] O Dupper 'Affirmative action and substantive equality: the South African experience' (2002) *South African Mercantile Law Journal* 275.

[48] *President of the Republic of South Africa v Hugo* 1997 4 SA 1 (CC) para 112 confirms a commitment to substantive equality. The Court held that there 'are at least two factors relevant to the determination of unfairness: it is necessary to look at the group or groups which have suffered discrimination in the particular case and at the effect of the discrimination on the interest of those concerned. The more vulnerable the group adversely affected by the discrimination, the more likely the discrimination will be held to be unfair. Similarly, the more invasive the nature of the discrimination upon the interests of the individuals affected by the discrimination, the more likely it will be held to be unfair;' TP Van Reenen 'Equality, discrimination and affirmative action: an analysis of section 9 of the Constitution of South Africa' (1997) *SA Public Law* 153.

In *President of the Republic of South Africa v Hugo* the Constitutional Court explains the principle as follows:[49]

> We need ... to develop a concept of unfair discrimination which recognises that although a society which affords each human being equal treatment on the basis of equal worth and freedom is our goal, *we cannot achieve that goal by insisting upon identical treatment in all circumstances before that goal is achieved*. Each case, therefore, will require a careful and thorough understanding of the impact of the discriminatory action upon the particular people concerned to determine whether its overall impact is one which furthers the constitutional goal of equality or not.[50]

Further confirmation of substantive equality is to be found in section 9(2)[51] which provides that equality includes full and equal enjoyment of all rights and liberties. In *Bhe v Magistrate, Khayelitsha*[52] the Constitutional Court emphasises that:

> [n]ot only is the achievement of equality one of the founding values of the Constitution, section 9 of the Constitution also guarantees the achievement of *substantive equality* to ensure that the opportunity to enjoy the benefits of an egalitarian and non-sexist society is available to *all including those who have been subjected to unfair discrimination in the past.*[53]

From the discussion above and the applicable case law highlighted, it is clear that the right to substantive equality is in accordance with the social model of disability within the human rights perspective. Substantive equality takes the circumstances of people with disabilities into account and requires equality of outcome, which inevitably means that the social environment must be adjusted to accommodate people with disabilities in order to achieve equality of outcome. In order to achieve the South African constitutional goal of equality, people with disabilities must be fully accommodated by society. Accommodation means that the social environment must be made accessible for people with disabilities by removing environmental and attitudinal barriers.

[49] *President of the Republic of South Africa v Hugo* 1997 4 SA 1 (CC) para 41.

[50] Our emphasis.

[51] See also the discussion in para 4.2.2.

[52] *Bhe v Magistrate, Khayelitsha* 2005 1 SA 850 (CC) para 50.

[53] Our emphasis.

Content of the equality clause

In terms of section 9(1) 'everyone' is equal before the law and has the right to equal protection and equal benefit of the law. Section 9(2) goes further in providing that equality includes the full and equal enjoyment of all rights and freedoms. The section further provides that legislative and other measures designed to protect or advance persons, or categories of persons, disadvantaged by unfair discrimination, may be taken in order to promote and achieve equality.[54] As it will be seen from later discussion in this chapter, the legislature introduced specific measures to protect disabled persons in particular as a designated group for purposes of equal treatment and affirmative action.[55]

Section 9(3) provides that the state may not unfairly discriminate directly or indirectly against anyone on one or more of the listed grounds. The grounds that are specifically mentioned in section 9(3) are 'race, gender, sex, pregnancy, marital status, ethnic or social origin, colour, sexual orientation, age, disability, religion, conscience, belief, culture, language and birth'. In this regard, Howell *et al*[56] state as follows:

> The Constitution's recognition that disabled people have been, and continue to be, discriminated against because of their disability, this means that disability has become an important consideration in new legislation and policy documents that make up South Africa's legal and policy framework. As a 'historical moment' in the history of the disability rights movement in South Africa, this recognition reflects the struggle of disabled people to be treated equally to all other people.

According to section 9(4), no person may unfairly discriminate directly or indirectly against anyone on one or more grounds in terms of subsection 9(3). This section therefore also prohibits any other person, such as private individuals and institutions, such as employers, from discriminating unfairly against someone else on one or more of the said grounds.

[54] See SR Van Jaarsveld & BPS Van Eck *Kompendium van Arbeidsreg* (2006) 137 and the discussion in para 5.3 below.

[55] See the discussions of the Employment Equity Act 55 of 1998 and affirmative action in paras 5 and 5.3 below.

[56] Howell *et al* (n 9 above 47).

Section 9(4) further requires that 'national legislation must be enacted to prevent or prohibit unfair discrimination'.[57]

According to section 9(5), discrimination on one or more of the grounds listed in subsection 9(3), is unfair unless it is established that the discrimination is fair. In terms of this provision, discrimination based on disability is unfair unless it has, been established that such discrimination is fair by reason of, for instance, valid inherent requirements for the work concerned. The question arises as to what is understood under the concept 'discrimination'.

The concept 'discrimination'

Mere differentiation between persons or groups of persons based on factors such as disability does not necessarily amount to discrimination. Unfair discrimination only takes place if the manner in which the differentiation is made amounts to unfair discrimination. It is also clear in terms of section 9(3) that 'unfair discrimination' is prohibited and not discrimination *per se*. Should discrimination be established on any of the grounds listed in section 9(3), such discrimination would be presumed to be unfair unless the contrary is proved.[58]

In what circumstances differentiation would amount to unfair discrimination, is a complex question. In *Prinsloo v Van der Linde*,[59] the Constitutional Court for the first time examined the concepts differentiation and discrimination. The essential question which had to be decided was whether the presumption of fault created in terms of the Forest Act[60] was not in conflict with the fundamental rights contained of the interim Constitution. The rights in question were the right to equality before the

[57] See the discussions of the Employment Equity Act 55 of 1998 in paras 5 and 5.2 below. The Promotion of Equality and Prevention of Unfair Discrimination Act 4 of 2000 (PEPUDA) was enacted in terms of sec 9(4) to prevent or prohibit unfair discrimination. Although not a disability specific piece of legislation, PEPUDA is a very important piece of legislation for the protection of people with disabilities, since sec 9 of the act specifically prohibits unfair discrimination on the ground of disability. Sec 9 of PEPUDA also strengthens the argument of accommodation of people with disabilities in terms of the social model of disability. However, PEPUDA does not fall within the scope of this chapter since PEPUDA *does not prohibit unfair discrimination in the workplace*. Unfair discrimination in the workplace falls within the scope of the Employment Equity Act as discussed in paras 5 and 5.2 below.

[58] Currie & De Waal (n 24 above) 239; and Van Reenen (n 48 above) 156.

[59] *Prinsloo v Van der Linde* 1997 6 BCLR 759 (CC); 1997 3 SA 1012 (CC).

[60] Forest Act 122 of 1984.

law; the right to equal protection by the law; the prohibition of discrimination; and the right to be considered not guilty until guilt is proved.[61]

The prohibition of discrimination in terms of the interim Constitution,[62] and also in terms of the Constitution,[63] does not constitute a prohibition on unfair differentiation or distinction but of 'unfair discrimination'. In this regard, the Court refers to the history of South Africa and the view that 'discrimination has acquired a particular pejorative meaning relating to the unequal treatment of people based on attributes and characteristics attaching to them.'[64] In this light, unfair discrimination means 'treating persons differently in a way which impairs their fundamental dignity as human beings, who are inherently equal in dignity.'[65]

In *Prinsloo,* the Court uses human dignity as criterion to determine unfair discrimination. The Court endorses the view that[66]

> [a]t the heart of the prohibition of unfair discrimination lies a recognition that the purpose of our new constitutional and democratic order is the establishment of a society in which all human beings will be accorded equal dignity and respect regardless of their membership of particular groups.

According to the Court, equality therefore means nothing 'if it does not represent a commitment to recognising each person's equal worth as a human being, regardless of individual differences.'[67] On this basis, the Court decided that differentiation amounted to unfair discrimination if the differentiation which was made infringed upon the human dignity of the person or persons concerned.[68] The fact that human dignity plays such an important role is of significant importance to persons with disabilities since such an interpretation accords with the social model of disability. In *Harksen v Lane,*[69] the

[61] Secs 8(1), 8(2) and 25(3)(c) of the interim Constitution.

[62] Sec 8(2) of the interim Constitution.

[63] Secs 9(3), 9(4) of the interim Constitution.

[64] *Prinsloo v Van der Linde* 1997 6 BCLR 759 (CC); 1997 3 SA 1012 (CC) (n 59 above) para 31.

[65] Van Jaarsveld & Van Eck (n 54 above).

[66] As above, para 32.

[67] As above.

[68] As above.

[69] *Harksen v Lane* 1998 1 SA 300 (CC) para 52.

Constitutional Court held that certain factors had to be taken into account in order to determine whether discrimination was unfair.[70] These factors are set out as follows by the Court:[71]

> (a) the position of the complainants in society and whether they have suffered in the past from patterns of disadvantage ... (b) the nature of the provision or power and the purpose sought to be achieved by it. If its purpose is manifestly not directed ... at impairing the complainants in the manner indicated above, but is aimed at achieving a worthy and important societal goal, such as. . . the furthering of equality for all, this purpose may. . . have a significant bearing on the question whether complainants have in fact suffered the impairment in question; ... (c) with due regard to (a) and (b) above ... the extent to which the discrimination has affected the rights or interests of complainants and whether it has led to an impairment of their fundamental human dignity.

Harksen further formulated the stages in which an enquiry into alleged unequal treatment and unfair discrimination must be instituted.[72] These stages are also relevant in determining whether there was any unfair discrimination against persons with disabilities. The stages are the following:[73]

[70] The same factors were taken into account in *WH Bosch v The Minister of Safety and Security & Minister of Public Works* Case no. 25/2005 9. In the mentioned case, people with disabilities had no access to the first floor of the police station where they had to apply for firearm licences. The factors laid down in *Harksen* will obviously play an important role when equality courts have to determine whether in such case, there was unfair discrimination against people with disabilities.

[71] *Harksen* case (n 69 above) para 51.

[72] As above, para 53. This was confirmed in *National Coalition for Gay & Lesbian Equality v Minister of Justice* 1999 1 SA 6 (CC) para 17. In the next paragraph, para 18, the steps are slightly refined and reduced to three main steps. Venter (n 44 above) summarises them as follows: 1) Does the act in question differentiate between people or categories of people? 2) If so, does such differentiation amount to unfair discrimination? 3) If unfair discrimination is established, can the act in question be justified in terms of section 36 (the limitation clause) of the Constitution?

[73] Regarding the analyses, see also IM Rautenbach 'Die Konstitusionele Hof se riglyne vir die toepassing van die reg op gelykheid' (2001) *Tydskrif vir Suid-Afrikaanse Reg (TSAR)* 329, and G Carpenter 'Equality and non-discrimination in the new South African constitutional order: the early cases – part 1' (2001) *Tydskrif vir Hedendaagse Romeins-Hollandse Reg* 409; 'Equality and non-discrimination in the new South African constitutional order: important trilogy of decisions – part 2' (2001) *Tydskrif vir Hedendaagse Romeins-Hollandse Reg* 619; 'Equality and non-discrimination in the new South African constitutional order: the sage continues – part 3' (2002) *Tydskrif vir Hedendaagse Romeins-Hollandse Reg* 37 and 'Equality and non-discrimination in the new South African constitutional order: update – part 4' (2002) *Tydskrif vir Hedendaagse Romeins-Hollandse Reg* 177.

(i) It must be established whether the relevant legislation or conduct of the respondent differentiates or distinguishes between persons or categories of persons. If so, it must be established whether there is a rational link between the differentiation and a legitimate government purpose. If no such link can be identified, the differentiation would be irrational and arbitrary, and would justify a conclusion that it constitutes an infringement of section 9(1)[74] that provides for equality and equal protection and benefit of the law. However, even though the differentiation serves a legitimate purpose, it might still possibly constitute an infringement of section 9(2), which provides for protection against unfair discrimination.

(ii) If the first part of the enquiry should indicate that the differentiating measure in question was not an arbitrary measure, and did in fact serve a legitimate purpose, the court must, secondly, determine whether the said differentiating measure amounted to unfair discrimination. To this end, a two stage analyses is necessary:

a) It must first be established whether the differentiation amounts to discrimination. If the differentiation is based on one or more of the grounds contemplated in section 9(3), for instance disability, a presumption of discrimination arises.

b) If the differentiation amounts to discrimination, it must be established whether the discrimination amounts to *un*fair discrimination. If the discrimination is found to have been based on one of the grounds listed in section 9(3), such as disability, a presumption of *unfair* discrimination arises. The respondent must then show that the discrimination was fair.[75] If the discrimination is not based on any of the grounds referred to in section 9(3), the complainant must show that the differentiation was unfair. The test for *un*fairness focuses mainly on the effect of the discrimination on the complainant or others in his/her situation.

Impairment of the victim's dignity is essential[76] in order to determine whether the alleged discrimination was indeed unfair.

[74] *Harksen* case (n 69 above) para 53.

[75] The presumption in terms of sec 9(5) of the Constitution. See also *Hoffmann v South African Airways* 2001 1 SA 1 (CC).

[76] According to C Albertyn & G Goldblatt B 'Facing the challenge of transformative difficulties in the development of an indigenous jurisprudence of equality' (1998) *South African Journal on Human Rights* 248–249, dignity is central to the equality question.

In *Harksen*[77] – as in *Prinsloo*[78] – the determining factor which rendered the discrimination unfair was evidently the impact which it had on the victim. This is a subjective factor which involved the dignity of the victim in answering the question whether or not the discrimination was indeed unfair.[79] This approach to discrimination accords with the social model of disability.[80]

Differentiation on any ground envisaged in section 9(3) of the Constitution is presumed to be unfair unless the contrary is proved.[81] The Constitutional right to equality must in view of the discussion above be interpreted contextually. In the interpretation of unfair discrimination against any person with a disability, the extent to which the victim's dignity has been regained plays an important role.[82] Such interpretation of the right to equality in the South African constitutional dispensation accords with the social model of disability in human rights context.

The constitutional right to fair labour practices

Section 23(1) of the Constitution guarantees everyone's right to fair labour practices. From this provision, it is clear that every employee, employer, or other organisation or institution that is involved in labour relations has the right to fair labour practices in terms of the Constitution.[83] It goes without saying that disabled employees are also entitled to protection in terms of this provision.

In *NEHAWU v University of Cape Town,*[84] the Constitutional Court interpreted this right as follows:

[77] *Harksen* case (n 69 above) para 51.

[78] *Prinsloo* case (n 59 above), para 32.

[79] In *Bhe v Magistrate of Khayelitsha* 2005 1 SA 580 (CC), 2005 1 BCLR (CC), the Court found that the rules of customary law regarding birthright infringed upon both the right to equality and the right to dignity.

[80] The importance of human dignity was also emphasised in *WH Bosch v The Minister of Safety and Security & Minister of Public Works* Case no. 25/2005 (9) when the Equality Court in Port Elizabeth held that '[t]here is no price that can be attached to dignity or a threat to that dignity. There is no justification for the violation or potential violation of the disabled person's right to equality and maintenance of his dignity that was tendered or averred by the respondent. ... The court therefore found the discrimination to have been unfair.'

[81] Sec 9(5) of the Constitution and *Harksen v Lane* (n 69 above).

[82] *Standard Bank of South Africa v CCMA* 2008 4 BLLR 371; and Van Niekerk *et al* (n 40 above) 33.

[83] Van Jaarsveld & Van Eck (n 54 above) 137.

[84] *NEHAWU v University of Cape Town* 2003 *Industrial Law Journal* 95 (CC) 110H–111A.

> [t]he concept of fair labour practice is incapable of precise definition ... [It should be] given content by legislation and thereafter be left to gather meaning ... from the decisions of specialist courts and tribunals. ... In giving content to this concept the courts and tribunals will have to seek guidance from domestic and international experience. Domestic experience is reflected both in the equity based jurisprudence generated by the unfair labour practice provisions of the 1956 LRA [Labour Relations Act] as well as the codification of unfair labour practice in the LRA.

As mentioned above, it is not appropriate for an aggrieved person to approach the courts based on an infringement of a constitutional principle if specific legislation has already given effect to the relevant human right.[85] However, the Constitution does play a significant role whenever legislation that gives effect to a human right is being interpreted and when the common law must be developed in the absence of existing legislative provisions giving effect to constitutional principles.

As pointed out by the Labour Court in *Standard Bank of South Africa v CCMA & Others*,[86] the employment rate of people with disabilities is less than one third, and even in this modern era, there are '[m]any employers [that still] tend to exclude and marginalise employees with disabilities' with the result that 'more disabled people are dismissed than accommodated'.

The most significant labour laws that provide protection to persons with disabilities are the Employment Equity Act 55 of 1998 (EEA) and the Labour Relations Act 66 of 1995 (LRA) and the codes that have been published in terms of these laws. These acts and codes give effect to the equality clause,[87] the right to fair labour practices[88] as well as the international and foreign norms in respect of fair labour treatment of people with disabilities.[89]

[85] See para 4.1 above.

[86] 2008 4 BLLR (LC) 356, 368–369.

[87] Sec 9 of the Constitution.

[88] Sec 23(1) of the Constitution.

[89] Supranational instruments (n 1 above).

The Employment Equity Act

Introduction

The EEA is not a disability specific piece of legislation. It strives towards the attainment of two goals, namely to prohibit unfair discrimination and to promote the implementation of affirmative action measures to eradicate inequalities that were institutionalised by previous political policies.[90] Chapter of the EEA gives effect to the first goal and it broadly coincides with the principles of formal equality as enshrined in section 9(1), (3) and (4) of the Constitution. It provides that everyone at the workplace is equal before the law and that unfair discrimination on a list of grounds, including disability, is proscribed.[91] Chapter gives effect to the second goal, namely the constitutional promise of substantive quality and affirmative action that is contained in section 9(2) of the Constitution.[92]

The EEA stipulates that codes of good practice in respect of vulnerable groups, such as persons with HIV/aids,[93] may be published. For purposes of this contribution, the Code of Good Practice: Key Aspects on the Employment of People with Disabilities (Disability Code)[94] is of special importance. Although the Disability Code is not an authoritative summary of the law, courts and tribunals must take it into account when provisions of the EEA are being interpreted and it provides guidance to employers in respect to the development and implementation of disability equity policies at the workplace.[95]

Item 6 of the Disability Code requires employers to make 'reasonable accommodation' for people with disabilities. Reasonable accommodation

[90] Sec 2(b) of the EEA; Venter (n 44 above) 7.

[91] See para 4.2.2.

[92] In this regard, also see the discussion regarding the concept of 'equality' in para 4.2.1.

[93] The Code of Good Practice on Key Aspects of HIV/Aids and Employment was published in *Government Gazette* 21815 of 1 December 2000.

[94] The Disability Code was published in terms of sec 54 of the EEA in *Government Gazette* 23702 of 19 August 2002. It is to be noted that in 2004, the Department of Labour issued additional guidelines in the 'Technical Assistance Guidelines on the Employment of People with Disabilities' that must be read in conjunction with the EEA and the Disability Code. These guidelines are practical in nature and are based on the prohibition on unfair discrimination and affirmative action measures.

[95] Item 3(1) of the Disability Code. See also the 'South Africa country profile: Promoting the employability and employment of people with disabilities through effective legislation (Southern Africa)' prepared by the ILO Skills and Employability Department funded by Irish Aid (June 2006) 10 available at http://www.ilo.org/public/english/employment/skills/disability/download/sthafrcp.pdf (accessed 19 May 2008).

does not only mean that obstacles should be eliminated at the workplace, but it also requires positive measures to be taken in order to adapt policies, practices and the working environment in promoting accessibility at the workplace[96] of disabled persons. The Disability Code further explains that safeguards against unfair discrimination should be implemented throughout the full cycle of employment – from recruitment to promotions and termination of employment.[97]

Unfair discrimination

Section 6(1) of the EEA prohibits unfair discrimination at the workplace. It states that:

> [n]o person may unfairly discriminate, directly or indirectly, against an employee, in any employment policy or practice, on one or more grounds, including race, gender, sex, pregnancy, marital status, family responsibility, ethnic or social origin, colour, sexual orientation, age, *disability*, religion, HIV status, conscience, belief, political opinion, culture, language and birth.[98]

This prohibition applies to all employees and job applicants irrespective of the size of the employer's undertaking.[99] Section 6(2) provides that it is not unfair discrimination if an employer differentiates on the basis of a valid 'inherent requirement' of the job or in the event of the implementation of affirmative action measures in accordance with the EEA.

The EEA defines 'people with disabilities' as 'people who have a long-term or recurring physical or mental impairment which substantially limits their prospects of entry into, or advancement in, employment'.[100] The Disability Code contains guidelines regarding the interpretation of this

[96] Item 6 of the Disability Code. The Code provides examples of reasonable accommodation. This could entail the adaptation of computer hard- and software, the provision of training and evaluation material, and amendments to work time and leave. See also C Ngwena 'Equality for people with disabilities in the workplace: an overview of the emergence of disability as a human rights issue' (2004) *Journal for Juridical Science* 179.

[97] n 96 above.

[98] Our emphasis.

[99] Sec 4(1) provides that Chapter II of the EEA applies to 'all employees and employers' and also covers any 'employment policy or practice' which includes 'recruitment procedures, advertising and selection criteria'.

[100] Sec 1 of the EEA.

definition and in *IMATU v City of Cape Town*[101] the Labour Court, for the first time, had the opportunity to consider the definition in the EEA in the context of the Disability Code. The facts in this case were briefly as follows:

Murdoch (the employee) was a type 1 insulin controlled diabetic who applied to the City of Cape Town (the employer) to be transferred to a vacant position of fire-fighter. The employer contended that the employee did not meet the inherent requirements of the job due to the fact that he was prone to a possible debilitating hypoglycaemic attack. This, according to the employer, had the potential of endangering the population, his colleagues and his own life. The employee argued that the employer was merely discriminating against him on grounds of his disability.

The Court in the first instance considered whether the situation was covered under one of the listed grounds, namely 'disability', of section 6(1). The Court held that 'persons with disabilities' is not defined in terms of the EEA but nevertheless took the definition and explanation thereof into account as contained in the Disability Code. Item 5 of the Disability Code provides that:

> [t]he scope of protection for people with disabilities in employment focuses on the *effect of a disability on the person in relation to the working environment, and not on the diagnosis of the impairment*. People are considered as persons with disabilities who satisfy all the criteria in the definition:
> (i) having a physical or mental impairment;
> (ii) which is long term or recurring; and
> (iii) which substantially limits their prospects of entry into, or advancement in employment.[102]

The Court held that the employee's diabetes did not limit his long-term prospects of employment and that his situation was not covered by the definition of disability. However, the Court found that the EEA did not contain a restricted number of grounds and that the employer's differentiation was comparable to some of the other grounds covered by section 6(1). The Court held that the employee's condition could be categorised as potentially discriminating.

It is significant to note that item 5 of the Disability Code tends to support the social model of disability, rather than the more limiting medical model,

[101] 2005 11 BLLR 1084 (LC).

[102] Our emphasis.

in determining disability. According to the Disability Code, a diagnosis should be made of the effect that the impairment may have on the person in relation to the work environment.[103] However, this introductory part is, followed by a relative restrictive definition of disability, which in our view, is open to an interpretation in line with the medical model of disability.

One can support the decision in the *IMATU* case in as much as it held that employers should not be permitted to impose a 'blanket ban' on persons with impairments of whatever nature; and that each case should be scrutinised on merit before a decision as to compliance with the inherent job requirements, can be made. The Court's decision was, however, based on the American Supreme Court of Appeal decision in *Sutton v United Airlines Inc*[104] and reliance on this case is questionable. The American Court adopted a particularly limited approach in determining who should qualify for protection as a disabled person in terms of the American Disabilities Act of 1990 (ADA).[105] By emphasising the disabled person's impairment instead of the potential discrimination they would be subjected to, the Court relied on the medical model of disability, thereby deviating the focus away from the social model in terms of which discrimination would have been emphasised.[106]

The American Congress found that *Sutton*[107] and subsequent cases had frustrated its original intention to afford broad protection to persons with disabilities. These decisions unnecessarily excluded numerous persons from the protection of the ADA[108] and pursuant to this, Congress adopted the Americans with Disabilities Amendments Act.[109]

[103] O Dupper *et al Essential Discrimination Law* (2004) 163.

[104] *Sutton v United Airlines Inc* 527 US 471 (1999).

[105] Americans with Disabilities Act of 1990, codified by 42 U.S.C. § 12101 *et seq*. of 26 July 1990.

[106] Areheart (n 7 above) 40.

[107] *Sutton v United Airlines Inc* (n 104 above).

[108] In para 2(a)(4) and (6), *Public Law* 110–325 of 25 September 2008, it was mentioned that '[c]ongress finds that the holdings of the Supreme Court in *Sutton v United Air Lines, Inc.* ... and its companion of cases have narrowed the broad scope of protection intended to be afforded by the ADA, thus eliminating protection for many individuals whom Congress intended to protect ... as a result of these Supreme Court cases, lower courts have incorrectly found in individual cases that people with a range of substantially limiting impairments are not people with disabilities'.

[109] See sec 12101 that deals with the 'Findings and purpose of ADA Amendments Act of 2008', *Public Law* 110–325, para 2 of 25 September 2008. 'Day in Washington – Home of the Disability Policy Podcast' http://dayinwashington. com/?p=141 (accessed 31 May 2008).

It is submitted that South African courts should be careful when interpreting the disability concept, and not to become entrapped in superficial comparative studies of foreign case law.[110] Even though the ADA is regarded an impressive piece of legislation, there are shortcomings in the American system that should not be transplanted into our system.

Affirmative Action

In respect of the second goal, Chapter of the EEA places an obligation on 'designated employers' to implement affirmative action measures in respect of persons from the 'designated groups'.[111]

Designated employers are defined as municipalities, organs of state, employers with 50 or more employees and employers with less than 50 employees but with a total annual turnover higher than that of a small business in terms of the EEA.[112] The designated groups that must enjoy the benefit of affirmative action are black people, women and persons with disabilities.[113]

The reason why designated employers are duty-bound to favour disabled persons when making appointments and considering promotions, is that there are strong indications that unemployment, low salaries and stereotyping is a common occurrence amongst persons with disabilities.[114] Designated

[110] J Langa in *MEC for Education: KwaZulu-Natal v Pillay* 2008 2 BCLR 99 (CC) para 49 stated that '[w]hile foreign jurisprudence is useful, the context in which a particular pronouncement was made needs to be carefully examined. See also O'Regan J in *NK v Minister of Safety and Security v Jordaan* 2005 *Industrial Law Journal* 1205 (CC) para 35 where she states that '[i]t is for this very reason that our Constitution contains an express provision authorising courts to consider the law of other countries when interpreting the Bill of Rights. It is clear that in looking to the jurisprudence of other countries, all the dangers of shallow comparativism must be avoided'. See also G Carpenter 'The Equality Act in the Constitutional Court' '*MEC for Education: KwaZulu-Natal v Pillay* 2008 2 BCLR 99 (CC)' (2008) *SA Public Law* 200; C Ngwena 'Deconstructing the definition of 'disability' under the employment equity act: legal deconstruction' (2007) *South African Journal on Human Rights* 151; and K Malan 'Regsvergelyking in fundamentele regte litigasie' (1997) *Tydskrif vir Hedendaagse Romeins-Hollandse Reg* 217.

[111] Sec 13 of the EEA.

[112] Sec 1 of the EEA.

[113] Sec 1 of the EEA. Black persons are further defined as 'a generic term which means Africans, Coloured and Indians'.

[114] In a 2002 South African Human Rights Commission's report under the title 'Towards a barrier-free society: A Report on accessibility and built environment' http://www.sahrc. org. za/towards_barriers_free_society.pdf (2002) 22 (accessed 28 May 2008), it is mentioned that 'as a result, people with disabilities experience high unemployment levels and, if they are employed, often remain in low status jobs and earn lower than average remuneration. In terms of the Act, all legal entities that employ more that 50 people must submit Employment Equity Plans to the Department of Labour, showing how many people with disabilities are employees and what positions they hold'.

employers do not have a choice whether they want to implement affirmative action measures or not.[115] Such employers must, in consultation with their employees, devise an affirmative action plan and, depending on the size of the undertaking, must annually or biannually report to the Department of Labour on their progress in pursuance of their affirmative action plans.[116] The plan must contain details regarding 'preferential treatment and numerical goals' aimed at attaining equitable representation at the workplace.[117] In other words, the EEA does not set quotas. Employers formulate their own goals in the affirmative action plan and they must strive to attain these goals.

In the implementation of such a plan, an employer may, for example, favour persons with disabilities above other more suitable candidates who are not disabled in an attempt to reach goals in respect of representivity.[118] Chapter of the EEA, that relates to formal equality, expressly provides that the implementation of affirmative action measures that coincide with the goals of the EAA does not constitute unfair discrimination against other candidates.[119]

The EEA does not establish an enforceable right against an employer in favour of disabled employees who are not enjoying the benefits of affirmative action, by way of, for example, appointment or promotion. It does, however establish a duty on employers to institute affirmative action measures and affords such employers a valid defence against allegations of unfair dis-

[115] Sec 13(1) of the EEA provides that '[e]very designated employer *must*, in order to achieve employment equity, implement affirmative action measures' [our emphasis].

[116] Sec 13(2) of the EEA describes the duties on designated employers. Sec 21 provides that employers with more than 150 employees must submit reports annually and employees with less than 150 employees must report every second year.

[117] Sec 15(2) of the EEA.

[118] In *Department of Correctional Services v Van Vuuren* 1999 *Industrial Law Journal* 297 (LAC) the Labour Appeal Court considered the following set of facts: Ms Van Vuuren, a white female, was 'strongly recommended' for a position by an interviewing panel whereas four other candidates were merely 'recommended'. The employer decided to appoint a black person who was only 'recommended' based on an affirmative action policy that had been implemented. The employer admitted that the black candidate was appointed only because of his race. Having found that the employer had not deviated from the collectively agreed upon affirmative action policy, the Court held that the decision to appoint the black man was just and fair. It held that the decision was 'dictated by weighing up the comparative past inequalities suffered by the respondent and the other applicants'.

[119] Sec 6(2)(a) of the EEA.

crimination against those who may feel that they have been prejudiced by such affirmative action measures.[120]

The Labour Relations Act

Introduction

One of the primary goals of the LRA is to give effect to section 23(1) of the Constitution. This much is made clear in section 1(a) where it is stated that it is the purpose of the LRA to give effect to the fundamental rights contained in the Constitution and the obligations incurred by the state as a member of the International Labour Organisation. As mentioned previously, section 23(1) states that 'everyone' has the right to fair labour practices and it is clear that it also applies to persons with disabilities. This constitutional right to fair labour practices is wide and non-specific and it should not be confused with the definition of 'unfair labour practice' as contained in the LRA that only covers specific practices perpetrated by employers.[121]

Broadly speaking, the LRA protects employees against unfair dismissal and specific unfair labour practices,[122] safeguards all workers' right to freedom of association,[123] promotes collective bargaining[124] and enshrines every worker's right to strike.[125]

For purposes of this discussion, the focus falls on protection afforded to disabled employees in respect of unfair labour practices perpetrated against them and unfair dismissal on grounds of incapacity due to injury and illness.[126]

[120] In *Harmse v City of Cape Town* 2003 *Industrial Law Journal* 1130 (LC) and *Dudley v City of Cape Town* 2004 *Industrial Law Journal* 305 (LC), opposing points of view were adopted regarding the question whether the EEA established an enforceable right in favour of employees from the designated groups. However, in *Dudly v City of Cape Town* 2008 12 BLLR 1155 (LAC), the Labour Appeal Court settled the debate when it held that the EEA did not create such a right, but that it did establish a defence in favour of employers who applied affirmative action.

[121] Van Niekerk *et al* (n 40 above) 166–167.

[122] Chapter VIII of the LRA.

[123] Chapter I of LRA.

[124] Chapter II of LRA.

[125] Chapter IV of LRA.

[126] Sec 185 of LRA.

Protection against unfair labour practices

In terms of section 186(2) of the LRA, the term 'unfair labour practice' means any unfair act or omission that arises between an employer and an employee relating to the unfair conduct of the employer relating to the 'promotion, demotion, probation … or training of an employee or relating to the provision of benefits'. The definition also covers the 'unfair suspension' or 'other unfair disciplinary action short of dismissal' of an employee.[127] From this definition, it is clear that a disabled employee would have the option of referring a dispute to the Commission for Conciliation, Mediation and Arbitration (CCMA) based on, for example, non-promotion, demotion or the unfair provision of benefits should it relate to an employee's disability. It is, however, submitted that it would be more appropriate to refer such a dispute to the Labour Court under the provisions of the EEA that was specifically enacted to deal with unfair discrimination disputes.

Protection against unfair dismissal

Section 186(1) of the LRA describes a number of occurrences that would be covered by the term 'dismissal'. It includes the termination of a contract of employment by an employer: with or without notice;[128] the non-appointment of employees on fixed term contracts after such an expectation has been created by the employer;[129] the refusal of an employer to allow an employee to resume employment after taking maternity leave;[130] and the termination of the contract by an employee because the employer made continued employment intolerable.[131]

The LRA sets two main requirements before a dismissal can be deemed to be fair. A dismissal is deemed to be unfair if the employer fails to prove that there was a fair reason for dismissal (also referred to as substantive fairness) and that the dismissal was effected in accordance with a fair procedure.[132] What is significant for purpose of this discussion is the fact that certain categories of dismissal are classified as being 'automatically unfair

[127] Also included in the definition is any 'occupational detriment' in contravention of the Protected Disclosures Act 26 of 2000. The Act is also referred to as the 'whistle blower's act'.

[128] Sec 186(1)(a) of the LRA.

[129] Sec 186(1)(b) of the LRA.

[130] Sec 186(1)(c) of the LRA.

[131] Sec 186(1)(d) of the LRA.

[132] Sec 188 of the LRA.

dismissal.'[133] Amongst others, it is automatically unfair should an employee be dismissed (with or without notice) on grounds of 'disability'. The LRA adds an important qualification to this protection in so far as it specifically states that the dismissal of an employee on a ground such as disability may be fair if it is based on the inherent requirements of a particular job.[134]

According to Van Jaarsveld & Van Eck[135] the following forms of disability can, amongst others, be encountered at the workplace, namely: physical disability due to illness and injury; mental incapacity due to stress, illness trauma etc.;[136] and chronic illnesses that result in continuous absence from work. Should a disabled employee be subjected to an automatically unfair dismissal, the employee would be entitled to lodge a claim for reinstatement or a compensation order up to a maximum of 24 months' remuneration calculated on the day of the dismissal.[137]

Taking both the EEA and the LRA into account, it is therefore clear that disabled employees are protected against unfair discrimination when they apply for work, when they qualify for promotion in terms of the provisions of the EEA and possibly also in terms of the LRA, and against unfair dismissal in terms of the LRA.[138]

Code of Good Practice: Dismissal

Schedule 8 of the LRA contains a Code of Good Practice: Dismissal (Dismissal Code),[139] which provides guidelines regarding substantive fairness and the different procedures that apply to the dismissal on different grounds. The grounds are misconduct,[140] incapacity based on poor work perfor-

[133] Sec 187(1)(f) of the LRA includes a list of grounds upon which an employee may not be dismissed. The other grounds include, but are not limited to race, age, gender, sex, political opinion etc.

[134] Sec 187(2)(a) of the LRA; J Grogan *Workplace law* (2005) 147; *Schmahmann v Concept Communication Natal (Pty) Ltd* 1997 *Industrial Law Journal* 1333 (LC); and *Archer v United Association of SA* 2005 *Industrial Law Journal* 790 (CCMA).

[135] Van Jaarsveld & Van Eck (n 54 above).

[136] *Spero v Elvey International (Pty) Ltd* 1995 *Industrial Law Journal* 1210 (IC); and *Automobile Association of SA v Govender* DA23/99) 2000 ZALAC 19 (20 September 2000).

[137] Sec 194(3) of the LRA. Van Jaarsveld & Van Eck (n 54 above) 168–169; *Van Niekerk v Minister of Labour* 1996 *Industrial Law Journal* 525 (K); *Walters v Transitional Local Council of Port Elizabeth* 2000 *Industrial Law Journal* 2723; and *POPCRU v SA Police Service* 2003 *Industrial Law Journal* 254.

[138] Van Jaarsveld & Van Eck (n 54 above) 168.

[139] Amended by Act 42 of 1996 and by Act 12 of 2002.

[140] Item 4(1) of the Dismissal Code.

mance,[141] incapacity on grounds of ill health or injury[142] and the operational requirements of the employer.[143] Any person considering the fairness of a dismissal, whether it be the chair of disciplinary or incapacity enquiry, or a presiding officer of a tribunal or court, is compelled to take the Dismissal Code into account before making a decision.[144]

The Dismissal Code provides that employers must distinguish between temporary and permanent injury and illness and must also consider the extent of the employees' inability to render normal services. If the employee's absence is likely to be unreasonably long, the employer must investigate all the possible alternatives short of termination, such as adapting the employee's duties or securing alternative employment, before contemplating dismissal.[145] There is a more onerous duty on the employer to accommodate the employee who is injured at work or contracts a work-related illness.[146]

The Dismissal Code directs that an employer should adopt a staged enquiry before contemplating the dismissal of an employee on grounds of incapacity. During this process, the employee must be granted the opportunity to state a case and to be represented by a trade union official.[147] It is more appropriate to refer to this procedure as an incapacity enquiry rather than a disciplinary enquiry as this does not relate to misconduct.

In *Standard Bank Ltd v CCMA & Others,*[148] the Labour Court had the opportunity to consider the interaction between the Constitution, the EEA, the LRA and the four staged enquiry in terms of the Dismissal Code pertaining to the dismissal of an employee on grounds of a physical impairment.

In this case, the facts were briefly as follows: Ferreira (the employee) had 15 years of service with Standard Bank (the employer) when she sustained back injuries in a motor vehicle accident while she was on duty. After returning to work, the employee found that she could not cope with travelling and she was assigned to light administrative work like shredding of paper which she found demeaning. The employee applied for a more inspiring position which

141 Item 9 of the Dismissal Code.

142 Item 10 of the Dismissal Code.

143 This is also referred to as retrenchment. Secs 189 and 189A provide comprehensive requirements regarding the procedures that must be followed in this regard.

144 Sec 188(2) of the LRA.

145 Item 10(1) of the Dismissal Code.

146 Item 10(4) of the Dismissal Code. See also *Free State Consolidated Gold Mines (Operations) Bpk v Labuschagne* 1999 *Industrial Law Journal* 2823 (LAC).

147 Item 10(2) of the Dismissal Code.

148 *Standard Bank Ltd v CCMA & Others* 2008 4 BLLR 357 (LC).

would involve telesales but the employer declined her request to be furnished with a telephone headset. The employee applied to be boarded but the employer declined this and decided to terminate her services on grounds of continuing absenteeism.

The Court noted that a claim of unfair dismissal based on incapacity involves a number of constitutional rights, including the right to dignity, equality, fair labour practices and the right to choose an occupation freely.[149] Central to these rights is the right to human dignity. Of significance, for purpose of this discussion is the fact that the Court noted that the inclusion of disabled persons into the main stream is not merely about establishing equality, but about remedying the dignity of disabled persons. The Court held that:[150]

> [d]ignity, for employees with disabilities, is about being independent socially, and most of all, economically, about managing their normal day to day activities with minimum hardship for themselves and others and about contributing to and participating in society. It is about self-respect and self worth.

Many employers tend to discriminate against disabled employees, not because they cannot do the work, but because their disability is seen as an abnormality.[151] Labour legislation gives effect to constitutional principles and to this end, the EEA prohibits unfair discrimination, and the LRA and the Dismissal Code protect disabled employees against unfair dismissal.

In terms of the Dismissal Code, employers should follow a four-staged enquiry before dismissing an employee on grounds of disability. Firstly, the question is whether the employee is unable to perform his or her work.

[149] As above, para 60. The Court held that '[v]arious foreign and international human rights and labour instruments seek to re-enforce the protection of people with disabilities and to prevent discrimination against them. The overarching policy underpinning the protection of disabled people is to give effect to human rights.'

[150] As above, para 65. The Court considered a number of other cases, such as the *Hoffmann* case, where the role of dignity was recognised in circumstances when it still had to be decided whether discrimination had in fact occurred.

[151] As above, para 61. The Court held that '[t]heir employment rate is less than a third of the general population. Many employers tend to exclude and marginalise employees with disabilities not merely because the disability impairs the employee's suitability for employment, but also because the employer regards the disability as an abnormality or flaw. When the attitude that disability is the problem of the disabled individual, not society, that the workplace is hazardous for disabled people and that they need to be looked after combines with paternalism, charitableness, ignorance and misinformation about disabilities, the result is that more disabled people are dismissed than accommodated. Some employers may find it more convenient to budget for a disability dismissal than to attempt to accommodate an employee.'

Secondly, if the answer to this question is in the affirmative, the next question is to what extent the employee is unable to do his or her work? Thirdly, the employer must consider whether the employee's working conditions can be adapted, and lastly, if this is impossible, whether there is any alternative work which the employee could be required to do. If these steps were not followed, the dismissal would not only be unfair, but would also automatically constitute, unfair dismissal. The Court stressed that an employer would also be permitted to terminate an employee's services if the disabled employee was incapacitated.[152] However, the dismissal of an employee who is disabled but not incapacitated is one of the worst forms of discrimination possible.

Having considered the provisions of the EEA, the LRA and the Dismissal Code, the Court held that the employer had not properly considered the nature and extent of the employee's disability and had not considered granting the employee extended periods of unpaid leave. The employer also turned down her suggestions of buying a headset and special chair. By failing to make reasonable efforts to accommodate the employee, who was injured while on duty, the employer had unfairly discriminated against her and had dismissed her in bad faith. The employer also transgressed the prescribed four-staged enquiry before taking the decision to dismiss the employee.

Despite the above, the dismissal of a disabled employee can still be fair if the employee's disability is making it impossible for the employee to meet the inherent requirements of the job. The Court held that in the case of incapacity, an employee's dismissal may be fair if the obligation to accommodate the employee imposes unreasonable hardship on the employer. However, the onus rests on the employer to prove that a reasonable accommodation could not justifiably be made.[153]

Conclusion

From the aforegoing discussion, the conclusion can be drawn that the rights of employees with disabilities are protected quite comprehensively in South Africa. Their protection is not only guaranteed by the legislative instrument with the highest status in the country, the Constitution, but also by a number

[152] See also *Association of Professional Teachers v Minister of Education* 1995 *Industrial Law Journal* 1048 (IC); *Mahlanyana v Cadbury (Pty) Ltd* 2000 *Industrial Law Journal* 2274 (LC); and *Ackerman v United Cricket Board of SA* 2004 *Industrial Law Journal* 353 (CCMA).

[153] *Standard Bank Ltd v CCMA & Others* (n 148 above), para 92.

of labour laws. Disabled persons' right to equality, the right to dignity and the right to fair labour practices have been given human right status and the EEA and the LRA give effect to the overarching constitutional principles. It is submitted that both the constitutional framework and the labour laws fall within the scope of the social model of disability. In applying the social model of disability, disabled employees' dignity is respected and disabled employees are not merely identified based on their physical and psychological impairments, but on the discrimination that they could possibly be subjected to by the barriers established by their environment.

However, there are indications that the South African courts should be careful when interpreting the concept 'disability' not to get entangled in superficial comparative studies of foreign case law that may result in a restrictive interpretation of 'disability' which does not accord with contemporary South African human rights concepts. A restrictive interpretation, such as the one applied in *IMATU,* limits the scope of the concept 'disability' and reverts to the medical model of disability that focuses on the nature of the impairment and not the distress caused by the discrimination.

However, discrimination against disabled employees cannot be limited or removed by labour legislation alone. It is also important that an attitudinal change towards disabled employees at the workplace must be brought about.[154] Such attitudinal change can be expressed in legal terms as the recognition of human rights, and more specifically, the recognition of the dignity of the disabled employees by reasonably accommodating them at the workplace.[155] The emphasis is therefore on a fundamental mind shift away from the medical model of disability to the social model of disability and the human rights perspective afforded by the latter model.[156] It is for this reason that the judgement in *Standard Bank Ltd* is of importance to persons with disabilities and welcomed in the South African jurisprudence. The Court acknowledged the fact that inclusion of a disabled employee in the main stream of human activities is not merely about establishing equality, but also about reinstating the *dignity* of the person with a disability.

[154] Preamble to the CRPD.

[155] Southern African Regional Poverty Network website regarding 'Report of the Taylor Committee into social security systems for SA – Essential reading on poverty issues; Committee Report No 9: Social security for people with disabilities' http://www.sarpn.org.za/CountryPovertyPapers/SouthAfrica/ taylor/report9.php (accessed 1 May 2008).

[156] Foreword to the 1997 White Paper for an 'Integrated National Disability Strategy' (n 7 above).

8

The promotion and protection of disability rights in the African human rights system

Japhet Biegon

Introduction

It is estimated that 80 million people experience some form of disability in Africa.[1] The majority of these people live in dire conditions. A recent situational analysis of the lived realities of Persons with Disabilities (PWDs) in Southern Africa shows that they are the 'poorest of the poor', have limited access to education and employment opportunities, and often suffer stigma and discrimination.[2] In almost all African cities and towns, it is commonplace to find PWDs walking about or lined up on the streets begging for alms. Amongst PWDs, children and women with disabilities are the most vulnerable. Many children with disabilities are often hidden away from the public by their parents or relatives. This practice is premised on the notion harboured in many African traditional societies that disability is a curse or punishment from the gods.[3] According to Chimedza and Peters, in the traditional Shona and Ndebele cultures, for instance, the birth of a child with disabilities is associated with witchcraft, promiscuity by the mother

1 'Disability in Africa' available at www.ascleiden.nl/Library/Webdossiers/DisabilityIn Africa.aspx (accessed on 6 December 2010).

2 Report of the Disability Rights Roundtable (co-hosted by the Centro de Direitos Humanos, Eduardo Mondlane University and the Centre for Human Rights, University of Pretoria), Maputo, Mozambique, 26 May 2010 (on file with the author).

3 However, it has been argued that the hiding away of children with disabilities may be ascribed to overprotection rather than shame or guilt. See J Kisanji 'Growing up disabled' in P Zinkin & H McConadine *Disabled children and developing countries* (1995) cited in H Combrink 'The hidden ones: Children with disabilities in Africa and the right to education' in J Sloth-Nielsen (ed) *Children's rights in Africa: A legal perspective* (2008).

during pregnancy and punishment by ancestral spirits.[4] For women with disabilities, the intersection between their gender and disability constantly expose them to double discrimination. They are always susceptible to physical and sexual abuse, which in turn puts them at risk of contracting HIV and other sexually transmitted diseases. Moreover, women who give birth to children with disabilities are prone to be blamed for such births and consequently abandoned by their spouses. Not surprisingly, many women with disabilities are single parents.

Yet it is only until recently that the plight of PWDs began to receive the appropriate attention in Africa (and indeed in the world). Historically, PWDs have been treated not as right-bearers in their own capacity, but merely as a people deserving of pity, charity, and medical attention.[5] The upshot is that disability issues have traditionally operated outside the African human rights system. However, developments at the international level culminating in the adoption of the United Nations Convention on the Rights of Persons with Disabilities (CRPD) in 2006, have seen the gradual migration of disability issues into the human rights arena. Disability is now viewed with a human rights lens. This approach puts emphasis on the dignity of the individual. He or she is at the centre of all decisions that affect him or her. The focus is extended beyond the individual and into the society's response to the individual and disability. In a nutshell, a human rights-based approach to disability entails seeing PWDs as right-holders.[6]

Still, there is a general low level of visibility of disability issues across the African continent. The African human rights system has generally been underused in advancing disability rights. As such, the emancipation of PWDs is not consistently framed in a human rights language. Progress towards such a framing is slow. A handful of African countries have enacted disability

4 R Chimedza & S Peters 'Disabled peoples' quest for social justice in Zimbabwe' in F Armstrong & L Barton (eds) *Disability, human rights and education* (1999).

5 These perceptions gave rise to two (now out of place) models of disability: medical and charity models of disability. The medical model views PWDs predominantly as patients in need of treatment. As such, it locates the problem within the person rather than in society. The charity model views PWDs as victims to be pitied and offered help in the form of charity, alms and services. See A Harris & S Enfield *Disability, equality and human rights: A training manual for development and humanitarian organizations* (2003) 14–18.

6 G Quinn & T Degener 'The moral authority for change: Human rights values and the worldwide process of disability reform' in G Quinn & T Degener *Human rights and disability: The current use and future potential of United Nations human rights instruments in the context of disability* (2002).

legislation that treat PWDs as right-bearers and/or responds to their needs from a human rights perspective. At the continental level, the Organisation of African Unity (now African Union) began to take serious cognisance of the plight and rights of PWDs in the late 1990s. As a result, a number of human rights treaties adopted under the auspices of the OAU/AU have paid some focus on disability rights. Disability issues have also started to feature in the agenda of African human rights treaty bodies and in the activities of some regional economic communities (RECs). A significant development in this regard relates to the initiative by the African Commission on Human and Peoples' Rights to draft an African autochthonous treaty on the rights of PWDs. Thus, despite the late and slow entry of disability issues into the African human rights system, there is now a fledgling African regional disability law regime. This contribution traces the development of this regime, critically examines its normative content and institutional structure, and considers the viability or otherwise of formulating an African regional treaty for the promotion and protection of disability rights.

Historical development of disability rights in Africa: from invisibility to relative limelight

Disability rights under the OAU

The development of disability rights in Africa is intricately tied to the broader development of human rights within the Organisation of African Unity (OAU) and its successor, the African Union (AU).[7] It is now an open secret that for the most part of its existence, the OAU showed little concern for or commitment to human rights.[8] The OAU dedicated much of its time and energy to safeguarding and consolidating the independence, sovereignty and territorial integrity of its member states, and fighting neo-colonialism.[9] Thus, the principles of state sovereignty and non-interference in domestic affairs were so firmly embedded in the philosophy underlying the OAU such that the concept of human rights was never truly considered as an organising principle of the institution. All that was required of member states under the

[7] See generally R Murray *Human rights in Africa: From the OAU to the African Union* (2004)1–48.

[8] For a general account of the OAU see G Naldi *The Organization of African Unity: An analysis of its role* (1999).

[9] OAU Charter, preamble, para 6. See Murray (n 7 above) 7; Naldi (n 8 above) 2–18.

OAU Charter was to have due regard to the Universal Declaration of Human Rights (UDHR).[10] Until the doctrines of state sovereignty and non-interference began to be eroded in the 1970s, the OAU had neither the mechanism for the promotion and protection of human rights nor the political will to include rights issues in its agenda.

Therefore, it comes as no surprise that disability issues featured only remotely in the first two or so decades of OAU's existence. The UDHR to which OAU member states were required to have due regard only made a single reference to disability.[11] The neglect of disability issues by the OAU during this period was not an isolated case. On the contrary, it was a reflection of the global picture that was obtaining then. The UN equally ignored PWDs in its first three decades of operation.[12] It was only in 1971 that the UN first formulated an instrument on a disability issue: the Declaration of the Rights of Mentally Retarded Persons.[13] Four years later, the UN adopted the Declaration on the Rights of Disabled Persons,[14] which articulated the rights of PWDs generally. These two declarations not only ushered the humble beginnings of the adoption of international instruments on disability, but they also formed part of a growing global attention to human rights in the 1970s. In particular, the UN heightened its involvement in human rights even as it encouraged the establishment of regional human rights systems.

In Africa, gross human rights violations occurring in Central African Republic, Equatorial Guinea and Uganda in the 1970s pushed the OAU towards focusing on human rights. Taking cue from developments in international law, the 'Africa Regional Conference on the International Year of the Disabled Persons' was held in 1980, the outcome of which was the recommendation to establish the African Rehabilitation Institute (ARI). In 1981, the OAU adopted the African Charter on Human and Peoples' Rights (African Charter or Charter)[15] marking the first time that the institution

[10] OAU Charter, art 2(1)(e).

[11] Article 25 of the UDHR states that, 'Everyone has ... the right to security in the event of unemployment, sickness, *disability*, widowhood, old age, or other lack of livelihood in circumstances beyond his control'. My emphasis.

[12] T Degener 'International disability law – a new legal subject on the rise: The interregional experts' meeting in Hong Kong, December 13–17, 1999' (2000) 18 *Berkeley Journal of International Law* 180–187.

[13] G.A Res. 2027, U.N. GAOR, 26th Sess., U.N. Doc 20.7.1 (i)–(vi) (1971).

[14] G.A. Res. 2433, U.N. GAOR, 30th Sess., 2433rd mtg., U.N. Doc. 20.7.1 (i)–(vi) (1975).

[15] OAU Doc CAB/LEG/67/3 rev. 3 adopted on 26 June 1981 and entered into force 21 October 1986.

formally began to view disability as a human rights issue. In reflection of the fact that the global evolution of disability law was at its infancy stage at the time of its adoption, the Charter, like the UDHR, had only a single cursory reference to the rights of PWDs. The two UN declarations on disability adopted in the 1970s appear to have had little influence, if any, in the drafting of the African Charter.

After its adoption, it took five years before the African Charter came into force, during which period UN activities in the field of disability gained momentum. The year 1981 was declared the UN International Year of Disabled Persons and the decade 1983–1993 the UN Decade of Disabled Persons (hereinafter UN Decade). Most importantly, the World Programme of Action Concerning Disabled Persons (WPA)[16] was adopted in 1983, followed a year later by the appointment of a Special Rapporteur for Human Rights and Disability. Although a proposal to adopt a UN Convention on the Elimination of All Forms of Discrimination Against Disabled Persons had failed in 1987 supposedly because of 'treaty fatigue',[17] the UN Standard Rules on the Equalization of Opportunities for Persons with Disabilities was adopted in 1993 as a 'compensatory alternative.'[18]

The coming into force of the African Charter in 1987 also coincided with the establishment of ARI as a specialised agency of the OAU. Headquartered in Harare, ARI engages in manpower development and research in the field of rehabilitation and disability prevention.[19] Despite the global shift towards a human rights-based approach to disability, the Institute's mandate is largely based on a social welfare conception of disability. The Institute has four regional offices in Southern, Western, Central and Eastern Africa.

At the end of the UN Decade, the rights of PWDs had become a subject of discussion in international fora. Around this time, the discourse and activities relating to disability at the international level began to influence general human rights standard setting. In 1989, the UN adopted the Convention of the Rights of the Child (CRC)[20] which paid a particular attention to children with disabilities.[21] Similarly, the African Charter on the Rights

[16] UN General Assembly Resolution 37/52, 3 December 1982.

[17] G Quinn 'Disability and human rights: A new field in the United Nations' in C Krausse & M Scheinin *International protection of human rights: A textbook* (2009) 247–252.

[18] Degener (n 12 above) 189.

[19] See www.africanrehab.org.zw (accessed 14 February 2011).

[20] 1577 UNTS 3 adopted on 20 November 1989 and entered into force 2 September 1990.

[21] CRC, art 23.

and Welfare of the Child (African Children's Charter)[22] adopted in 1990 singled out children with disabilities as a category in need of protection. The end of the UN Decade also coincided with the wave of democratisation that was sweeping across the continent in the 1990s,[23] bringing with it a more favourable environment for the agitation of respect for and protection of human rights. The OAU started to be more involved in human rights issues. In April 1999, the OAU held the first Ministerial Conference on Human Rights,[24] the output of which was the Grand Bay (Mauritius) Declaration and Plan of Action.[25] This document, as rightly pointed out, 'indicated a shift from human rights being seen as the domain of the African Commission in Banjul to a more integrated perspective within the OAU itself, and marked an important turning point in the OAU's recognition of its role in this regard'.[26]

The OAU's apparent embrace of human rights within its ambit provided the much needed impetus for a regional focus on disability. The 1999 OAU Ministerial Conference on Human Rights highlighted the plight of PWDs in Africa.[27] It urged all African states to work towards ensuring the full respect of the rights of PWDs.[28] Two days after the conclusion of the Ministerial Conference on Human Rights, the OAU Labour and Social Affairs Commission (LSAC) opened its 22nd Ordinary Session in Widhoek, Namibia, a session in which the plight and rights of PWDs in Africa was discussed. The conclusion of the discussion was a recommendation that the period 1999–2009 be proclaimed as the African Decade of Disabled Persons (hereinafter African Decade). In its 23rd session held in Algiers, Algeria, in April 2000, LSAC adopted the recommendation, which was subsequently endorsed by both the OAU Council of Ministers and the Assembly of State and Government in July 2000 in Lome, Togo.

The African Decade was proclaimed with two broad goals in mind: to give fresh impetus to the implementation of the WPA in Africa beyond

[22] OAU Doc CAB LEG/24.9/49 adopted on 11 July 1990 and entered into force on 29 November 1999.

[23] See generally P Huntington 'Democracy's third wave' in L Diamond & F Plattner (eds.) *The global resurgence of democracy* (1993) 3.

[24] The Conference was held in Grand Bay, Mauritius.

[25] Reprinted in C Heyns & M Killander (eds) *Compendium of key human rights documents of the African Union* (2010) 155.

[26] Murray (n 7 above) 27.

[27] Grand Bay Declaration and Plan of Action, para 7.

[28] As above.

1992; and to strengthen regional cooperation to resolve issues affecting the achievement of the goals of the WPA.[29] It was essentially a reaction to the perceived failure of the UN Decade to deliver tangible gains for PWDs on the continent. That the recommendation to proclaim the African Decade was initiated by LSAC is particularly revealing. It shows that at this point in time, the OAU regarded disability more as a social welfare issue than as a human rights issue. Not surprisingly, therefore, there is nothing to show that the African Commission, which was more than ten years old at that time, participated in the process leading to the proclamation of the African Decade. However, despite the fact that the African Decade was predominantly founded on a social welfare perspective, three principles – equality, full participation and empowerment of PWDs – which states were urged to internalise and foster during the African Decade, had a human rights tinge.

Disability rights under the AU

The proclamation of the African Decade occurred at a time when the process of transforming the OAU to the AU was already afoot. In July 2000, the AU Constitutive Act[30] was adopted. Less than a year later, the Act came into force. Inaugurated in 2002 in Durban, South Africa, the AU, unlike the OAU, has a clearly defined human rights mandate.[31] The AU Constitutive Act states that one of the objectives of the AU is to 'promote and protect human and peoples' rights in accordance with the African Charter on Human and Peoples' Rights and other relevant human rights instruments'.[32] With such clarity of purpose and mandate, the AU began to engage in human rights activities right at its inaugural session. At its very first ordinary session, the AU Executive Council adopted the Continental Plan of Action for the African Decade of People with Disabilities (CPOA). This instrument was designed to provide guidance to governments and other stakeholders engaged in furthering the goals of full participation, equality and empowerment of PWDs in Africa.

The years immediately following the proclamation of the African Decade and the adoption of the CPOA regrettably went without much progress in

[29] Declaration of the African Decade, para 1.

[30] OAU Doc. CAB/LEG/23.25 adopted on 11 July 2000 in Lomé, Togo and entered into force on 26 May 2001.

[31] See E Baimu 'The African Union: Hope for better protection of human rights in Africa?' (2001) 1 *African Human Rights Law Journal* 299.

[32] AU Constitutive Act, art 3(h).

the continental promotion of disability rights. In May 2003, two important events returned the disability issue on the spotlight. Firstly, the first AU Ministerial Conference on Human Rights in Africa was held in Kigali, Rwanda. With great concern, the Ministers noted 'the plight of the vulnerable groups including persons with disability in general'.[33] They called upon member states to provide adequate support to ARI, and perhaps more importantly, 'to develop a Protocol on the protection of the rights of people with disabilities and the elderly'.[34] Secondly, the Disability African Regional Consultative Conference was held in Johannesburg, South Africa. In the conference, a decision was made to set up a secretariat that would facilitate the implementation of the CPOA by governments, disability peoples' organisations (DPOs) and non-governmental organisations (NGOs). Following this decision, the Secretariat of the African Decade of Persons with Disabilities (SADPD) was established in 2004 with its headquarters in Cape Town, South Africa. In recognition of the fact that disability is a cross-cutting issue, SADPD runs five key programmes in the following areas: HIV and AIDS, youth and children, gender, law and policy, and livelihood opportunities and poverty reduction. These programmes are up and running in five African countries (Ethiopia, Kenya, Rwanda, Senegal and South Africa) while national African Decade Steering Committees have been established in 16 other countries.[35]

Through the determined efforts of key stakeholders, the AU has somewhat maintained a focus on the rights and plight of PWDs. In what signifies a steady shift towards a human rights approach to disability, human rights documents adopted under the AU have provisions relating to PWDs.[36] These documents include the Protocol to the African Charter on Human and Peoples' Rights on the Rights of Women in Africa (African Women's Protocol),[37] African Youth Charter,[38] and the African Charter on Democracy, Elections and Governance (African Charter on Democracy).[39] In 2009, to

[33] Kigali Declaration, para 19.

[34] Kigali Declaration, para 20.

[35] Burkina Faso, Burundi, Cameroon, Cape Verde, Egypt, Ghana, Gambia, Guinea, Mali, Mauritania, Namibia, Senegal, South Africa, Tanzania, Togo and Zambia.

[36] For a compilation of AU human rights documents, see Heyns & Killander (n 25 above).

[37] Adopted on 11 July 2003 in Maputo, Mozambique and entered into force on 25 November 2005.

[38] Adopted on 2 July 2006 in Banjul, The Gambia and entered into force on 8 August 2009.

[39] Adopted on 30 January 2007. The Charter will come into force after the 15th ratification.

further maintain focus on disability issues, the AU declared 2010–2019 as the second African Decade on the Rights of Disabled Persons.[40] Some of the organs of the AU are also now engaged in the promotion of disability rights. The Pan-African Parliament (PAP), for instance, deals with disability issues through its Committee on Gender, Family, Youth and People with Disabilities although something concrete is yet to emanate from this Committee. RECs have also started to focus on disability rights. Perhaps most significantly, the African Commission has also turned its focus to disability rights. It established the Working Group on the Rights of Older Persons and People with Disabilities in Africa and conferred it with the mandate to draft a concept paper that will serve as the basis for the adoption of a Draft Protocol on Ageing and People with Disabilities.

In concluding, it is fitting to note that although old notions about disability still persist across the continent, the now accepted human rights based approach to disability is gradually displacing the medical and charity models. Clearly, disability issues have walked a long arduous path out of invisibility into relative limelight. In effect, the African regional normative framework for the promotion and protection of disability rights has developed in a piecemeal and *ad hoc* manner. Specific provisions which seek to address the particular plight of PWDs are not embodied in a single treaty – a feat only achieved recently at the international level – but are rather scattered in various regional and subregional treaties. In the section that follows, I analyse the extent to which these provisions secure the rights of PWDs in Africa.

Africa regional disability law regime: a fragmented edifice

Regional instruments

Naturally, the discussion here begins with an analysis of the African Charter. It is the principal instrument upon which the African human rights system is founded. But more importantly, as noted earlier, the African Charter was the first African instrument to categorise PWDs as a specially protected group. The African Charter is basically a catalogue of substantive rights that accrue

[40] AU Executive Council Resolution EX.CL/477 (XIV), adopted during the 14th ordinary session of the African Heads of State and Government, 26–30 January 2009, Addis Ababa, Ethiopia.

to individuals and peoples in Africa.[41] It is unique in several respects including in its embodiment of an African conception of human rights,[42] the inclusion of both civil and political rights and socio-economic rights in the same document, and the recognition of peoples' rights. Ideally, it is needless to say that PWDs enjoy all the rights catalogued under the African Charter in parity with all other persons. However, this fact is not immediately manifest from a textual reading of the African Charter. Article 2 of the Charter guarantees non-discrimination in the enjoyment of the Charter rights but in keeping with the time of its adoption, it does not specifically list disability as a prohibited ground of discrimination. Article 2 reads:

> Every individual shall be entitled to the enjoyment of the rights and freedoms recognised and guaranteed in the present Charter without distinction of any kind *such as* race, ethnic group, colour, sex, language, religion, political or any other opinion, national and social origin, fortune, birth or *other status.*

The failure of article 2 to specifically refer to disability as a prohibited ground of discrimination is not entirely fatal. The use of the words 'such as' to introduce the listed grounds indicates that the list was never intended to be exhaustive. And most significantly, in addition to the listed grounds, article 2 also prohibits discrimination on the basis of 'other status', which undeniably includes disability. That said, it should be noted that it is one thing to guarantee formal equality in the enjoyment of rights as article 2 does, and another thing to ensure the substantive and equal enjoyment of those rights in practice. The emancipation of vulnerable groups, for example women, children and PWDs, demand that individuals belonging to these groups are not just discriminated against, but that positive actions (such as affirmative action) are also taken to ensure that they have the capacity and space to enjoy the guaranteed rights. Article 18 of the Charter recognises this fact as it singles out women, children, the aged and the disabled as protected groups. In relation to PWDs, article 18(4) provides that '[t]he aged and the *disabled* shall also have the right to *special measures of protection* in keeping with their physical and moral needs'.[43]

[41] For a detailed analysis of the substantive provisions of the African Charter, see F Ouguergouz *The African Charter on Human and Peoples' Rights: A comprehensive agenda for human dignity and sustainable democracy in Africa* (2003).

[42] See eg M Mutua 'The Banjul Charter and the African cultural fingerprint: An evaluation of the language of duties' (1995) 35 *Virginia Journal of International Law* 339.

[43] My emphasis.

By requiring states to take 'special measures of protection' that are responsive to the 'physical and moral needs' of PWDs, article 18(4) reinforces the break with formal equality and puts emphasis on substantive equality. However, article 18(4) lumps together PWDs with the aged thereby conflating the rights and situation of two distinct groups that should otherwise be treated separately. Nevertheless, article 18(4) did set the stage for further elaboration of the rights of PWDs in treaties adopted subsequent to the African Charter, in particular the African Children's Charter, African Women's Protocol, and the African Youth Charter. These three treaties do not focus on the rights of PWDs in general but rather on specific categories thereof, that is, children with disabilities, women with disabilities and youth with disabilities.

The African Children's Charter is a regional legal response to the specific plight of the African child whose needs and interests were not adequately catered for and reflected in the CRC.[44] As earlier noted, both the African Children's Charter and the CRC were adopted when disability issues were beginning to receive more attention on the international platform. As such, they both have provisions that specifically focus on the rights of children with disabilities. In this regard, article 13 of the African Children's Charter builds upon and goes further than article 18(4) of the African Charter in its scope of protection of disability rights. Article 13(1) begins by providing that a child with disabilities has the right to special measures of protection. These measures should be provided not only in keeping with the physical and moral needs of the child, but also 'under conditions which ensure his dignity, promote his self-reliance and active participation in the community'. Articles 13(2) and (3) enumerate specific positive actions that the state is obliged to take, subject to availability of resources, in ensuring the protection of children with disabilities. In particular, the state should ensure that a child with a disability has effective access to training, preparation for employment and recreation opportunities. These activities should be conducted in a manner conducive to the child achieving the fullest possible social integration, individual development and his or her cultural and moral development. A child with a disability should also be allowed access to public highways, buildings and other places to which he or she may legitimately want to have access to.

[44] For a detailed discussion of the African Children's Charter, see D Chirwa 'The merits and demerits of the African Charter on the Rights and Welfare' (2002) 10 *International Journal of Children's Rights* 157; D Olowu 'Protecting children's rights in Africa: A critique of the African Charter on the Rights and Welfare of the Child' (2002) 10 *International Journal of Children's Rights* 127.

Unlike the African Children's Charter, the African Women's Protocol was not adopted as a reaction to the normative inadequacies of the UN equivalent instrument, in this case the Convention on the Elimination of all Forms of Discrimination against Women (CEDAW),[45] but as a response to the ineffective enforcement of women's rights in the region.[46] The Protocol is nevertheless more elaborate than CEDAW in the range of substantive rights it guarantees the African woman.[47] Its provision on women with disabilities, which is conspicuously absent under CEDAW,[48] is indicative of this attribute. In terms of article 23(1) of the Protocol, state parties have generally undertaken to 'ensure the protection of women with disabilities' and particularly to 'take specific measures ... to facilitate their access to employment, professional and vocational training as well as their participation in decision-making'. Article 23(2) further requires states to 'ensure the right of women with disabilities to freedom from violence, including sexual abuse, discrimination based on disability and the right to be treated with dignity'.

The third vulnerable group to which special attention is drawn consists of youth with disabilities. They are covered under the African Youth Charter which highlights the situation of African youth and itemises their rights and duties. Pursuant to article 24 of the Charter, youth with disabilities are, firstly, guaranteed the right to special care and to equal and effective access to education, training, healthcare services, employment, sport, physical education, cultural and recreational activities. Secondly, state parties are obliged

[45] 1249 UNTS 13 adopted on 18 Dec 1979 and entered into force on 3 September 1981.

[46] See African Women's Protocol, preamble, para 11 where state parties express concern that 'despite the ratification of the African Charter on Human and Peoples' Rights and other international human rights instruments by the majority of state parties, and their solemn commitment to eliminate all forms of discrimination and harmful practices against women, women in Africa still continue to be victims of discrimination and harmful practices'.

[47] Some of the issues covered in the African Women's Protocol and not in the CEDAW include polygamy, medical abortion, domestic violence, and HIV and AIDS. For detailed analyses of the African Women's Protocol, see F Viljoen 'An introduction to the Protocol to the African Charter on Human and Peoples' Rights on the Rights of Women in Africa' (2009) 16 *Washington & Lee Journal of Civil Rights and Social Justice* 11; D Olowu 'A critique of the rhetoric, ambivalence and promise in the Protocol to the African Charter on Human and Peoples' Rights on the Rights of Women in Africa' (2006) *Human Rights Review* 78; D Chirwa 'Reclaiming (wo)manity: The merits and demerits of the African Protocol on Women's Rights' (2006) 53 *Netherlands International Law Review* 63.

[48] To fill this gap, the CEDAW Committee adopted, in 1991, General Comment No 18 on disabled women.

to work towards eliminating any obstacles that may have negative implications for the full integration of youth with disabilities. Despite its positive stance, the African Youth Charter refers to youth with disabilities as 'physically and mentally challenged youth', a reference which puts emphasis on the impairment of the individual and may thus be understood as being derogatory.

With increasing visibility, disability rights have found normative expression even in 'unlikely quarters', that is, in instruments whose focus is not human rights *per se*. A case in point in this regard is the African Charter on Democracy. Article 8 thereof enjoins state parties to adopt legislative and administrative measures to guarantee the rights of, amongst others, people with disabilities. State parties have further undertaken under article 43 of the Charter to ensure PWDs' access to education. The Charter has not come into force and its influence is therefore still limited.

Subregional instruments

Although they were initially designed to foster economic integration, RECs[49] are also expanding their respective mandates to cover human rights in general and disability issues in particular.[50] Indeed, the founding instruments of some of the RECs, for example, the East African Community Treaty (EAC Treaty) and the Treaty of the Southern African Development Community (SADC Treaty)) have specific provisions on PWDs. Under the EAC Treaty, the EAC states have undertaken to closely co-operate amongst themselves in the development and adoption of a common approach towards the disadvantaged and marginalised groups including persons with disabilities.[51] Thus, in December 2009, the EAC held a meeting the agenda of which was 'matters relating to persons with disabilities in the region'.[52] Despite its noble gesture, the EAC Treaty does not view disability as a human rights issue as such, but rather as a social welfare issue.[53] For this reason, actions

[49] For purposes of harmonisation, the AU has formally recognised eight RECs: Economic Community of West African States (ECOWAS), East African Community (EAC), Southern African Development Community (SADC), Intergovernmental Authority on Development (IGAD), Common Market for Eastern and Southern Africa (COMESA), Arab Maghreb Union (UMA), Community of Sahel-Saharan States (CEN-SAD), and the Economic Community of Central African States (ECCAS).

[50] See generally F Viljoen 'The realization of human rights in Africa through sub-regional institutions' (2001) 7 *African Yearbook of International Law* 186.

[51] EAC Treaty, art 120(c).

[52] S Ebobrah 'Human rights developments in African sub-regional economic communities during 2009' (2010) 10 *African Human Rights Law Journal* 233–239.

envisaged under the Treaty in respect to PWDs are primarily social welfare actions such as rehabilitation and provision of foster homes.

The SADC Treaty provides that SADC and its members shall not discriminate against any person on grounds of, *inter alia*, disability.[54] This provision is laudable for it marks the first time that disability is expressly included in a general non-discrimination clause. The SADC member states have also adopted the Charter of Fundamental Social Rights in SADC,[55] which bind them to adopt 'additional concrete measures' aimed at improving the social and professional integration of PWDs.[56] While the Charter understandably does not define PWDs, it exceptionally brings within its protection the widest range of PWDs, 'whatever their origin and nature of their disability'.[57]

In 2008, SADC member states adopted the Protocol on Gender and Development with a view to 'consolidate and create synergy between the various commitments on gender and equality and equity made at regional, continental and international levels into one comprehensive regional instrument that enhances the capacity to report effectively on all instruments and also addresses new challenges'.[58] Under the Protocol, member states have undertaken to adopt legislation and related measures to protect persons with disabilities.[59] Curiously, although the SADC Gender Protocol is a 'women's rights instrument', it focuses on persons with disabilities generally as opposed to women with disabilities as would have been ordinarily expected. Thus, in comparison to the African Women's Protocol, the SADC Gender Protocol fails to draw a special attention to women with disabilities who are often, as earlier mentioned, the victims of double discrimination.[60] Moreover, the SADC Gender Protocol has not yet come into force and its potential to

[53] This inclination is evident from article 120 which is titled 'social welfare' and under which partner states have undertaken to cooperate amongst themselves 'in the field of social welfare'.

[54] SADC Treaty, art 6(2).

[55] Adopted on 26 August 2003 in Dar es Salaam, Tanzania. The Charter entered into force on the same day.

[56] SADC Social Charter, art 9.

[57] As above.

[58] SADC Gender Protocol, preamble, para 8.

[59] SADC Gender Protocol, art 9.

[60] For a detailed comparison between the African Women's Protocol and the SADC Gender Protocol, see M Forere & L Stone 'The SADC Protocol on Gender and Development: Duplication or complementarity of the African Union Protocol on Women's Rights? (2009) 9 *African Human Rights Law Journal* 434.

promote and protect disability rights in particular and women's rights in general is currently limited.[61]

Unlike the EAC Treaty and the SADC Treaty, the Treaty of the Economic Community of West African States (ECOWAS Treaty) does not make any reference to the rights of PWDs. However, one of the fundamental principles of the Community is the 'recognition, promotion and protection of human and peoples' rights in accordance with the provisions of the African Charter on Human and Peoples' Rights'.[62] In this regard, ECOWAS member states are required to recognise, promote and protect disability rights in accordance with article 18(4) of the African Charter. It is noteworthy that the ECOWAS Community Court of Justice has incorporated a human rights mandate into its jurisdiction and as such, it has developed a burgeoning jurisprudence based on the African Charter.[63]

Seen as a whole, the provisions analysed above form what could be described as the African regional disability law regime. This regime is fragmented not merely because its normative standards are scattered in multiple instruments, but more notably because these instruments are mixed in their approach to disability and scope of protection offered to PWDs. Nevertheless, the regime has huge potential for promoting and protecting disability rights on the continent. Disappointingly, this potential remains largely untapped as a result of inaction or indifference by institutions with the mandate to promote and protect disability rights on the continent.

Regional institutional framework for the promotion and protection of disability rights in Africa

Two kinds of institutions are mandated to deal with disability rights at the African regional level. Firstly, there are those institutions that have developed within the institutional political structures of the OAU/AU. These are the LSAC and ARI. Secondly, there are those institutions that have been established under regional human rights treaties and they are, therefore, the main bodies that constitute the African human rights system's institutional architecture. There are three such bodies: the African Commission on Human

[61] The Protocol will come into force after two-thirds of SADC member states have ratified it.

[62] ECOWAS Treaty, art 4(g).

[63] See S Ebobrah *A critical analysis of the human rights mandate of the ECOWAS Community Court of Justice* (2008).

and Peoples' Rights (African Commission) established under the African Charter;[64] the African Committee of Experts on the Rights and Welfare of the Child (African Children's Committee) established under the African Children's Charter;[65] and the African Court on Human and Peoples' Rights (African Court) established by the Protocol to the African Charter on Human and Peoples' Rights on the Establishment of an African Court on Human and Peoples' Rights (African Court Protocol).[66] Although they operate under the financial sponsorship of and ultimately report to the AU, these three institutions are composed of individuals who serve in their individual capacities, independently of both the AU and their respective states. I refer to the former kind of institutions as 'AU-based institutions' and the latter as 'treaty-based institutions'.

The ensuing discussion is limited to the role of the treaty-based institutions in promoting and protecting disability rights. Suffice it to note, however, that although they virtually strive towards more or less the same goal, a strong operational synergy has not been developed between the AU- and the treaty-based institutions. Just as the normative regime is fragmented so is the institutional framework. This lack of institutional harmony and coordination does not come as a surprise to a keen observer of the African human rights system.[67] Over the years, there has been a proliferation of institutions for the promotion and protection of human rights on the continent.[68] These institutions have been created without giving much thought as to their possible interaction in practice. Similarly, without considering possibilities for collaboration with existing human rights mechanisms, AU organs and other continental initiatives such as the New Partnership for Africa's Development (NEPAD) have also taken up the role of monitoring respect for human rights on the continent.[69]

[64] African Charter, art 30.

[65] African Children's Charter, art 32.

[66] Adopted on 10 June 1998 in Addis Ababa, Ethiopia and entered into force on 25 January 2004.

[67] See eg K Kithure 'The African human rights system: unnecessary overlaps or useful synergies?' (2006) 12 *East African Journal of Peace and Human Rights* 319.

[68] See A Lloyd & R Murray 'Institutions with responsibility for human rights protection under the African Union' (2004) 48 *Journal of African Law* 165.

[69] See C Doebbler 'A complex ambiguity: The relationship between the African Commission on Human and Peoples' Rights and other African Union initiatives affecting respect for human rights' (2003) 13 *Transnational Law and Contemporary Problems* 7.

The end result is a system lacking in coherence; composed of institutions with overlapping, sometimes conflicting, mandates and functions. These institutions scramble for the meager AU resources and are, therefore, perennially underfunded and understaffed.

In existence now for 25 years, the African Commission, a body of 11 members,[70] is the oldest of the three treaty-based institutions. It is charged with the function of supervising state compliance with the African Charter and the African Women's Protocol.[71] In this regard, the Commission has two core functions: the examination of state reports[72] and the determination of communications alleging human rights violations by state parties.[73] The African Children's Committee performs similar tasks with respect to the African Children's Charter.[74] It is also composed of 11 members who possess, amongst other attributes, 'competence in matters of the rights and welfare of the child'.[75] While the African Commission and the African Children's Committee are quasi-judicial bodies, the African Court is a judicial body with the mandate to exercise jurisdiction over all cases and disputes concerning the interpretation of the African Charter and 'any other relevant human rights instrument ratified by states concerned'.[76] Essentially, the African Court complements the protective mandate of the African Commission (and arguably that of the African Children's Committee).[77]

The role of the three treaty-based institutions in promoting and protecting disability rights has been dismal so far. The African Children's Committee and the African Court have just recently started to operate and they have, as such, done little to discharge their overall mandate leave alone focusing on disability rights. Despite its comparatively long existence, it is only until 2009 that the African Commission started to focus on disability issues as a matter of priority. Until then, reference and focus on disability issues in the activities of the Commission were infrequent and superficial, almost always appearing as an afterthought. For instance, the African Commission has adopted numerous thematic resolutions elaborating the provisions of the

[70] African Charter, art 31.

[71] African Charter, art 45; African Women's Protocol, arts 26 & 32.

[72] African Charter, art 62; African Women's Protocol, art 26.

[73] African Charter, arts 47–59; African Women's Protocol, art 32.

[74] African Children's Charter, arts 42–45.

[75] African Children's Charter, art 33.

[76] African Court Protocol, art 3.

[77] African Court Protocol, art 2.

African Charter.[78] However, not a single of these resolutions has focused on disability rights. In the same vein, state reporting on implementation of disability rights in terms of articles 18(4) of the African Charter has been inconsistent at best. While some few states have been minded to indicate the policy and legislative steps they have taken to implement disability rights, others have been silent on this aspect.

Moreover, despite the fact that it has developed a sizeable body of jurisprudence through its communications procedure,[79] the African Commission has received and determined only a single case alleging the violation of the rights of PWDs: *Purohit and Others v The Gambia*.[80] This case concerned the automatic and indefinite institutionalisation of mentally disabled persons under the Gambian Lunatics Detention Act (LDA), which practice, the complainants averred, constituted discrimination on the basis of disability. The issues dealt with in the case included the right of mentally disabled persons to challenge their detention, the conditions under which they are detained, and their right to vote. The decision of the Commission in this case is one of the most progressive although it is not widely known.

Four particular points made by the Commission in this case are worth highlighting. Firstly, the Commission affirmed disability as a prohibited ground of discrimination notwithstanding that it is not explicitly mentioned under article 2 of the African Charter. In this regard, the Commission stated that '[a]rticle 2 lays down a principle that is essential to the spirit of the African Charter and is therefore necessary in eradicating discrimination in all its guises'.[81] Secondly, the Commission reaffirmed that all human beings regardless of their mental capabilities or disabilities are entitled to be treated with dignity which is an inherent basic right.[82] As such, reference to mentally

[78] See, for instance, Resolution on the adoption of the Declaration of Principles on Freedom of Expression in Africa (2002); Resolution on Guidelines and Measures for the Prohibition and Prevention of Torture, Cruel, Inhuman or Degrading Treatment or Punishment in Africa (2002); Principles and Guidelines on the Right to a Fair Trial and Legal Assistance in Africa (2003); Resolution on the Right to a Remedy and Reparation for Women and Girls Victims of Sexual Violence (2007). For the full list and text of the resolutions of the African Commission, see www.achpr.org/english/_info/index_resolutions_en.html (accessed 11 January 2011).

[79] For the full list and text of the decisions of the African Commission see www.achpr.org/english/_info/Decision_Communications.html (accessed on 11 January 2011). See also *African Human Rights Law Reports* (2000–2008) available online at www. chr.up.ac.za/index.php/ahrlr-downloads.html (accessed 11 January 2011).

[80] *Purohit and Others v The Gambia* (2003) AHRLR 96 (ACHPR 2003).

[81] *Purohit*, para 49.

[82] *Purohit*, para 57.

disabled persons as 'lunatics' and 'idiots' under the LDA was found to be both dehumanising and an insult to their dignity.[83] Moreover, drawing inspiration from the UN Declaration on the Rights of Disabled Persons,[84] the Commission stated that it:

> maintains that mentally disabled persons would like to share the same hopes, dreams and goals and have the same rights to pursue those hopes, dreams and goals just like any other human being. Like any other human being, mentally disabled persons or persons suffering from mental illnesses have a right to enjoy a decent life, as normal and full as possible, a right which lies at the heart of the right to human dignity. This right should be zealously guarded and forcefully protected by all states party to the African Charter in accordance with the well established principle that all human beings are born free and equal in dignity and rights.[85]

Thirdly, the Commission held that mentally disabled persons are entitled to participate in electoral processes of states in which they are citizens. It stated that the right to political participation under the African Charter is extended to 'every citizen' and its denial can only be justified by reason of legal incapacity which may not necessarily mean mental incapacity. Finally, in relation to the right to health, the Commission read into article 16 of the African Charter 'the obligation on [the] part of states to take concrete and targeted steps, while taking full advantage of its available resources, to ensure that the right to health is fully realised in all its aspects without discrimination of any kind'.[86]

That only a single case has been lodged with the Commission alleging the violation of disability rights is a reflection of the general invisibility of the Commission. The majority of PWDs in Africa are yet to consider the Commission as a possible forum for the ventilation of their rights partly because they are not even aware of its existence. PWDs, mainly drawn from the Gambia, have recently started to participate in the sessions of the Commission. However, their participation is hindered by the fact that the medium of communication is not attuned to suit their needs. For instance, the Commission does not translate its proceedings into sign language, a fact

[83] *Purohit*, para 59.

[84] Pursuant to article 60 of the African Charter, the Commission is obliged to 'draw inspiration from international law on human and peoples' rights'.

[85] *Purohit*, para 61.

[86] *Purohit*, para 84.

that has forced those with hearing disabilities to come into the sessions along with their own translators. This is undoubtedly an expensive venture which only a handful of PWDs can afford. In sum, the African Commission is still far away from mainstreaming disability issues in its working ethos notwithstanding that it has embarked on formulating an African regional treaty on disability rights, an issue that I now turn to.

Towards an African regional treaty on disability rights: underlying issues

The drafting process

This idea to formulate an African regional treaty on the rights of PWDs was first expressed in 2003 during the first AU Ministerial Conference on Human Rights in Africa which called upon AU member states to develop a Protocol on the protection of the rights of people with disabilities and the elderly. Probably because this call was addressed to the entire membership of the AU and not to a particular organ or institution of the organisation, it was not taken up until 2009 when the African Commission took the initiative on its own volition. However, the Commission's initiative was an afterthought. Although article 18(4) of the African Charter makes reference to both older persons and PWDs, the African Commission initially established and appointed a focal point on older persons only.[87] This omission was rectified in 2009 during the Commission's 45th ordinary session when it transformed the Focal Point on the Rights of Older Persons to a five-member Working Group on the Rights of Older Persons and People with Disabilities in Africa.[88] The Working Group was mandated, *inter alia*, to '[h]old comprehensive brainstorming sessions to articulate the rights of older persons and people with disabilities' and '[d]raft a Concept of the Draft Paper for consideration by the African Commission that will serve as a basis for the adoption of the Draft Protocol on Ageing and People with Disabilities'.

In terms of its mandate, the Working Group organised an expert seminar on the rights of older persons and PWDs in Accra, Ghana, between 26 and

[87] Resolution on the Establishment and Appointment of Focal Point on the Rights of Older Persons in Africa.

[88] Resolution on the Transformation of the Focal Point on the Rights of Older Persons in Africa into a Working Group on the Rights of Older Persons and People with Disabilities in Africa, ACHPR/Res143 (XXXXV) 09.

28 August 2009. The outcome of this seminar was two draft protocols, one on the rights of older persons and the other on the rights of PWDs. In respect to the latter (hereinafter the Accra Draft), a sub-committee was established during the seminar and tasked with the role of enhancing the draft. In August 2010, the changes made to the Accra Draft by the sub-committee were presented to the Working Group in a meeting held in Balaclava, Mauritius.[89] However, the finalisation and adoption of the draft was postponed to 2011. The Working Group also recommended that its membership be expanded in order to 'balance geographical and gender representation, as well as [to] enhance the work of the Working Group'. The African Commission accepted this recommendation during its 48th ordinary session,[90] but the additional members of the Group are yet to be appointed. The Accra Draft is by and large a replica of the CRPD and its relevant provisions for the present discussion will be discussed below in detail.

Is an African treaty on disability rights necessary?

Although the process of formulating an African disability treaty is underway, it is nevertheless important to inquire whether it is at all necessary to have such a treaty considering that there is already a global treaty on disability rights from which PWDs in Africa can potentially draw protection. This inquiry is especially imperative in light of the fact that the Commission's initiative to formulate the treaty was based on the recommendation of a purely political forum, the AU Ministerial Conference on Human Rights in Africa, and not on an initial objective feasibility study. The Ministerial Conference's call for a protocol on the protection of PWDs was made at a time when a similar treaty at the global level had not yet been conceived. Thus, the need to have a specific binding instrument focusing on PWDs was then apparent. However, by 2009, when the Commission established the Working Group on the Rights of Older Persons and People with Disabilities, a global disability convention was already in force, arguably filling the normative gap that had hitherto prompted calls for an African disability treaty. Perhaps in light of this development, the Commission mandated the Working Group to draft a concept paper that would serve as a basis for

89 Report of the Meeting of the Working Group on Older Persons and People with Disabilities in Africa, Balaclava, Mauritius, 9–11 August 2010 (Hereinafter Balaclava Report).

90 Resolution to increase members of the Working Group on Older Persons and People with Disabilities in Africa.

adopting a continental treaty on PWDs. However, there is no indication that the concept paper was ever drafted. Instead, the Working Group immediately proceeded to draft a protocol, a task that is, strictly speaking, not expressly spelt out in the Resolution that established the Working Group.

Regrettably too, the Accra Draft, prepared by the Working Group during the aforementioned expert seminar in Accra, is not a product of a broad-based consultative process. Key stakeholders have lamented about this fact. In a communiqué prepared and released during the 48th session of the Commission, SADPD and other DPOs expressed their concern that the process leading to the adoption of the Accra Draft 'was not sufficiently inclusive of the participation of expert opinions of Persons with Disabilities'.[91] Earlier on, during the Balaclava meeting, the Commission's chairperson, Reine Alapini-Gansou, had expressed similar sentiments noting that the Accra Draft was 'very raw' and that its finalisation would require the input of other stakeholders including PWDs.[92] In essence, little discussion has gone into both the idea of and the resultant draft treaty on disability rights in Africa. The exclusion of stakeholders in the formulation of the Accra Draft is particularly striking when the CRPD's drafting process is recalled. As Kanter rightly points out, the meetings at which the CRPD was drafted was 'the most inclusive in the UN's history' with the effect that 'the influence of NGOs can be seen in the actual language of the treaty'.[93]

Regional human rights treaties are ideally relevant, when juxtaposed to their global counterparts, only in so far as they address peculiar regional issues or problems in addition to reflecting regional philosophical and cultural underpinnings of the notion of human rights. They either fill normative gaps evident in the global framework or strengthen the monitoring or enforcement mechanism. In a sense, regional human rights treaties, individually and collectively, complement or supplement the global system. It is on this understanding that the majority of African specific human rights treaties have been formulated and adopted. The OAU Convention Governing

[91] 'Communiqué on the Draft Disability Protocol' available at www.africandecade.org/humanrightsafrica/newsletter.2010-11-17.1543715827 (accessed 7 December 2010). See also 'Call for an inclusive disability protocol in Africa' available at www.jollofnews.com/call-for-an-inclusive-disability-protocol-in-africa.html (accessed on 7 December 2010).

[92] Balaclava Report (n 89 above).

[93] A Kanter 'The promise and challenge of the United Nations Convention on the Rights of Persons with Disabilities' (2006–2007) 34 *Syracuse Journal of International Law and Commerce* 287–294.

the Specific Aspects of Refugee Problems in Africa,[94] for instance, sought to address a peculiar refugee problem in Africa, that is, the mass movement of persons across an international border as a result of 'external aggression, occupation, foreign domination or events seriously disturbing public order' in their country of origin. Thus, the OAU Refugee Convention complements the UN Refugee Convention, which restricts the definition of a 'refugee' to a person who flees his country of origin for 'fear of persecution'. In this context, the justification for having an African disability treaty lies in asserting that the proposed treaty is intended to address or reflect a peculiar African issue(s) or position(s) that is not addressed or reflected in the CRPD.

Arguably, due to a host of factors including abject poverty, the scourge of war, and the AIDS pandemic, the condition of PWDs in Africa is generally worse as compared to that of PWDs in other regions of the world. Still, the question must be posed: Is there an African conception of disability rights that is distinct from the global conception as mirrored in the CRPD? From the onset, it must be noted that Africa is not a homogenous entity; it is a continent with a mosaic of cultures and religions that make it difficult, if not undesirable, to draw general conclusions about the values to which it subscribes. This caveat notwithstanding, there are several factors that have informed the text of human rights treaties in Africa, chief among which is the communal nature of many African societies.

Africa's conception of human rights lays emphasis on a communal-based society in which individuals are not only entitled to rights, but they also bear duties.[95] According to Cobbah, 'African worldview is tempered with the general guiding principle of the survival of the entire community and a sense of cooperation, interdependence and collective responsibility'.[96] This conception finds expression in the totality of values underlying the CRPD,[97]

[94] OAU Doc CAB/LEG/24.3, adopted 10 September 1969, entered into force 20 June 1974.

[95] See Mutua (n 42 above); B Mezmur 'The dutiful child: The implications of article 31 of the African Children's Charter' (2008) 52 *Journal of African Law* 159.

[96] J Cobbah 'African values and the human rights debates: An African perspective' (1987) 9 *Human Rights Quarterly* 309.

[97] The CRPD is animated by eight general principles: respect for inherent dignity, individual autonomy including the freedom to make one's own choices, and independence of persons; non-discrimination; full and effective participation and inclusion in society; respect for difference and acceptance of persons with disabilities as part of human diversity and humanity; equality of opportunity; accessibility; equality between men and women; and respect for the evolving capacities of children with disabilities and respect for the right of children with disabilities to preserve their identities. CRPD, art 3.

and particularly in its call for the full and effective participation and inclusion of PWDs in society and respect for difference and acceptance of PWDs as part of human diversity and humanity.[98] In a sense, the CRPD calls for the actualisation of the African notion of *ubuntu* or *batho* in respect to PWDs. *Ubuntu* is about humanity, diversity and interdependence.[99] According to Nobel Peace laureate, Desmond Tutu, *ubuntu* carries with it a sense of interdependence and in this context, 'a person is a person through other persons'.[100] Thus, one is expected to view and treat a person with disabilities as a reflection or extension of oneself.

It may be felt that the CRPD contradicts Africa's conception of human rights in one particular respect: its call for 'individual autonomy including the freedom to make one's own choices, and independence of persons'.[101] On this basis, for instance, the CRPD provides for the right to privacy,[102] which is arguably incompatible with a communal-based conception of society. Here, it is important to note that while Africa's worldview celebrates interdependence, it does not negate the concept of individual autonomy and independence.

In a communal setting, the individual is allowed personal space although he or she is required to constantly weigh his or her actions against the interests of the community. That Africa's conception of human rights is not on a collision course with the values of autonomy and independence is evident from national constitutions that guarantee autonomy rights such as privacy.[103] Indeed, the African Commission has read into the African Charter the existence of the right to privacy,[104] while the African Children's Charter expressly provides for this right.[105] Thus, a proper construction of the CRPD would support the view that the Convention upholds interdependence just as it upholds independence.

In Dhanda's view, while CRPD is an agency for PWDs to manage their own affairs, '[t]his agency is not grounded in the paradigm of independence

[98] CRPD, art 3(c) & (d).

[99] See D Cornell & K van Marle 'Exploring ubuntu: Tentative reflections' (2005) 5 *African Human Rights Law Journal* 195.

[100] D Tutu *No future without forgiveness* (1999) 31.

[101] CRPD, art 3(a).

[102] CRPD, art 22.

[103] See eg the Constitution of the Republic of South Africa (1996), art 14.

[104] *SERAC & Another v Nigeria* (2001) AHRLR 60 (ACHPR 2001), para 61.

[105] African Children's Charter, art 10.

but in that of interdependence'.[106] She explains her point as follows:

> The interdependence paradigm lays down that capacity and support can be co-terminus. A person with disability does not have to pronounce himself incapable in order to obtain support. Consequently the CRPD recognises that a person with disability may need support to exercise capacity, yet the obtaining of the support is no reason to conclude that capacity does not exist. This paradigm of interdependence which allows both autonomy and support to co-exist is a major advance that the Convention has made in establishing rights regime for persons with disabilities.

The CRPD not only embodies African values but it also addresses a wide range of concerns and issues that are relevant to Africa. Issues captured within the remit of the CRPD include: the plight of both women and children with disabilities;[107] the protection and safety of PWDs in situations of armed conflict, humanitarian emergencies and occurrences of natural disasters;[108] and protection of PWDs from exploitation, violence and abuse.[109] However, the CRPD is not flawless. It fails to address two particular issues that are relevant to the promotion and protection of PWDs in Africa. Firstly, the CRPD does not expressly deal with the link between disability and HIV. Yet it is now internationally recognised that PWDs as a population are at a higher risk of HIV exposure.[110] As noted earlier, PWDs, especially women and children, are susceptible to sexual violence which exposes them to a higher risk of contracting HIV. They also have limited access to HIV education, information and prevention services. Moreover, people living with HIV may develop cognitive and physical disability. A recent study on HIV prevalence in South Africa shows that the prevalence rate among PWDs is higher than the national average.[111] Despite the omission to draw attention to the link between disability and HIV, the principles underlying the CRPD and the rights enumerated therein are applicable to PWDs living with HIV.

[106] A Dhanda 'Constructing a new human rights lexicon: Convention on the Rights of Persons with Disabilities' (2008) 8 *SUR International Journal on Human Rights* 43 47–48.

[107] CRPD, arts 6 & 7.

[108] CRPD, art 11.

[109] CRPD, art 16.

[110] L Gerntholtz *et al Disability rights and HIV/AIDS in Eastern and Southern Africa: A review of international, regional and national commitments on disability rights in the context of HIV/AIDS in Eastern and Southern Africa* (2010) 3.

[111] O Shisana *et al South Africa HIV prevalence, incidence, behavior and communication survey 2008: A turning tide among teenagers* (2009).

Secondly, the CRPD fails to comprehensively highlight the effect of harmful traditional practices and beliefs on the rights of PWDs. The Convention simply stipulates that states should take appropriate measures to modify or abolish 'customs and practices that constitute discrimination against persons with disabilities'.[112] As mentioned earlier, African traditional societies associate disability with witchcraft and punishment from the gods. Thus, PWDs, especially children, are often subjected to unspeakable rituals in a bid to purge them of disability. In this light, a provision akin to article 5 of the African Women's Protocol which enumerates states' obligations in the elimination of harmful practices would have been more responsive to the situation of PWDs in Africa. But still, as experienced has shown, the elimination of harmful traditional practices and beliefs lies in changing attitudes through non-legal means as opposed to purely legal prescriptions.[113]

The upshot of the foregoing sentiments is that while the need for an African treaty on disability rights cannot be merely dismissed, it is also not absolutely necessary. This conclusion becomes clearer when one reads through the Accra Draft. The Accra Draft simply duplicates the provisions of the CRPD albeit with some changes. Regrettably, the effect of these changes, as will be discussed below, is to weaken the protection afforded to PWDs under the CRPD. The only justification given in the preamble of the Draft is that the proposed treaty 'will promote the rights of persons with disabilities to enable them enjoy all their human rights fully'. As matters stand today, there is nothing on the contrary to indicate that this promotional role cannot be achieved through the CRPD or the continental disability law regime discussed earlier.

As illustrated by the *Purohit* case, the provisions of existing regional and subregional treaties can be innovatively interpreted and applied to protect and promote the rights of PWDs in Africa. Moreover, when interpreting the provisions of these treaties, international instruments on disability rights may be utilised as interpretative guides. In this regard, it is noteworthy that the African Charter expressly obliges the African Commission to 'draw inspiration from international law on human and peoples' rights'.[114] In particular, the Commission may draw inspiration, *inter alia*, from instruments adopted by the UN and its specialised agencies. The Commission is further

[112] CRPD, art 4(b).

[113] See B Ibhawoh 'Between culture and constitution: Evaluating the cultural legitimacy of human rights in the African state' (2000) 22 *Human Rights Quarterly* 838.

[114] African Charter, art 60.

obliged to take into consideration, 'as subsidiary measures to determine principles of law', other general or specialised international conventions laying rules expressly recognised by member states of the AU.[115] Thus, in the *Purohit* case, the Commission heavily relied on a number of UN documents in elaborating the content of article 18(4) of the African Charter.[116] In a similar fashion, the CRPD and other international instruments may be relied upon to elaborate the specific rights of PWDs in Africa.

The point being made here is that rather than formulating a new treaty, energy should be directed towards facilitating the promotion and enforcement of existing norms, and encouraging African states, that have not yet done so, to ratify the CRPD.[117] The invisibility and lack of enforcement of disability rights on the continent has been more as result of inaction of or indifference by the bodies charged with promoting and protecting these rights, rather than as a result of lack of a normative framework.[118] Although treaties still form the backbone of international human rights law, they are not necessarily the pragmatic means of protecting the rights of vulnerable groups especially when time is of the essence. Generally, it takes a complex and protracted process to formulate a treaty, and even when a treaty has been adopted, it always takes years before it comes into force. African states are not known to be enthusiastic about ratifying and domesticating treaties they have themselves adopted. The African Charter, which was adopted in 1981, only came into force five years later in 1986. Only a single African country, Nigeria, has domesticated the African Charter in its legal order.[119] The African Children's Charter took even a longer time – nine years – before it came into force. Apart from the African Charter, no other African human rights treaty has attracted universal ratification.

[115] African Charter, art 61.

[116] The Commission made reference to the following UN documents: UN Standard Rules on the Equalisation of Opportunities for Persons with Disabilities; Vienna Declaration and Programme of Action; UN Principles for the Protection of Persons with Mental Illness and the Improvement of Mental Health Care; UDHR; and the Declaration on the Rights of Disabled Persons.

[117] So far, 25 African states have ratified the CRPD. Of these, 13 have also ratified the CRPD Protocol.

[118] See A Dube 'Protection of the rights of persons living with disabilities under the African human rights system' available at www.up.ac.za/dspace/bitstream/2263/5441/1/dube-2007.pdf (accessed 14 February 2011) similarly expressing sceptical views about formulating a disability-specific treaty in Africa.

[119] See African Charter on Human and Peoples' Rights (Ratification and Enforcement) Act, Cap 10 Laws of Federation of Nigeria 1990.

The limitations inherent in formulating and applying human rights treaties have prompted analysts to prefer the use of existing normative frameworks to protect vulnerable groups over formulating new treaties. Viljoen, for instance, has argued that much time and energy should not be spent in campaigns to convince states to convert the UN Declaration on the Rights of Indigenous Peoples into a binding treaty.[120] He suggests that even in the absence of such a treaty, 'there are existing legal avenues that could be explored' and that '[s]trategically, because time is of the essence, these avenues may hold the most promise in the short term'.[121] Practitioners too have taken a similar stance. When the UN Representative of the Secretary-General on Internally Displaced Persons, Francis Deng, was asked to develop a normative framework for internally displaced persons, he opted to formulate a set of guiding principles as opposed to a treaty.[122] The resultant guiding principles were extracted from existing international human rights, humanitarian and refugee law.[123] It has been suggested that this approach could also be used in relation to street children[124] and irregular migrants.[125] In a nutshell, where there are existing norms that can be constructively applied, in one way or the other, to a particular vulnerable group, it is increasingly less appealing, even unwise, to embark on formulating a new treaty to protect that group. A new treaty is only necessary where it can be shown that there exist fundamental gaps in the existing normative framework.

Indeed, a comparative textual analysis of the Accra Draft vis-à-vis the CRPD reveals that the latter is better placed to secure disability rights than the former. In its attempt to model its provisions along the lines of the CRPD, the Accra Draft significantly dilutes the scope of protection granted to PWDs. Several glaring gaps are visible in the Draft even to the inattentive reader. Two examples will serve to poignantly illustrate this assertion. Firstly, while the CRPD emphasises that PWDs should enjoy or exercise all human

[120] F Viljoen 'Reflections on the legal protection of indigenous peoples' rights in Africa' in S Dersso (ed) *Perspectives on the rights of minorities and indigenous peoples in Africa* (2010) 75, 93.

[121] As above.

[122] See generally S Bagshaw *Developing a normative framework for the protection of internally displaced persons* (2005).

[123] See UN Guiding Principles on Internal Displacement, E/CN.4/1998/53/Add.2 (1998).

[124] M Pare 'Why have street children disappeared? – The role of international human rights law in protecting vulnerable groups' (2003) 11 *The International Journal of Children's Rights* 1.

[125] A Betts 'Towards a "soft law" framework for the protection of vulnerable irregular migrants' (2010) 22 *International Journal of Refugee Law* 209.

rights and fundamental freedoms 'on an equal basis with others',[126] this emphasis is omitted throughout the Accra Draft. The omission is unfortunate considering that one of the primary reasons for adopting a treaty for the protection of a vulnerable group is that members of such a group should henceforth have a consolidated normative basis for enjoying rights in parity with others.

Secondly, the Accra Draft cuts off the nexus between the concept of 'discrimination' and the notion of 'reasonable accommodation'. Under the CRPD, discrimination on the basis of disability includes 'denial of reasonable accommodation'.[127] Here, reasonable accommodation refers to taking necessary and appropriate modification and adjustments to ensure to PWDs the enjoyment of rights on an equal basis with others.[128] The notion of reasonable accommodation goes beyond taking positive measures at a general level. It requires the state to directly respond to the needs of individual PWDs with the implication that the failure to do so may trigger a suit against the state.[129] The Accra Draft shies away from imposing such an obligation. It gives in to the failed argument raised during the drafting of the CRPD that the notion of reasonable accommodation could become a 'Trojan horse for the enforceability of more and more slices of social and economic rights'.[130] The drafters of the Accra Draft seem to have been sympathetic to the now common argument that African states lack adequate resources to enforce socio-economic rights. While it is true that this may be the case, African states are nevertheless not precluded from taking measures to reasonably accommodate PWDs living within their territories. As the African Commission stated in the *Purohit* case, states should take 'concrete and targeted steps' to ensure the enjoyment of socio-economic rights, particularly by vulnerable groups such as PWDs.[131]

In addition to replicating its normative provisions, the Accra Draft also apes the institutional framework created under the CRPD. It proposes to create a Committee on the Rights of Persons with Disabilities in Africa. Considering the dismal performance of existing institutions in promoting

[126] CRPD, art 2.

[127] See above.

[128] See above.

[129] Quinn (n 17 above) 258.

[130] See above.

[131] *Purohit* case, para 84.

and protecting disability rights, this proposal is not without merit. The failure of existing institutions to focus on disability rights is partly due to lack of expertise in these institutions' membership. Thus, a committee of persons with competence in disability rights, as the Accra Draft suggests, will ensure that the promotion and protection of disability rights on the African continent is constantly monitored. At a practical level, however, the proposed Committee will only further intensify fragmentation of Africa's human rights institutional framework. As observed earlier, proliferation of human rights institutions in Africa has led to a financially malnourished system. Thus, to cut on costs, the AU has, for example, adopted a treaty that will see the merging of the African Court on Human and Peoples' Rights with the African Court of Justice.[132] Thus, the success of the proposed committee will largely turn on the political will of the member states to adequately fund its operations.

Concluding remarks

Africa has come a long way in the promotion and protection of disability rights. Important steps have been taken that have resulted in the gradual voyage of disability issues from invisibility to relative limelight. Although traces of mischaracterisation of disability as a medical or charity issue still subsist, disability issues are slowly but steadily being framed in a human rights language. Regional human rights treaties with provisions on various categories of PWDs attest to this paradigm shift. However, the existing regional disability law regime is fragmented not least because the provisions relating to PWDs are scattered in numerous instruments. Nevertheless, the regime can and should be used constructively, in conjunction with the CRPD, to advance disability rights on the continent. In this regard, resources and time should be directed towards two goals: enforcing existing norms and encouraging African states that have not done so, to ratify and domesticate the CRPD. Executing these twin goals should take preference over formulating an African-specific disability treaty, which is not only a protracted and complex process, but it may also lead to the watering down of the scope of protection already afforded to PWDs under the CRPD.

[132] See Protocol on the Statute of the African Court of Justice and Human Rights, 2008, adopted at the 11th session of the AU Assembly of Heads of State and Government.

In the end, however, the stubborn challenge lies in changing attitudes, traditions and beliefs that foster a view of PWDs as lesser human beings. To surmount this challenge, effective and appropriate awareness raising campaigns are imperative. Government agencies in concert with DPOs should take the lead in this regard. Moreover, strategic alliances should be established between DPOs and mainstream NGOs. These alliances will go a long way in establishing a forceful disability rights movement in Africa.

9

International financial institutions and the attainment of the UN Millennium Development Goals in Africa with specific reference to persons with disabilities

Tobias van Reenen & Helene Combrinck

Introduction

> This report shows how much progress has been made. Perhaps most important, it shows that the [Millennium Development] Goals are achievable when nationally owned development strategies, policies and programmes are supported by international development partners.[1]

In September 2000, world leaders signed the Millennium Declaration, an agreement described as a common vision for 'a more peaceful, prosperous and just world'.[2] This Declaration, and the time-bound goals and targets developed from it (known as the Millennium Development Goals),[3] have played a pivotal role in helping to concentrate international attention on issues of development and poverty reduction.[4] The eight Millennium Development Goals (MDGs) are the following: *eradicating hunger and poverty; achieving primary universal education; promoting gender equality and empowering women; reducing child mortality; improving maternal health; combating HIV/*

1 B Ki-Moon 'Foreword' in United Nations 'The Millennium Development Goals report' (2010) 3.

2 United Nations Millennium Declaration (resolution 55/2 adopted by the General Assembly on 8 September 2000) UN Doc A/RES/55/2 dated 18 September 2000 para 1.

3 See discussion below.

4 Amnesty International 'Combating exclusion: Why human rights are essential for the MDGs' (2010) 12 *SUR – International Journal on Human Rights* 55.

AIDS, malaria and other diseases; ensuring environmental sustainability; and developing a global partnership for development.

Ten years later, in 2010, it is reported that collective global efforts towards the objectives set out in the Declaration have made inroads in many areas.[5] However, the 2008-2009 economic downturn and food and energy crises have had a profound impact on the prospects of achieving the MDGs in all the regions by the current target date of 2015.[6]

Persons with disabilities make up an estimated 15 per cent of the world's population.[7] The Millennium Declaration, and the associated MDGs, do not make reference to 'disability' or 'persons with disabilities'.[8] This has meant that disability was initially almost invisible in the monitoring of progress in the implementation of the MDGs. The past five years, however, have seen increasing efforts at the international level to integrate the interests and concerns of persons with disabilities into the implementation framework of the Millennium Declaration. These efforts were given considerable impetus in 2006 with the adoption by the UN General Assembly of the Convention on the Rights of Persons with Disabilities (CRPD),[9] which has been described as both a human rights treaty and a development tool.[10]

Many states may find it difficult to attain all the MDGs by 2015. Certain states might partially achieve a few of the envisaged eight goals; other states might reach none. In anticipation of this situation, it has already been argued that states should aim at accomplishing the 'easier' MDGs (for example, the eradication of extreme poverty and hunger and the reduction of child mortality) as a matter of priority in order to at least be able to report some demonstrable progress.

It is not difficult to predict that certain states will claim the lack of resources as the principal reason for their failures. Although this might be a credible reason in some instances, such failures might also be ascribable to

[5] United Nations 'The Millennium Development Goals report' (2010) 4.

[6] For a useful progress update, see World Bank & International Monetary Fund 'Global monitoring report' (2010) 12–26.

[7] See also World Health Organisation & World Bank 'World report on disability' (2011) 27–29. Available at http://www.who.int/disabilities/world_report/2011/summary.pdf (accessed 8 September 2011).

[8] The reasons are discussed below.

[9] Convention on the Rights of Persons with Disabilities (adopted on December 2006) UN Doc A/61/611 (CRPD).

[10] Report of the Secretary-General 'Status of the Convention on the Rights of Persons with Disabilities and the optional protocol thereto' UN Doc 63/264 dated 11 August 2008.

poor governance and planning in the case of other states that do indeed have adequate resources at their disposal. In extreme cases, states' failure might even be the result of 'benign' or even intentional neglect.

The implications of this state of affairs for persons with disabilities are obvious. Since disability was not included in the initial formulation and setting of the MDGs, it is highly unlikely that it will henceforth receive prioritised attention, despite the commitments by states at the recent 2010 MDG Summit.

Both the CRPD and the Millennium Declaration support an international development framework where international financial institutions such as the World Bank and the International Monetary Fund (IMF) play a significant role. This chapter accordingly investigates the potential contribution of these financial institutions towards the attainment of the MDGs in Africa with inclusion of the rights of persons with disabilities.[11]

Background: The Millennium Declaration and the Millennium Development Goals

The Millennium Declaration was adopted in 2000 at a special meeting of the UN General Assembly attended by 147 heads of state or government. In terms of this statement, governments undertook a number of key objectives relating to, amongst others, development and poverty eradication,[12] protecting our common environment,[13] and human rights, democracy and good governance.[14] Importantly, particular attention is paid to meeting the special needs of Africa.[15]

[11] The United Nations Development Programme (UNDP) divides its annual Human Development Index into four categories: 'very high human development', 'high human development', 'medium human development' and 'low human development'. In order to gain a sense of the position among African countries, it is instructive to note that in 2010, there were no African countries in the 'very high human development' category, and only three in that of 'high human development'. Ten countries resorted under 'medium human development', while the balance of African countries (35) was classified under 'low human development' – UNDP 'The real wealth of nations: Pathways to human development' (2010) 144–147. Available at http://hdr.undp.org/en/reports/global/hdr2010/ (accessed 8 September 2011).

[12] Millennium Declaration (n 2 above) paras 11–20.

[13] Millennium Declaration (n 2 above) paras 21–23.

[14] Millennium Declaration (n 2 above) paras 24–25.

[15] Millennium Declaration (n 2 above) paras 27–28.

Following the acceptance of the Declaration, the UN Secretariat subsequently convened the Inter-Agency and Expert Group on MDG Indicators (IAEG).[16] This IAEG developed a comprehensive set of eight goals, 18 targets and 48 indicators with which to track the achievement of the commitments undertaken in the Millennium Declaration. The resulting framework of goals, targets and indicators were named the Millennium Development Goals (MDGs).[17] The Goals are specifically designed to address the needs of the world's poorest citizens and most marginalised populations.[18]

Since the adoption of the Millennium Declaration, the General Assembly has periodically reviewed progress made and obstacles encountered in achieving the MDGs.[19] These reviews included a World Summit held on 2005,[20] a High-level Event[21] in 2008 and a High-level Plenary Meeting of the General Assembly in 2010.[22]

The 2011 MDG progress report points out that the world is facing historic development challenges, ranging from natural disasters, to sharp food and fuel increases, and profound change in the Middle East.[23] It notes that despite high average growth in the developing world, it is crucial to provide opportunities to those that are being left behind. While wealthier economies are experiencing slower growth, development assistance needs remain high.

[16] Secretariat for the Convention on the Rights of Persons with Disabilities 'Mainstreaming disability in MDG policies, processes and mechanisms: Development for all' (Report of the Expert Group Meeting) (2009) paras 13, 17–18. Both the Economic Commission for Africa (ECA) and the World Bank are members of the Inter-Agency and Expert Group on MDG Indicators (IAEG). Other key mechanisms tasked with overseeing implementation include the Millennium Development Gaps Task Force, the Millennium Campaign and the United Nations Development Group.

[17] At the World Summit held in 2005, world leaders committed to four new targets, in addition to those contained in the Millennium Declaration – see the 2005 World Summit Outcome in A/RES/60/1 of 16 September 2005.

[18] Report of the UN Secretary-General 'Fifth quinquennial review and appraisal of the World Programme of Action concerning Disabled Persons' UN Doc A/63/183 dated 28 July 2008, Annex II, para 1.

[19] An annual progress report is compiled by the IAEG; the MDG Gap Task Force also publishes an annual update report.

[20] The 2005 World Summit was held from 14 to 16 September at United Nations Headquarters in New York – see http://www.un.org/summit2005/ (accessed 15 April 2011).

[21] See 'High-level Event, New York, 25 September 2008' available at http://www.un.org/millenniumgoals/2008highlevel/index.shtml (accessed 15 April 2011).

[22] This meeting was held from 20–22 September 2010 – see http://www.un.org/en/mdg/summit2010/ (accessed 20 March 2011).

[23] World Bank & International Monetary Fund 'Global Monitoring Report' (2011) xi.

As can be expected, poor countries and regions tend to be behind in their progress towards attaining the MDGs,[24] with the low-income countries lagging on all the MDGs. While poverty in Sub-Saharan Africa has fallen steeply with the acceleration of growth since 2000, the region is not on track to meet the poverty reduction goal (MDG 1). Seventeen countries in Africa are far from halving extreme poverty, even though the aggregate goals will be reached.[25]

However, the picture in Sub-Saharan Africa is not uniformly bleak, as this monitoring report explains – the region has shown some encouraging results.[26] Progress is quite good on extreme poverty, hunger, gender parity in primary education, and access to safe drinking water. Goals related to child and maternal mortality, access to sanitation, and primary education completion require enhanced efforts.

The reports compiled in preparation for the 2010 review process were unanimous that the global financial disruptions of 2008-2009 caused major setbacks in progress towards the achievement of the MDGs, and that the full impact was at the time difficult to calculate. For example, the global crisis severely reduced the external resources of developing countries by drastically curtailing their export revenues and their access to private capital flows. The resulting decline in economic activity sharply increased poverty and impaired public services to the poor.[27] Many developing and transition economies lost output, income and employment.[28]

The 2010 regional progress report prepared in respect of Africa showed that most African countries are making steady progress towards almost all the MDGs.[29] Most countries have consistently advanced toward all the targets of the MDGs in spite of the international economic downturn. Key areas of progress included a reduction in the proportion of undernourished people on the continent (i.e. towards achievement of MDG 1) and the region is also

[24] World Bank & International Monetary Fund (n 23 above) 2.

[25] World Bank & International Monetary Fund (n 23 above) xi.

[26] World Bank & International Monetary Fund (n 23 above) 16.

[27] World Bank & International Monetary Fund (n 6 above) 21.

[28] United Nations 'The global partnership for development at a critical juncture' (2010) 2. Available at http://www.un.org/millenniumgoals/pdf/10-43282_MDG_2010%20(E)%20WEBv2.pdf (accessed 8 September 2011).

[29] United Nations Economic Commission for Africa *et al* 'Assessing progress in Africa toward the Millennium Development Goals: MDG Report 2010' (2010) 1. Available at http://www.uneca.org/cfm/2010/documents/English/AssessingProgress-inAfrica-towardsMDG.pdf (accessed 8 September 2011).

well positioned to meet the goals of universal primary education and gender equality (MDG 2 and MDG 3 respectively). In terms of health, 'commendable progress' has been made in reducing tuberculosis, while the proportion of children sleeping under insecticide-treated bed-nets is increasing, aiding in the drive to combat malaria.[30]

Significantly, the financial and economic crises that had troubled Africa in the recent past had not eroded the high-level political commitment to the MDGs. African governments have adopted a broad range of policy instruments to minimise the impacts of these financial and economic crises.[31] The role played by Africa's development partners is noteworthy: the G20 agreed to a request from the IMF's to raise its capital base and a consequence, the IMF increased its lending to Africa almost fivefold. The World Bank and the African Development Bank (AfDB) also provided countercyclical funding to the region.[32] In addition, the African Development Bank developed innovative financing instruments to assist countries to mitigate the adverse impact of the crisis.

However, formidable challenges still lie ahead: the impact of the international financial implosion on African economies (and their ability to attain the MDGs) will continue to be felt for many years to come. Uncertainty over the pace of recovery in the industrialised economies will continue to have an effect on the economies of developing countries.

With fours years remaining to the MDGs' end-date and with the rate of progress on most of the goals slower than desired, the African progress report predicts that it is unlikely that the region as a whole will achieve all of the goals by 2015, if current trends and practices persist. It does add that in some instances, this will not be for lack of effort, but rather due to 'structural, cultural rigidities in African society'.[33] Inadequate financing is noted as a further constraint.

[30] United Nations Economic Commission for Africa *et al* (n 29 above) 2.

[31] The report cites the examples of South Africa and Morocco, which drew on their foreign reserves to cushion the shock; Nigeria 'rescued' some of its banks; whilst Uganda, Kenya, and Tanzania raised public expenditure on infrastructure by 20–30 per cent to enhance economic growth (n 29 above) 2.

[32] The World Bank tripled its lending to Africa in 2009 compared to the pre-crisis level, to reach a total of US$ 8.25 billion. Of this, US$7.89 billion was channeled through the International Development Association (IDA), and US$362 million through the International Bank for Reconstruction and Development.

[33] United Nations Economic Commission for Africa *et al* (n 29 above) 3.

The Millennium Development Goals and disability

The MDGs have been described as an established, unifying set of developmental objectives for the global community.[34] However, these goals (and the accompanying sets of targets and indicators for measuring progress) do not make explicit mention of persons with disabilities or the issue of disability. This omission is remarkable, especially in the light of an emerging body of research showing the inter-relation between poverty and disability.[35]

As recently observed by Mitra *et al*, disability and poverty are complex, dynamic and intricately linked phenomena: the onset of disability may increase the risk of poverty and poverty may increase the risk of disability.[36] Although these connections are commonly taken for granted and noted in literature,[37] there has been little systematic empirical research on these linkages.[38] However, the mutually reinforcing nature of these causal links between disability and poverty, complicated by variations in defining[39] and measuring disability and a lack of reliable statistical information, make it this empirical understanding difficult to reach.[40] Researchers agree that the available empirical evidence differs greatly between developed and developing countries.[41]

Groce and Trani argue that the reasons for persons with disabilities having been overlooked in the MDGs include the fact that development experts and organisations often assume that the needs of people with disabilities will be taken care of by some disability-specific group or programme; yet

34 Secretariat for the Convention on the Rights of Persons with Disabilities (n 16 above).

35 See NE Groce & JF Trani "Millennium Development Goals and people with disabilities' (2009) 374 *The Lancet* 1800.

36 S Mitra *et al* 'Disability and poverty in developing countries: A snapshot from the World Health Survey' (2011) 1. World Bank discussion paper, No 1109 available at http://siteresources.worldbank.org/SOCIALPROTECTION/Resources/SP-Discussion-papers/Disability-DP/1109.pdf (accessed on 8 September 2011). See World Health Organisation & World Bank (n 7 above) 39–40.

37 See eg L Swartz & M MacLaclan 'From the local to the global: The many contexts of disability and international development' in M MacLaclan & L Swartz (eds) *Disability and international development* (2009) 2.

38 Mitra *et al* (n 36 above) 1; J Braithwaite & D Mont 'Disability and poverty: A survey of World Bank poverty assessments and implications' (2009) 3 *Alter* 220.

39 See Mitra *et al* (n 36 above) 3–6; Braithwaite & Mont (n 38 above) 220–221.

40 Mitra *et al* (n 36 above) 3–6; Braithwaite & Mont (n 38 above) 220–221.

41 Mitra *et al* provide a helpful review of recent literature relating to both developed countries and developing countries: see Mitra *et al* (n 36 above) 12–16.

disability-specific programmes are rare.[42] A second reason that has been advanced is the lack of available data – at both at international and national level – on disability.[43]

It has been observed that reaching the MDGs is unlikely to be achieved unless the rights and needs of persons with disabilities are considered in the process of development.[44] This is because of the close interlinkages between disability and the eight 'Goals'. It is noteworthy that nearly all the Goals have both a causal and consequential relationship to disability.

For example, in the case of the *sixth Goal*,[45] (which is of particular importance in sub-Saharan Africa),[46] there is growing evidence indicating that persons with disabilities are at equal or increased risk of exposure to all known risk factors for HIV infection.[47] Similar to efforts to improving maternal health (*Goal 5*), campaigns to halt these epidemics, strongly reliant on print media, frequently do not effectively reach persons with disabilities, thus placing them at higher risk.[48] This coincides with inadequate access to health care services, including both prevention and support services.[49] Conversely, both AIDS and other diseases may, in and of themselves, be disabling.[50] In this context, the intersections of gender and disability are important: women with disabilities are often at higher risk of violence and sexual assault,[51] in turn rendering them more susceptible to HIV infection.[52]

[42] Groce and Trani (n 35 above) 1800.

[43] See Secretariat for the CRPD (n 16 above) para 51.

[44] JD Wolfensohn 'Poor, disabled and shut out' *Washington Post* 3 December 2002.

[45] MDG 6 is to combat HIV/AIDS, malaria and other diseases.

[46] At the time of writing, sub-Saharan Africa continues to bear an inordinate share of the global HIV burden. Although the rate of new HIV infections has decreased, the total number of people living with HIV continues to rise. In 2009, that number reached 22.5 million, 68% of the global total. Sub-Saharan Africa has more women than men living with HIV. See UNAIDS 'Report on the Global AIDS epidemic' (2010) 25.

[47] Report of the Secretary-General 'Realizing the Millennium Development Goals for persons with disabilities through the implementation of the World Programme of Action concerning Disabled Persons and the Convention on the Rights of Persons with Disabilities' UN Doc A/64/180 dated 27 July 2009. para 24; also para 23.

[48] World Bank 'Millennium Development Goals (MDGs) and Persons with Disabilities' (undated) available at http://go.worldbank.org/D4RRSK0N10 (accessed 17 June 2011).

[49] Report of the Secretary-General (n 47 above), para 24.

[50] World Bank (n 48 above).

[51] NE Groce 'Global survey on HIV/AIDS and disability' (2004) 10.

[52] See eg R Jewkes *et al* 'Factors associated with HIV sero-status in young rural South African women: Connections between intimate partner violence and HIV' (2006) 35 *International Journal of Epidemiology* 1467.

Looking at *Goal 7*,[53] it is estimated that 80 per cent of all people in the world with disabilities live in rural areas of developing countries and have limited or no access to the services they need, including water and sanitation.[54] In line with this goal, consideration of environmental factors and disability are particularly important when addressing urban design and in rapidly aging societies:[55] inaccessible environments prevent persons with disabilities from taking part in economic and social activities. On the other hand, environmental dangers such as pollutants and poor road design can result in many types of disabilities.[56]

The 2008 report of the UN Secretary-General sets out 'disability indicators' for each of the MDGs and targets.[57] It further discusses practical difficulties with the indicators themselves as well as with monitoring and evaluation of the indicators,[58] and is therefore a useful tool towards inclusion of disability at national level.

Making progress: From invisibility to recognition

Following the adoption of the Millennium Declaration in 2000, a series of significant conferences and meetings on disability and the MDGs took place within the disability community leading to calls for action to mainstream disability and include persons with disabilities.[59] However, very little of this discussion within the disability community was permeating the work of experts within the 'MDG community', especially at the highest levels. This limitation was symptomatic of the more general exclusion of persons with disabilities from global development initiatives.

Encouraging signs of progress in this regard at the United Nations level came in September 2005 with the UN World Summit Outcome document, which recognised the need for persons with disabilities to be guaranteed full

[53] MDG 7 is to ensure environmental sustainability.

[54] Report of the Secretary-General n 47 above, para 25. Similarly, restricted access to water and sanitation services leads to a much higher risk for persons with disabilities of contracting diseases.

[55] World Bank (n 48 above).

[56] World Bank (n 48 above).

[57] Report of the UN Secretary-General (n 18 above).

[58] Report of the UN Secretary-General (n 18 above) 26–39.

[59] Secretariat for CRPD (n 16 above), para 7.

enjoyment of their rights without discrimination.[60] (It will be recalled that the World Summit was the first five-year progress review by the General Assembly of the MDGs.) This was followed in December of the same year by an important General Assembly resolution relating to the implementation of the World Plan of Action concerning Disabled Persons,[61] which urged governments to address the situation of persons with disabilities in the implementation of all human rights treaties to which they were parties and in efforts taken towards achieving the MDGs.[62]

At its sixty-third session in 2008, the General Assembly considered a report of the Secretary-General reviewing the World Programme of Action concerning Disabled Persons.[63] This report concluded that there was an urgent need to reinforce the disability perspective in reviews of progress and challenges encountered in implementing the MDGs.[64] It also indicated that the upcoming periodic review of the MDGs in 2010 would provide a crucial entry point to include the concerns of persons with disabilities in the implementation of the Goals by 2015.[65] This led the General Assembly to a key resolution that formally brought persons with disabilities within the ambit of the MDGs at the UN level.[66]

[60] UN General Assembly Resolution 60/1 'World Summit Outcome' (adopted on 16 September 2005) UN Doc A/RES/60/1 dated 24 October 2005 para 129.

[61] UN General Assembly Resolution 37/52 'World Programme of Action Concerning Disabled Persons' UN GAOR 37th Session Supp No 51(adopted on 3 December 1982) UN Doc A/RES/37/52.

[62] UN General Assembly Resolution 60/131 'Implementation of the World Programme of Action concerning Disabled Persons: Realizing the Millennium Development Goals for persons with disabilities' (adopted 16 December 2005) UN Doc A/RES/60/131 dated 26 January 2006 para 11.

[63] Report of the UN Secretary-General (n 18 above).

[64] Report of the UN Secretary-General (n 18 above) paras 4, 79.

[65] Report of the UN Secretary-General (n 18 above) para 4.

[66] UN General Assembly Resolution 63/150 'Realizing the Millennium Development Goals for persons with disabilities through the implementation of the World Programme of Action concerning Disabled Persons and the Convention on the Rights of Persons with Disabilities' (adopted on 18 December 2008) UN Doc A/RES/63/150 dated 11 February 2009.

This was followed by a succession of reports[67] and General Assembly resolutions,[68] culminating in the outcome document of the 2010 review process[69] and a subsequent resolution. Given the amount of preparatory work that preceded the Review process, the final document was somewhat disappointing. 'Disability' is mentioned only three times in the document: under the heading of reviewing successes and challenges; the document notes that policies and actions must focus 'on the poor and those living in the most vulnerable situations, including persons with disabilities', so that they benefit from progress towards achieving the MDGs.[70]

Secondly, members commit themselves to accelerating progress in order to achieve Millennium Development Goal 1 (the eradication of poverty), including through –

(a) pursuing 'job-intensive, sustained, inclusive and equitable economic growth and sustainable development' to promote full and productive employment and decent work for all, including for women, indigenous people, young people, people with disabilities and rural populations;[71] and

(b) making special efforts to meet the nutritional needs of women, children, older persons and persons with disabilities, as well as those living in vulnerable situations, through targeted and effective programming.[72]

Significantly, the document notes that more attention should be given to Africa, especially those countries most off track to achieve the MDGs by

[67] See Report of the UN Secretary-General (n 18 above); Report of the Secretary-General 'Keeping the promise: realizing the Millennium Development Goals for persons with disabilities towards 2015 and beyond' UN Doc A/65/173 dated 26 July 2010.

[68] UN General Assembly Resolution 64/131 'Realizing the Millennium Development Goals for persons with disabilities' (adopted on 18 December 2009) UN Doc A/RES/64/131 dated 3 February 2010; UN General Assembly Resolution 64/154 'Convention on the Rights of Persons with Disabilities and the Optional Protocol thereto' (adopted on 18 December 2009) UN Doc A/RES/64/154 dated 26 March 2010.

[69] UN General Assembly Resolution 65/1 'Keeping the promise: United to achieve the Millennium Development Goals' (adopted on 22 September 2010) UN Doc A/RES/65/1 dated 19 October 2010.

[70] UN General Assembly Resolution 65/1 (n 69 above) para 28. In this respect, it is noted that there is a particular need to provide more equitable access to economic opportunities and social services.

[71] Report of the UN Secretary-General (n 18 above), para 70(d).

[72] Report of the UN Secretary-General (n 18 above), para 70(v).

2015.[73] Progress has been made in some African countries, but the situation in others remains a grave concern, not least because the continent is among the hardest hit by the global financial and economic crisis. It further notes that while aid to Africa has increased in recent years, it still lags behind the commitments that have been made. A strong appeal is therefore made for the delivery of those commitments.[74]

The outcome document also advocates, among other mechanisms, the consideration of enhanced approaches to sovereign debt restructuring mechanisms based on existing frameworks and principles as an important role for the Bretton Woods institutions.[75] It calls on all countries to contribute to the ongoing discussion in the International Monetary Fund, the World Bank and other forums on the need for, and feasibility of, a more structured framework for international co-operation in this area. It stresses the need for further reform and modernisation of the international financial institutions to better enable them to respond to and prevent financial and economic emergencies, effectively promote development and better serve the needs of member states.[76]

Finally, another theme that emerges strongly from the outcome document is the need to improve national-level capacity to monitor and report on progress, gaps and opportunities through better generation and use of sex- and age-disaggregated data, including with the support of the international community.[77] It is unfortunate that the document does not make specific reference to the need for disability-specific data at both national and international level.

As noted above, given the important strides made in previous Resolutions adopted by the General Assembly and the preparations towards the 2010 review process, the subdued way in which 'disability' ultimately featured in the outcome document is somewhat disappointing. While the commitments undertaken in respect of MDG 1 relating to persons with disabilities are undoubtedly significant, especially in the light of the previous silence of Millennium Development instruments regarding disability, the impression cannot be avoided that this document views persons with disabilities in a one-dimensional perspective of vulnerability – rather than taking the more

[73] Report of the UN Secretary-General (n 18 above), para 33.

[74] Report of the UN Secretary-General (n 18 above), paras 33 & 78(g).

[75] Report of the UN Secretary-General (n 18 above), paras 33 & 78(r).

[76] Report of the UN Secretary-General (n 18 above) above, para 33 para 40(h).

[77] See Resolution 65/1 (n 60 above) para 33 paras 23(s), 68 & 72(h).

balanced approach earlier underwritten by the General Assembly that persons with disabilities are recognised as both agents and beneficiaries in all aspects of development.[78]

Certain of these concerns were addressed in a subsequent Resolution adopted by the General Assembly in December 2010,[79] which again accentuated the importance of the agency of persons with disabilities in development and also expressed concern about the lack of data and information on disability and the situation of persons with disabilities at the national level.[80] The resolution sets on a number of steps for member states to take towards realising the MDGs for persons with disabilities; these include for member states (together with international organisations, regional organisations, regional integration organisations, financial institutions, the private sector and civil society) to explicitly include and mainstream disability issues and persons with disabilities in national plans and tools designed to contribute to the achievement of the Goals.[81]

Developing the normative framework

It is useful at this point to briefly gain an overview of the normative framework underpinning disability and international development.

From a human rights perspective, one of the first significant developments at the international level was the adoption of the World Programme of Action concerning Disabled Persons (WPA) in 1982.[82] The Programme was adopted during the International Decade of Disabled Persons (which was designated from 1982 to 1991). Quinn and Degener explain that the WPA represented a landmark in that it embodied the 'slow but sure shift' away, during the

78 UN General Assembly Resolution 64/131 (n 68 above), Preamble.

79 UN General Assembly Resolution 65/186 'Realizing the Millennium Development Goals for persons with disabilities towards 2015 and beyond' (adopted on 21 December 2010) UN Doc A/RES/65/186 dated 4 February 2011.

80 UN General Assembly Resolution 65/186 (n 79 above), preamble. The resolution explains that this situation contributes to the invisibility of persons with disabilities in official statistics, presenting an obstacle to achieving development planning and implementation that is inclusive of persons with disabilities.

81 UN General Assembly Resolution 65/186 (n 79 above) para 5.

82 World Programme of Action concerning Disabled Persons (WPA) (n 61 above).

1980s, from the so-called 'caring' approach to disability (also referred to as the medical and charity models) to a rights-based model.[83]

The broad objectives of the WPA are: disability prevention; rehabilitation; and equalisation of opportunities. This equalisation of opportunities is described in the document as the process through which the 'general system of society', such as the physical and cultural environment, housing and transportation, social and health services, educational and work opportunities, cultural and social life, including sports and recreational facilities, are made accessible to all.[84]

Part of the WPA addresses the implementation of the Programme. Among the measures set out here, the Programme envisages the development of long-term programmes at national level to achieve its objectives, and specifies that such programmes should be an integral part of the country's general policy for socio-economic development.[85]

A second major development was the adoption in 1993 by the General Assembly of the Standard Rules on the Equalisation of Opportunities for Persons with Disabilities.[86] Although these rules do not have legal effect, Lord *et al* explain that they represented a significant step towards outlining a comprehensive framework for addressing the rights of persons with disabilities.[87]

The Standard Rules address the question of equalisation of opportunities under the following headings: preconditions for equal participation; target areas for equal participation; implementation measures; and the monitoring mechanism. Of particular interest to the present discussion are Rules 21 and 22, which deal with cooperation between States and in the international community. Rule 21 sets out the responsibility of States in the realm of technical and economic cooperation and may therefore be regarded as an important antecedent of Article 32 of the CRPD.[88] Interestingly, the Standard

[83] G Quinn & T Degener 'Human rights and disability: The current use and future potential of United Nations human rights instruments in the context of disability' (2002) para 2.2; J Lord *et al Disability and international cooperation and development* (2010) 3. For a helpful overview of the different approaches to disability, see Quinn & Degener (2002) chapter 1.

[84] WPA (n 61 above), para 12.

[85] WPA (n 61 above), para 88.

[86] UN General Assembly Resolution 48/96 'UN Standard Rules on the Equalisation of Opportunities for Persons with Disabilities' (adopted 20 December 1993) UN Doc A/RES/48/96.

[87] Lord *et al* (n 83 above) 4

[88] Lord *et al* (n 83 above) 4.

Rules accept the notion of conditioning development aid programmes to the achievement of equality goals.[89]

The third component of what has been described as 'the international disability architecture'[90] is of course the CRPD. The document contains an explicit social development dimension, firstly in its recognition that the majority of persons with disabilities live in conditions of poverty, and that there is accordingly a critical need to address the negative impact of poverty on persons with disabilities.[91] It also emphasises the importance of 'mainstreaming disability issues' as an integral part of sustainable development strategies.[92]

Secondly, article 32 expressly addresses the obligations of Member States in respect of international cooperation.[93] They are required to cooperate internationally through partnerships with other States, with relevant international and regional organisations and civil society in support of national measures to give effect to the CRPD. Article 32 proposes a range of measures that Member States may take, including –

(a) ensuring that international cooperation is inclusive of and accessible to persons with disabilities;
(b) facilitating and supporting capacity-building, including through the exchange and sharing of information, experiences, training programmes and best practices; and
(c) facilitating cooperation in research and access to scientific and technical knowledge.

Lord *et al* further present a cogent argument that the CRPD reflects the 'interdisciplinary and holistic' nature of development in that each individual article must be interpreted in light of the general principles articulated in article 3 and other thematic articles such as those on education, health, living in the community, adequate standards of living, and others.[94] This argument takes on particular importance in the low-resource settings

[89] Rule 21 paras 2 and 22(2); Lord *et al* (n 83 above).

[90] See UN Secretary-General (n 18 above) para 6.

[91] CRPD (n 9 above), Preamble para (t).

[92] CRPD (n 9 above), Preamble, para (g).

[93] The Preamble recognises the 'importance of international cooperation for improving the living conditions of persons with disabilities in every country, particularly in developing countries' – para (l).

[94] Lord *et al* (n 83 above) 5.

prevailing in many African countries and the concomitant limitations in respect of especially socio-economic rights. In this respect, Article 4(2) of the Convention should also be considered: with regard to economic, social and cultural rights, state parties agree to take measures to the maximum of their available resources and, *where needed, within the framework of international cooperation*, with a view to achieving progressively the full realisation of these rights.

In this way, the CRPD underscores the international commitment to development embodied in the Millennium Declaration and the MDGs, and in addition to the broad junction between the 'explicit social development dimension' of the CRPD and the Millennium Declaration, there are also specific instances where the two instruments amplify each other.[95] One example is article 32, discussed above, and MDG 8, which is to develop a global partnership for development.[96] A second example is that of education.[97]

Looking back on the advances that have been set out here, one is presented with an apparent contradiction: there has been an indisputable trajectory of progress in terms of recognition of the rights of persons with disabilities since the 1980s, culminating in the adoption of the CRPD in 2006 (and its coming into operation in 2008). At the same time, while the Millennium Declaration and the MDGs were silent on disability, issues of disability were increasingly included in monitoring and evaluation reviews from 2005 onwards. Although the 2010 review was disappointing, as pointed out, a

[95] There has been some debate about the relationship between the international human rights framework and the MDG agenda – see eg. P Alston 'Ships passing in the night: The current state of the human rights and development debate seen through the lens of the Millennium Development Goals' (2005) 27 *Human Rights Quarterly* 759–762; S Zaidi 'Millennium Development Goal 6 and the rights to health: Conflictual or complementary?' (2010) 12 *SUR International Journal on Human Rights* 124–125. A more comprehensive discussion of this issue is beyond the scope of this chapter.

[96] This confluence between article 32 and MDG 8 is further strengthened by the Accra Agenda for Action: developing countries and donors undertake to ensure that their respective development policies and programmes are designed and implemented in ways consistent with their agreed international commitments on 'gender equality, human rights, disability and environmental sustainability' – Third High Level Forum on Aid Effectiveness *Accra Agenda for Action* adopted in Accra, Ghana on 4 September 2008, para 13(c).

[97] Lord *et al* explain that article 24 of the CRPD would be bolstered by including disability as a target under MDG 2 on universal primary education. Empirical education data from across the world indicates that children with disabilities tend to have lower enrolment rates than children without disabilities; therefore, achieving MDG 2 will not be possible as long as children with disabilities are not specifically targeted in an effort to reach universal primary education – Lord *et al* (n 83 above) 6.

subsequent resolution was adopted and aimed at addressing certain disability-related concerns. However, in the face of these increments, one notes the stark reality of persons with disabilities still living in poverty, the majority in developing countries such as those on the African continent.

Significantly, the fundamental reasons for the failure to include persons with disabilities (or to mainstream disability) still persist. The reports and resolutions reviewed above set out a common call for action to address the exclusion of persons with disability, and are in agreement that concerted and combined efforts will be required at various levels. As exemplified by article 32 of the CRPD, it is generally understood that governments at national level will be the primary actors in these efforts to address exclusion;[98] however, international and regional organisations and institutions must also be involved. Given the prominent position that has been accorded to the international financial institutions, as discussed above, the question arises whether it may be possible for these institutions to play a more strongly 'human rights' oriented role towards achievement of the MDGs. This question will be addressed in the next section of this chapter.

The roles of the World Bank and the International Monetary Fund vis-à-vis the Millennium Development Goals

As noted above, the eighth MDG calls for the creation of a global partnership for development. Among the 18 targets and 48 indicators initially developed for tracking the progressive attainment of the goals, 6 of the former and 16 of the latter apply to this goal. In both instances, this amounts to one third (or 33%) of the total number of targets and indicators respectively. This high percentage emphasises the importance of the achievement of this goal for the other seven MDGs.[99]

It is evident that the degree of success or failure in attaining the targets of MDG 8 will have an impact on the attainment of the targets of the remaining

[98] Due to constraints of space, this chapter does not consider the role of the mechanism established to monitor compliance by State Parties with the CRPD, i.e., the Committee on the Rights of Persons with Disabilities (see art 34 of the Convention). In addition to considering periodic country reports, the Committee also receives communications under the Optional Protocol to the Convention.

[99] The complete list of targets and indicators is provided in the table on pages 229–230.

7 MDGs in developing and least developed countries. It is further evident that the major international trading, financing and lending institutions have a distinctive role to play in this regard. Since these institutions are based on the collaborative efforts of their member states, their outcome oriented involvement will be indicative of the seriousness of the latter to comply with Article 32 of the CRPD.

It is therefore instructive to develop an understanding of the operation of the main international financial institutions, that is, the World Bank and the IMF since these institutions are, due to their status as specialised agencies of the UN, considered to have leading roles to play in the pursuance of MDG 8.[100] Although the 'World Bank Group' consists of five closely related institutions, this discussion is confined to two of them, the International Development Association (IDA) and the International Finance Corporation (IFC).[101]

As the major international lending institution the World Bank is the primary source of the financial means for developing states that are experiencing fiscal shortfalls between their annual incomes[102] and their public expenditure commitments. The loans awarded by the Bank are channelled through its two funding institutions, that is, the IDA and the IFC.

The IDA promotes economic development in least-developed countries through providing (more) concessionary finance to such states than would normally be done in terms of the conventional loans system of the Bank.[103] The resources from which the loans are funded are derived from the contributions by developed and developing countries through their original (membership) subscriptions and their three-yearly replenishments contributions to the IDA fund.[104]

The IFC focuses on the promotion of joint private-publicly initiated development-oriented investments that often take the form of joint public-private partnership agreements between transnational companies and the governments of developing states. The IFC provides long-term capital loans to states to enable them to effect structural reforms to their economies with

[100] An examination of the international trade system is beyond the scope of the present discussion.

[101] Unless otherwise indicated, 'World Bank' or the 'Bank' as used here, refers to these two entities collectively.

[102] Composed of various forms of taxation and the yield by the GDP.

[103] World Bank assistance is generally long term and is funded both by member country contributions and through bond issuance.

[104] See the discussion in para 9 below.

a view to stimulating economic growth and to undertake projects aimed at reconstruction and development. The Bank may set conditions, standards and requirements for the qualification for loans as well as for the utilisation of the funds. The conditions are, among other things, employed to ensure the compatibility of state action with national and international law.[105]

Both IDA and IFC loans are subject to the Directives and the Operational Policies and Strategies of the Bank. The Inspection Panel of the Bank monitors its compliance with its own operational policies. This ensures a measure of public accountability by the Bank to its shareholders, which are states.[106] The IFC is not subject to the jurisdiction of the World Bank Inspection Panel, but it is subject to review by the Bank's Compliance Advisor/Ombudsman (CAO). It is evident that the various types of loans provided by the World Bank can have a determinant impact on the way that development takes place in the benefiting countries. In the context of the pursuance of the attainment of the MDGs, this is of great importance.

The IMF promotes international monetary cooperation and provides policy advice and technical assistance to help countries build and maintain strong economies. The Fund also makes loans and helps countries design policy programmes to solve balance of payments problems when sufficient financing on affordable terms cannot be obtained by such countries to meet net international payments. IMF loans are short and medium term and funded mainly by the pool of quota contributions that its members provide.

Although the basic missions and purposes of the WB and IMF differ, these institutions sometimes overlap in their approaches and mechanisms employed to support the pursuance of the MDGs at both the international and the national level.[107] The terms for their cooperation were set out in 1989 in a concordat to ensure effective collaboration in areas of shared responsibility. In our view, the following forms of cooperation, from among

[105] Aspects of conditionality relevant to the present discussion are considered in para 9 below.

[106] See DL Clark 'The World Bank and human rights: the need for greater accountability' (2002) 15 *Harvard Human Rights Journal* 206–226; N Birdsall 'Why it matters who runs the IMF and the World Bank', in G Ranis *et al* (eds) *Globalization and the nation state: The impact of the IMF and the World Bank* (2006) 429–451.

[107] International Monetary Fund Factsheet: 'The IMF and the World Bank', available at: http://www.imf.org/external/np/exr/facts/imfwb.htm (accessed 24 June 2011); International Monetary Fund Factsheet: 'The IMF and the Millennium Development Goals', available at http://www.imf.org/external/np/exr/facts/mdg.htm (accessed 24 June 2011).

the various initiatives taken by the two institutions, are important for assisting states in their pursuance of the MDGs:

> First, the meeting of IMF and World Bank Governors as part of the joint Development Committee whose purpose is to advise the two institutions on critical development issues and on the financial resources required to promote economic development in low-income countries; secondly, their collaboration through a Joint Management Action Plan (JMAP) (established in 2007) under which IMF and the Bank country teams discuss their country-level work programmes for purposes of identifying macro-critical sectoral issues, the division of work between them, and the planning of initiatives for the ensuing year(s);[108] thirdly, the joint IMF and WB analysis of the debt sustainability of heavily indebted poor countries (HIPC) under the Debt Sustainability Framework (DSF); and fourthly, their publication of the joint Global Monitoring Report (since 2004) which assesses the progress made, as well the contributions of the efforts at national and international levels, towards the achievement of the MDGs.

The place of disability in the development agenda of the World Bank[109]

The Bank's formal commitment to disability began in 2002 with the establishment of the Disability and Development Team (DDT) within the Social Protection Unit (SPU) of the Vice-President of the Bank. The primary focus of the team is the inclusion of disability in the international development agenda. This inclusion is generally not advanced through dedicated loan projects but integrated as parts of other projects. The Bank cites its mainstreaming approach as the reason why it has no data on the amounts of Bank resources dedicated to its disability-related work. According to its estimates, though, at least 4% of all Bank projects, representing 5% of its lending volume,

[108] A recent review of JMAP implementation underscored the importance of these joint country team consultations in enhancing collaboration. See World Bank and International Monetary Fund, 'Implementation of the Joint Management Action Plan on Bank-Fund Collaboration', prepared by the Bank's Poverty Reduction and Economic Management Network and the Fund's Strategy, Policy and Review Department, approved by O Canuto and R Moghadam, March 3, 2010. Available at: http://www.imf.org/external/np/pp/eng/2010/030310.pdf (accessed 27 June 2011).

[109] This paragraph is partially based on the information available at http://www.brettonwoodsproject.org/print.shtml?cmd[884]=x-545889 (accessed 15 November 2010).

have integrated disability as a component of their work over the period 2006–2010.

Much of the early work (2002–2004) involved improving the available disability-related data. The DDT has developed a toolkit containing thematic disability-related information, for example data collection, disability in the project cycle and disability law. The Team cooperates with country offices in the Poverty Reduction and Strategy Paper[110] (PRSP) formation process and in the areas of interface between disability and other matters that have captured the Bank's attention in recent years. The Bank's engagement with disabilities people organisations (DPOs) and civil society is done by the Team and the country offices.[111]

In 2004, the Bank established the Global Partnerships for Disability and Development (GPDD), an international consortium of development agencies, NGOs, governments and other interested parties. The GPDD has three principal aims: first, to accelerate the inclusion of people with disabilities and their families into development policies and practices; secondly, to increase collaboration among development agencies and organisations to reduce the extreme poverty and exclusion of the disabled; and thirdly, to serve as a clearing house for information on disability.[112] The Bank administers a Development Grant Facility and a Multi-Donor Trust Fund, established in 2005, the main purposes of which are to fund the activities of the GPDD.

[110] Poverty Reduction Strategy Papers (PRSPs) are in many ways the replacement for Structural Adjustment Programmes, and are documents required by the IMF and World Bank before a country can be considered for debt relief within the Heavily Indebted Poor Country (HIPC) Programme. According to the IMF, PRSPs are prepared by the member countries through a participatory process involving domestic stakeholders as well as development partners, including the World Bank and International Monetary Fund. Updated every three years with annual progress reports, PRSPs describe the country's macroeconomic, structural and social policies and programmes over a three year or longer horizon to promote broad-based growth and reduce poverty, as well as associated financing needs and major sources of financing. See http://www.imf.org/external/np/prsp/prsp.aspx (accessed 10 July 2011). Critics, however, argue that the criteria used to judge PRSPs by the World Bank and IMF are actually used to impose neo-liberal policies, and that these policies tend to increase poverty rather than decrease it. See eg., D Craig & D Porter 'Poverty Reduction Strategy Papers: A new convergence' (2003) 31(1) *World Development* 53–69 (available at: http://www.sciencedirect.com/science/article/pii/S0305750X0200147X (accessed 10 July 2011).

[111] See Lord *et al* (n 83 above).

[112] See http://www.gpdd-online.org/index.php?option=com content&view=article&id=41&ltemid=37 (accessed 5 November 2010).

The Bank further participates in inter-agency cooperation to ensure the implementation of the CRPD.[113] In addition, the Bank's regional and country offices may freely develop their own work programmes on disability. The approaches of these offices depend on the cultural, economic, social environments, and the financial situations in the regions and countries.[114]

Another example of inter-agency partnership in the field of disability is the Bank's recent publication, with the World Health Organisation, of the first-ever World Report on Disability.[115] Using data from the World Health Survey (2004) and the Global Burden of Disease study (2004 update), the report gives an overview of the status of disability in the world, including the first global estimates of the number of persons with disabilities since the 1970s.[116]

The Bank's 'mainstreaming' approach to the place of disability in the development agenda is confirmed in the content of the 2011 Global Monitoring Report.[117] The report contains one single explicit reference to 'disability' where it is linked to 'the indigenous and socially excluded'.[118] It must, consequently, be assumed that disability interests are included in the analyses and findings of this report.

[113] For example, by means of partnerships established through the Global Partnership for Disability and Development (GPDD) which is composed of national governments, development banks, UN agencies, DPOs, NGOs, universities, foundations, and enterprises, all committed to the GPDD objective to combat the social and economic exclusion and impoverishment of persons with disabilities and their families in developing countries. See Lord *et al* (n 83) above.

[114] See also further discussion in para 8 below.

[115] World Health Organisation & World Bank (n 7 above). The report was launched on 9 June 2011.

[116] The full report, also in alternative accessible formats, is available at www.who.int/disabilities/world_report/2011/en/index.html (accessed 9 July 2011).

[117] World Bank & International Monetary Fund (n 23 above).

[118] See chapter 4, which deals with 'Assisting Indigenous and Socially Excluded Populations' under the rubric of 'Vulnerable groups receive less schooling and underperform in school' – World Bank & International Monetary Fund (n 23 above) 123. A scanning of the report yielded no further references to 'disability' or 'persons with disabilities' or any links thereof to 'indigenous', 'marginalised' or 'vulnerable' or 'minority' communities, groups or people.

The place of human rights in the development agenda of the World Bank and the IMF

Although a cogent case has already been made earlier in this chapter for the recognition of the interdependence between human rights and development in order to effectively pursue the achievement of the MDGs,[119] it remains disputed whether, and to what extent, international financial institutions should play a role in the progressive development of international law, in this case promoting human rights in development.[120]

As international organisations, the Bank and the Fund are primarily bound by their founding charters, that is the international agreements (read 'treaties') by means of which they are established. In the case of the Bank, legal restrictions are placed upon it by its Articles of Agreement[121] on the factors that may be taken into account in decision-making by staff members. Political factors[122] are prohibited and only economic and efficiency considerations are permitted.[123]

Secondly, as 'secondary subjects' of international law, international organisations can be bound by obligations under the general principles of international law and can possess international rights and duties. In the third place, they are bound by the *ius cogens* (peremptory, non-derogable norms, including those pertaining to human rights obligations).[124] In the fourth place, as specialised agencies of the UN, the Bank and IMF are bound by the purposes, principles and norms of the UN Charter. In the view of Darrow, this includes the human rights purposes as stated in article 55 of the Charter as elaborated in the UDHR (1948) and the body of international human rights law built upon it.[125]

[119] See para 5 above.

[120] See eg M Darrow *Between light and shadow, the World Bank, the International Monetary Fund and international human rights law* (2003) 113–142; B Ghazi *The IMF, the World Bank Group and the question of human rights* (2005) 142–177.

[121] International Bank for Reconstruction and Development, Articles of Agreement, 22 July 1944, Stat 1440, 2 UNTS 134.

[122] Read: the stance of civil and political rights in borrowing countries.

[123] See art IV(10) and art III(5)(b).

[124] See A Cassese *International law* (2005)134–140, 198–210 ; MN Shaw *International law* (2003) 241–246; P Sands & P Klein (eds) *Bowett's law of international institutions* (2001) 442–464.

[125] Darrow (n 120 above) 168–183.

The Bank has obligations vis-à-vis its state members, which may include the enforcement of (non-Bank-related) treaty obligations among them. However, as far as membership to human rights agreements are concerned, there is a large divergence among Bank members. It remains open to debate whether the Bank should (or could) attempt to enforce such human rights related obligations through loan conditionality or through preferential assistance.[126] Although the Bank has adopted various environmental and social policies, it has, probably owing to the above-mentioned factors, not (yet) adopted a general operational policy on human rights. This has resulted in the *ad hoc* and discretionary incorporation of human rights in the decision-making by the Bank employees instead of the consistent, systematic incorporation thereof into everyday decision-making procedures with respect to grant-making and lending when they are engaged in individual country dialogues drafting Country Assistance Strategies.[127]

The lack of a human rights approach within the Bank has, for a number of reasons, been criticised as not keeping up with the dynamic of a rights based approach adopted by other major international development oriented institutions.[128] For example, the United Nations Development Programme (UNDP),[129] the United Nations Children's Fund (UNICEF), United Nations'

[126] D Bradlow 'Should the international financial institutions play a role in the implementation and enforcement of international humanitarian law?'(2002) 50 *University of Kansas Law Review* 695.

[127] See eg P Alston & M Robinson (eds) *Human rights and development: Towards mutual reinforcement* (2005); M Darrow & L Arbour 'The pillar of glass: human rights in the development operations of the United Nations' (2009) 103 *American Journal of International Law* 446, 487; GA Sarfaty 'Why culture matters in international institutions: The marginality of human rights at the World Bank' (2009) 103 *American Journal of International Law* 648. See also para 10 below.

[128] See eg Clark (n 106 above) 222–226.

[129] As the UN's global development network, the UNDP plays an explicitly articulated leading role in the pursuance of the MDGs. It publishes a number of significant reports on the MDGs. See http://www.beta.undp.org/undp/en/home/mdgoverview.html (accessed 2 July 2011). It is ironic that the UNDP has signed a co-operation agreement with the Islamic Development Bank in June 2011 aimed at promoting the work of both institutions in the areas of economic development and social progress whilst the World Bank itself continues to maintain an ambivalent approach towards human rights. See http://www.beta.undp.org/undp/en/home/presscenter/articles/2011/06/20/idb-andp-agree-to-deepen-cooperation.html (accessed 2 July 2011).

Entity for Gender Equity and the Empowerment of Women (UN Women),[130] UN–HABITAT,[131] the Global Environmental Facility (GEF),[132] have adopted either human rights policies or rights-based approaches to development.

All of these institutions have mechanisms in place for tracking their own and their member states' progress towards achieving the MDGs. It has been argued that the IFC (discussed above), has similarly adopted a human rights approach in its risk management strategies, although it has done so in a selective manner.[133] Moreover, private financial institutions have begun to follow suit by incorporating human rights considerations in their business practices.[134]

In addition to the legal restrictions mentioned above, the lack of a consistent systematic human rights approach by the Bank has been found to

[130] Two funds, first, a multi-donor initiative, the Fund for Gender Equality is dedicated to programmes that increase women's economic opportunities and/or political participation at local and national level; secondly, managed by UN Women on behalf of the UN system, the UN Trust Fund to End Violence against Women works to stop all of the diverse forms of gender-based violence that undercut women's rights around the world. See http://www.unwomen.org/how-we-work/?show=Grant-making_Funds (accessed 2 July 2011).

[131] A significant number of UN Habitat's programmes are directed towards the achievement of human rights oriented goals. See http://www.unhabitat.org/?gclid=CKzyntft56kCFUUHHAoduTUsVg (accessed 2 July 2011).

[132] The GEF was established as a pilot programme within the Bank in 1991. It moved out of the Bank to become a permanent, separate institution within the UN. The Bank still acts as trustee for GEF Trust Fund and provides administrative services to it. The GEF is the financial mechanism for the implementation of a number of significant global environmental conventions. The Instrument for the Establishment of the Restructured GEF (adopted in 1994 and amended in 2010) may be considered the statutes and by-laws of the GEF, and contains provisions for the governance, participation, replenishment, and fiduciary and administrative operations of the GEF. It also lays out the roles and countries through its Least Developed Countries Fund (LDCF) which focuses on reducing the vulnerability of those sectors and resources that are central to development and livelihoods, such as water; agriculture and food security; health; disaster risk management and prevention; infrastructure; and fragile ecosystems. The GEF has developed a system for Transparent Allocation of Resources (STAR) within its Resource Allocation Framework (RAF). See http://www.thegef.org/gef/whatisgef (accessed 2 July 2011).

[133] See eg S Herz *et al* 'The International Finance Corporation's performance standards and the Equator Principles: Respecting human rights and remedying violations', (CIEL) (August 2008). Available at: http://www.ciel.org/Publications/IFC_Aug08/Ruggie_Submission.pdf (accessed 2 July 2011).

[134] Their initiatives are mostly based on the Equator Principles (2006) which are modeled on the social and environmental policies of the International Finance Corporation (IFC) of the World Bank. Available at http://www.equator-principles.com/ (accessed 2 July 2011).

be possibly ascribable to a number of additional factors.[135] First, the differences and divergences in the interpretation and understanding of the core mandate(s) of the Bank of, especially, the general legal counsel of the Bank. During their terms of office, these influential officials exert a determining impact on the direction of the Bank. Some of them were (and perhaps are) more supportive than others of establishing a human rights culture within the Bank.The most concerted efforts at aligning the operation of the Bank with the general normative framework of international (human rights) law[136] happened during the successive terms of office of general counsel Shihata and Dañino between 2000 and 2006.

Secondly, the corporate culture prevailing in the World Bank seems to be overwhelming. This culture favours the dominant position of economists over that of lawyers. The interpretive frames of these two groups, shaped by their professional knowledge, expertise and training, determine their respective understanding of the value of human rights and development in general as either intrinsic or instrumental to the work of the Bank. Lawyers view human rights as intrinsically universal and indivisible and the need for their protection as an end in itself. Economists, on the other hand, value human rights as an instrumental, functional means of achieving developmental objectives, such as poverty reduction and economic growth. In their pragmatic pursuance of these objectives, economists are often concerned about trade-offs that may have to be made in promoting human rights, especially in low resource countries.[137] The provision of empirical evidence of the effective enhancement of development and growth through the protection of human rights through the use of indicators that can measure and explain the causal links between development and growth and human rights protection goes a long way in demystifying the concept for economists.[138]

Nevertheless, both the World Bank and the IMF maintain that they take human rights seriously and include them in their grant-making and

[135] See eg Sarfaty (2009) (n 127 above) 648–650; 659–667.

[136] Discussed, from a disability perspective, in para 5 above.

[137] This momentum did not last, however, and started to peter out with the departure of the latter. See Sarfaty (n 127 above) 667–683 and the authors cited there. See also L Baker *The World Bank and human rights* (Bretton Woods Project Paper May 2007), available at http://www.ifiwatchnet.org/sites/ifiwatchnet.org/files/The_World_Bank_and-human_rights-%20at%20issue.pdf (accessed 2 August 2010); RW Edwards 'The role of the general counsel of an international financial institution' (2008) 17 *Kansas Journal of Law & Public Policy*: 254, 270–271.

[138] See Darrow (n 120 above) 182–196; Baker (n 137 above) 1–2.

development lending decisions – in the case of the World Bank not as an enforcer of human rights, but as a facilitator in helping its members realise their human rights obligations.[139]

In a theoretical analysis of the possible grounds for providing Bank loans (or grants) to developing states, Abouharb and Cingranelli[140] have made some very insightful findings. Linking the perspectives of four, partly contradictory, theories with results from empirical research, they have found significant indications of the potential importance of economic or political conflict and the levels of respect for human rights in potential recipient states being used as criteria by the Bank. States associated with a higher level of probability of receiving Bank loans were those in economic need, had larger populations, had higher levels of government respect for, specifically, workers' rights, and had not recently received Bank Loans. On the other hand, states associated with a lower level of probability of receiving loans were those characterised by extended and high levels of domestic unrest.

While some of their previous research on the selection criteria of the IMF had shown a preference of the latter for more authoritarian states, they found no evidence, in the case of the Bank, of bias for or against democratic states, military over civilian governments, repressive over libertarian governments, or colonially or dependency-wise linked to the USA. Understanding the selection criteria of the Bank is of importance for the estimation of the potential effects of Bank loans. This cannot be done by simply comparing recipient to non-recipient states. It will require the 'disentanglement' of the actual selection criteria from the measurable impacts of a loan in the case of every given individualised country. The answer pivots on whether it was the loan or the pre-existing situation that accounts for the impact attributed to the Bank loan.

All things being equal, it is maintained that stable and accountable democratic government, reliable and well-maintained infrastructure, and predictable policies and practices might enhance states' eligibility for Bank loans. This is obviously important for African states in their pursuance of the MDGs.

[139] World Bank *Human Rights* (August 2009), available at http://web.worldbank.org/WBSITE/EXTERNAL/EXTSITETOOLS/0,,contentMDK:20749693~pagePK:98400~piPK:98424~theSitePK:95474,00html (accessed August 2010). Permanent URL for this page: http://go.worldbank.org/72L95K8TN0.

[140] MR Abouharb & DL Cingranelli 'When the World Bank says yes: Determinants of structural adjustment lending' in G Ranis *et al* (n 106 above) 204–230.

Loan conditionality, MDGs and disability

The purpose of this part of the chapter is to investigate whether, through the imposition of conditions on loans, the funding institutions and mechanisms of the Bank and Fund could and/or should have a beneficial impact on the performance of recipient states in their pursuance of their attainment of the MDGs with respect to persons with disabilities. The investigation is premised on the Country Assistance Strategy (CAS) of the Bank which adopts an explicit results framework that specifies the expected links between the Bank's interventions and long-term development goals, along with indicators to monitor results.[141]

The World Bank 'interventions' take place through loan disbursements by the IDA. IDA funds are derived from, among others, periodic (triennial) replenishment rounds by donor states. During the last replenishment round (IDA 15, July 2008–June 2011), donors emphasised that restoring momentum to the MDGs leading to 2015 would require ambitious efforts to deliver on the economic and access agenda for basic services (health, education and basic infrastructure) during the next replenishment cycle of the IDA (IDA 16, which covers July 2011–June 2014).

In order to convey the seriousness of the matter, the level(s) of concessional (read 'conditionalised') aid will reflect both donor and beneficiary commitment to the achievement of the MDGs by 2015. For the IDA 16 period, fragile and post-conflict countries, several of which are in Africa, will receive specific attention. Fragile states are, from the Bank's perspective, generally characterised by weak policies and institutions but their country contexts vary considerably and operational approaches will be aligned to take this into account.[142]

[141] This question almost inevitably leads to the debate on the economic efficiency and human development impact of the 'structural adjustment programmes' that have been imposed by the international financial institutions – a 'fierce debate', as Darrow observes, since the 1980s (n120 above, 68). It is however not possible to do justice to this complex discussion within the scope of this chapter. See in this regard, generally: DP OBrien 'Structural adjustment programs in Sub-Saharan Africa' (1995) 19 *Fletcher Forum for World Affairs* 115–130; S Wairimu Kang'ara 'When the pendulum swings too far: Structural adjustment programs in Kenya' (1998) 109 *Third World Legal Studies* 109–151; SM Kawewe & R Dibie 'The impact of economic structural adjustment programs [ESAPs] on women and children: Implications for social welfare in Zimbabwe' (2000) 79 *Journal of Sociology and Social Welfare* 79–107; J Morgan-Foster 'The relationship of IMF structural adjustment programs to economic, social and cultural rights: The Argentine case revisited' (2002) 24 *Michigan Journal of International Law* 577–646; Darrow (n 120 above) 68–72.

[142] World Bank & International Monetary Fund (n 23 above) 145.

Both World Bank and IMF loans are occasionally conditionalised. The overarching purpose of conditions is to bring about economic and/or monetary policy reform by developing countries in exchange for grants and concessionary finance from the Bank or the Fund.[143] Policy conditionality is premised upon the assumption that it will persuade (read 'compel') policy makers to carry out beneficial reforms which they would not have made in the absence of policy conditionality or, differently stated, will only make as a result of the conditionality.[144] The Bank makes use of various types of conditionality, or combinations of types of conditionality, in order to direct state action towards outcomes desired by the Bank.[145] The type of conditionality set by the Bank or accepted by a state may demonstrate commitment on either side. On the side of the state it may, for example, demonstrate commitment to sustainable macroeconomic stability. On the side of the Bank it may demonstrate a willingness to assist, encourage or even 'reward'.[146]

There are two ways in which policy conditionality might have a beneficial impact, notably in the short-term and in the long-term. First, in the short term the promise of resources may persuade policy makers to make beneficial policy changes during the lifetime of the policy conditionality. Secondly, the short-term implementation of beneficial reforms may alter the political environment in a way that favours the continuation of those policies in the long term. Conditionality will only have an impact if there is a tendency for the reforms to persist.

In order to analyse the short-term effects of policy conditionality, it is necessary to understand the political and economic motivations behind the economic policy choices that the World Bank aims at reforming. With respect to the long-term effects, it is consequently necessary to understand why short-term implementation of reform policies will alter the political environment in favour of those policies. It basically boils down to understanding why 'economically irrational interventions' do indeed have the capacity to

[143] International Monetary Fund 'Conditionality in Fund-Supported Programmes: Policy Issues' (2001), para 16.

[144] S Coate & S Morris 'Policy conditionality' in G Ranis *et al* (n 106 above) 36–37, 43. For a thought-provoking article on state compliance with international commitments, see HH Koh 'Why do nations obey international law?' (1997) 106 *Yale Law Journal* 2599–2659.

[145] An analysis and typology of the conditions are beyond the purpose of this chapter.

[146] A Drazen 'Conditionality and ownership in IMF lending: A political economy approach' in G Ranis (n 106 above) 75–77.

influence 'politically rational choices'. Without understanding policy persistence, it is impossible to predict the circumstances under which policy conditionality will have a long-term impact.[147]

Of the several theoretical and empirical analyses of policy conditionality, the methodological focus on theories of public choice arguably goes the furthest to provide a theoretical explanation for the reasons for policy choices in developing countries.[148] The dominant implicit assumption in discussions of policy conditionality is that bad policy choices are made either out of ignorance or consciously with the purpose of favouring some (commercial, social, political) interest group in exchange for some political favours at an opportune future moment. For assessing the effectiveness and efficiency of conditionality, the reason for preferring a particular choice is of lesser importance than the way in which the policy-maker responds to the removal of the freedom of policy-making via conditionality.[149]

A major practical problem for World Bank policy conditionality is the limited number of state actions that can be effectively monitored and consequently subjected to conditions in reform programmes. Linked to this limitation is the possibility of the constitutional sanctioning of extensive governmental intervention in the national economy. The reason, motive or purpose for the intervention is possibly another limiting factor. If it is *bona fide* assumed that governments of all sovereign states rule according to their understanding of the public interest and of (distributive) justice, a particular intervention might simply be the most appropriate transfer mechanism in pursuance of the latter. The perception that conditionality might reduce the public welfare will compromise its imposition. The impact of any conditionality will therefore depend on its flexibility as trade-off value.[150]

The key to the explanation of the persistence of the impact of conditionality is to identify the mechanism by which the introduction of the reform alters incentives in the political process in favour of preserving the reform. Offering a private investment theory of policy persistence, Coate and Morris argue that when an economic policy is introduced, agents will often align their responding actions in order to benefit from it. Any benefit derived is likely to serve as an incentive to ensure the preservation of the

[147] Coate & Morris (n 144 above) 36–37.

[148] J Svensson 'When is foreign aid policy credible? Aid dependence and conditionality' (2000) *Journal of Development Economics* 81–84.

[149] Coate & Morris (n 144 above) 37–38.

[150] Coate & Morris (n 144 above) 41–42, 48.

policy.[151] In situations where decisions are made by majority rule, Fernandez and Roderik have shown that uncertainties about gains and losses from policy reform can result in the reform not being undertaken, even if would be supported once introduced. The removal of the uncertainty would therefore favour the possibility of the introduction of the reform.[152] Although it is difficult to comprehend or explain, it has been found that a policy may persist, in the absence of gains, for non-economic, psychological, reasons, because interest groups might perceive the removal of a policy reform, once introduced, as a loss and would therefore oppose it.[153]

It may be that these non-quantifiable 'non-economic' gains include factors that are conducive to the sub-conscious psychological experience of being part of a morally 'sound' society that is respectful of the needs of all and tolerant of diversity.

Given the fact that the enforcement of the CRPD (and, for that matter, the MDGs) ultimately rests on the willingness of governments to 'buy into' the normative framework provided by the Convention and other human rights instruments and to comply with the commitments undertaken in terms of the Millennium Declaration, the device of loan conditionality provides an additional mechanism to encourage compliance with these obligations.

Conclusion and recommendations

> [T]the [2011 MDG] report shows that we still have a long way to go in empowering women and girls, promoting sustainable development, and protecting the most vulnerable from the devastating effects of multiple crises, be they conflicts, natural disasters or volatility in prices for food and energy. Progress tends to bypass those who are lowest on the economic ladder or are otherwise disadvantaged because of their sex, age, disability or ethnicity.[154]

[151] Coate & Morris (n 144 above) 44–46, 48.

[152] R Fernandez & D Roderik 'Resistance to reform: Status quo bias in the presence of individual-specific uncertainty' (1991) 81 *American Economic Review* 1150; see also Drazen (n 146 above) 75–77.

[153] D Kahneman *et al* 'The endowment effect, loss aversion and status quo bias' (1991) 5 *Journal of Economic Perspectives* 201–203.

[154] B Ki-Moon 'Foreword' in United Nations 'The Millennium Development Goals report' (2011) 3.

The reality of the national implementation by states of measures agreed upon in situations of international collaborative state action is that states will normally do so when it is either to their advantage or when they are 'compelled' to so. This is where international financial institutions such as the World Bank and the IMF can play an important role. The fact that the loans system of the Bank is developmentally oriented and that the Bank and IMF have the power to conditionalise their loans and financial assistance to states, implies that it is possible to 'guide' the 'directing' of funds by recipient states to identified projects. Through its inspecting and reporting systems, the Bank is able to monitor the compliance by states.

Since state practice has confirmed the general and widespread absence of voluntary measures that give adequate attention to the developmental rights, interests and needs of persons with disabilities, more stringent measures that induce states to do so might go a long way to rectify this situation. The reality remains that without spending directives from the international financial institutions, certain states might never summon the political will to allocate the funds for the purposes that it has been applied for or granted – or to mainstream disability in sustainable development strategies, as required in terms of the CRPD.

In addition to the conditioning mechanisms for new loans, the replenishment round of the IDA might be the perfect tools for (re-)directing state budgets and expenditure towards their pursuance of the attainment of the MDGs.[155] This might assist developing states, where the needs of persons with disabilities are often the most neglected, to direct funding to the redressing of the situation. Hopefully, the Bank will use the opportunity to encourage developing countries to do that.

[155] The sixteenth replenishment of the IDA is scheduled to run from July 2011 to June 2014.

Official list of MDG indicators

All indicators should be disaggregated by sex and urban/rural as far as possible
Effective 15 January 2008

Millennium Development Goals (MDGs)

Goals and Targets (from the Millennium Declaration)

Goal 1: Eradicate extreme poverty & hunger		Indicators for monitoring progress
Target 1.A Halve, between 1990 and 2015, the proportion of people whose income is less than one dollar a day	1.1 1.2 1.3	Proportion of population below $1 (PPP) per day[1] Poverty gap ratio Share of poorest quintile in national consumption
Target 1.B Achieve full and productive employment and decent work for all, including women and young people	1.4 1.5 1.6 1.7	Growth rate of GDP per person employed Employment-to-population ratio Proportion of employed people living below $1 (PPP) per day Proportion of own-account and contributing family workers in total employment
Target 1.C Halve, between 1990 and 2015, the proportion of people who suffer from hunger	1.8 1.9	Prevalence of underweight children under-five years of age Proportion of population below minimum level of dietary energy consumption
Goal 2: Achieve universal primary education		**Indicators for monitoring progress**
Target 2.A Ensure that, by 2015, children everywhere, boys and girls alike, will be able to complete a full course of primary schooling	2.1 2.2 2.3	Net enrolment ratio in primary education Proportion of pupils starting grade 1 who reach last grade of primary Literacy rate of 15-24 year-olds, women and men
Goal 3: Promote gender equality & empower women		**Indicators for monitoring progress**
Target 3.A Eliminate gender disparity in primary and secondary education, preferably by 2005, and in all levels of education no later than 2015	3.1 3.2 3.3	Ratios of girls to boys in primary, secondary and tertiary education Share of women in wage employment in the non-agricultural sector Proportion of seats held by women in national parliament
Goal 4: Reduce child mortality		**Indicators for monitoring progress**
Target 4.A Reduce by two thirds, between 1990 and 2015, the under-five mortality rate	4.1 4.2 4.3	Under-five mortality rate Infant mortality rate Proportion of 1 year-old children immunised against measles
Goal 5: Improve maternal health		**Indicators for monitoring progress**
Target 5.A Reduce by three quarters, between 1990 and 2015, the maternal mortality ratio	5.1 5.2	Maternal mortality ratio Proportion of births attended by skilled health personnel
Target 5.B Achieve, by 2015, universal access to reproductive health	5.3 5.4 5.5 5.6	Contraceptive prevalence rate Adolescent birth rate Antenatal care coverage (at least one visit and at least four visits) Unmet need for family planning
Goal 6: Combat HIV/AIDS, malaria & other diseases		**Indicators for monitoring progress**
Target 6.A Have halted by 2015 and begun to reverse the spread of HIV/AIDS	6.1 6.2 6.3 6.4	HIV prevalence among population aged15–24 years Condom use at last high-risk sex Proportion of population aged 15–24 years with comprehensive correct knowledge of HIV/AIDS Ratio of school attendance of orphans to school attendance of non-orphans aged 10–14 years
Target 6.B Achieve, by 2010, universal access to treatment for HIV/AIDS for all those who need it	6.5	Proportion of population with advanced HIV infection with access to antiretroviral drugs
Target 6.C Have halted by 2015 and begun to reverse the incidence of malaria and other major diseases	6.6 6.7 6.8 6.9 6.10	Incidence and death rates associated with malaria Proportion of children under 5 sleeping under insecticide-treated bednets Proportion of children under 5 with fever who are treated with appropriate anti-malarial drugs Incidence, prevalence and death rates associated with tuberculosis Proportion of tuberculosis cases detected and cured under directly observed treatment short course

Goal 7: Ensure environmental sustainability	Indicators for monitoring progress
Target 7.A Integrate the principles of sustainable development into country policies and programmes and reverse the loss of environmental resources	7.1 Proportion of land area covered by forest 7.2 CO2 emissions, total, per capita and per $1 GDP (PPP) 7.3 Consumption of ozone-depleting substances 7.4 Proportion of fish stocks within safe biological limits 7.5 Proportion of total water resources used
Target 7.B Reduce biodiversity loss, achieving, by 2010, a significant reduction in the rate of loss	7.6 Proportion of terrestrial and marine areas protected 7.7 Proportion of species threatened with extinction
Target 7.C Halve, by 2015, the proportion of people without sustainable access to safe drinking water and basic sanitation	7.8 Proportion of population using an improved drinking water source 7.9 Proportion of population using an improved sanitation facility
Target 7.D By 2020, to have achieved a significant improvement in the lives of at least 100 million slum dwellers	7.10 Proportion of urban population living in slums[2]
Goal 8: Develop a global partnership for development	**Indicators for monitoring progress**
Target 8.A Develop further an open, rule-based, predictable, non-discriminatory trading and financial system Includes a commitment to good governance, development and poverty reduction – both nationally and internationally	*Some of the indicators listed below are monitored separately for the least developed countries (LDCs), Africa, landlocked developing countries and small island developing States* Official development assistance (ODA) 8.1 Net ODA, total and to the least developed countries, as percentage of OECD/DAC donors' gross national income
Target 8.B Address the special needs of the least developed countries Includes: tariff and quota free access for the least developed countries' exports; enhanced programme of debt relief for heavily indebted poor countries (HIPC) and cancellation of official bilateral debt; and more generous ODA for countries committed to poverty reduction	8.2 Proportion of total bilateral, sector-allocable ODA of OECD/DAC donors to basic social services (basic education, primary health care, nutrition, safe water and sanitation) 8.3 Proportion of bilateral official development assistance of OECD/DAC donors that is untied 8.4 ODA received in landlocked developing countries as a proportion of their gross national incomes
Target 8.C Address the special needs of landlocked developing countries and small island developing States (through the Programme of Action for the Sustainable Development of Small Island Developing States and the outcome of the twenty-second special session of the General Assembly)	8.5 ODA received in small island developing States as a proportion of their gross national incomes Market access 8.6 Proportion of total developed country imports (by value and excluding arms) from developing countries and least developed countries, admitted free of duty 8.7 Average tariffs imposed by developed countries on agricultural products and textiles and clothing from developing countries
Target 8.D Deal comprehensively with the debt problems of developing countries through national and international measures in order to make debt sustainable in the long term	8.8 Agricultural support estimate for OECD countries as a percentage of their gross domestic product 8.9 Proportion of ODA provided to help build trade capacityDebt sustainability 8.10 Total number of countries that have reached their HIPC decision points and number that have reached their HIPC completion points (cumulative) 8.11 Debt relief committed under HIPC and MDRI Initiatives 8.12 Debt service as a percentage of exports of goods and services
Target 8.E In cooperation with pharmaceutical companies, provide access to affordable essential drugs in developing countries	8.13 Proportion of population with access to affordable essential drugs on a sustainable basis
Target 8.F In cooperation with the private sector, make available the benefits of new technologies, especially information and communications	8.14 Telephone lines per 100 population 8.15 Cellular subscribers per 100 population 8.16 Internet users per 100 population

The Millennium Development Goals and targets come from the Millennium Declaration, signed by 189 countries, including 147 heads of State and Government, in September 2000 (http://www.un.org/millennium/declaration/ares552e.htm) and from further agreement by member states at the 2005 World Summit (Resolution adopted by the General Assembly - A/RES/60/1, http://www.un.org/Docs/journal/asp/ws.asp?m=A/RES/60/1). The goals and targets are interrelated and should be seen as a whole. They represent a partnership between the developed countries and the developing countries "to create an environment – at the national and global levels alike – which is conducive to development and the elimination of poverty".

1 For monitoring country poverty trends, indicators based on national poverty lines should be used, where available.

2 The actual proportion of people living in slums is measured by a proxy, represented by the urban population living in households with at least one of the four characteristics: (a) lack of access to improved water supply; (b) lack of access to improved sanitation; (c) overcrowding (3 or more persons per room); and (d) dwellings made of non-durable material.

Permissions

All chapters in this book were first published in ADLA, by Pretoria University Law Press (PULP); hereby published with permission under the Creative Commons Attribution License or equivalent. Every chapter published in this book has been scrutinized by our experts. Their significance has been extensively debated. The topics covered herein carry significant findings which will fuel the growth of the discipline. They may even be implemented as practical applications or may be referred to as a beginning point for another development.

The contributors of this book come from diverse backgrounds, making this book a truly international effort. This book will bring forth new frontiers with its revolutionizing research information and detailed analysis of the nascent developments around the world.

We would like to thank all the contributing authors for lending their expertise to make the book truly unique. They have played a crucial role in the development of this book. Without their invaluable contributions this book wouldn't have been possible. They have made vital efforts to compile up to date information on the varied aspects of this subject to make this book a valuable addition to the collection of many professionals and students.

This book was conceptualized with the vision of imparting up-to-date information and advanced data in this field. To ensure the same, a matchless editorial board was set up. Every individual on the board went through rigorous rounds of assessment to prove their worth. After which they invested a large part of their time researching and compiling the most relevant data for our readers.

The editorial board has been involved in producing this book since its inception. They have spent rigorous hours researching and exploring the diverse topics which have resulted in the successful publishing of this book. They have passed on their knowledge of decades through this book. To expedite this challenging task, the publisher supported the team at every step. A small team of assistant editors was also appointed to further simplify the editing procedure and attain best results for the readers.

Apart from the editorial board, the designing team has also invested a significant amount of their time in understanding the subject and creating the most relevant covers. They scrutinized every image to scout for the most suitable representation of the subject and create an appropriate cover for the book.

The publishing team has been an ardent support to the editorial, designing and production team. Their endless efforts to recruit the best for this project, has resulted in the accomplishment of this book. They are a veteran in the field of academics and their pool of knowledge is as vast as their experience in printing. Their expertise and guidance has proved useful at every step. Their uncompromising quality standards have made this book an exceptional effort. Their encouragement from time to time has been an inspiration for everyone.

The publisher and the editorial board hope that this book will prove to be a valuable piece of knowledge for researchers, students, practitioners and scholars across the globe.

List of Contributors

Trynie Boezaart

Ann Skelton

Bonolo Ramadi Dinokopila

Jimcall Pfumorodze

Charles Manga Fombad

Victor Jere

Michael Ashley Stein

Janet E. Lord

Lorenzo Wakefield

Nkatha L. Murungi

Ilze Grobbelaar-du Plessis

Stefan van Eck

Japhet Biegon

Tobias van Reenen

Helene Combrinck

Index